African Voices, African Lives

D0148763

African Voices, African Lives explores the world of 'Mohammed', a Swahili peasant living on the coast of Tanzania. Through his own words – some written, some spoken – we glimpse the changing world he inhabits, which includes the invisible but ubiquitous spirits of land and sea, who play a significant role in his life. Other voices, too, are heard, principally those of Mohammed's wife 'Mwahadia', and one of their daughters, 'Subira', giving their own perspectives on events.

Pat Caplan, an anthropologist, has been working in this area for almost three decades during which time she has developed close personal ties with Mohammed and members of his family, as both she and they have moved through their respective life courses. Here she acts as translator, interpreter and facilitator of their voices, allowing them to speak, and at the same time utilising her own knowledge of Swahili society, gathered from intensive fieldwork over a long period, to provide relevant background and so assist the reader to a fuller understanding of the rich tapestries which are their lives.

By utilising a mixture of styles – narrative and life history, ethnographic observation, and the diary kept by Mohammed at the anthropologist's request – this book will make an important contribution to current debates in anthropology by grappling with issues of 'personal narratives', authorial authority and reflexive ethnographic writing.

Pat Caplan is Professor of Anthropology at Goldsmiths' College, University of London.

African Voices, African Lives

Personal narratives from a Swahili village

Pat Caplan

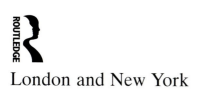

London and New York

First published in 1997
by Routledge
11 New Fetter Lane, London EC4P 4EE

Simultaneously published in the USA and Canada
by Routledge
29 West 35th Street, New York, NY 10001

© 1997 Pat Caplan

Typeset in Times Ten and Frutiger by
Keystroke, Jacaranda Lodge, Wolverhampton

Printed and bound in Great Britain by
Biddles Ltd, Guildford and King's Lynn

British Library Cataloguing in Publication Data
A catalogue record for this book is available from the British Library.

Library of Congress Cataloguing in Publication Data
Caplan, Patricia.
    African voices, african lives: personal narratives from a Swahili
village / Pat Caplan.
        p.   cm.
    Includes bibliographical references and index.
    1. Swahili-speaking peoples—Social conditions. 2. Swahili-
speaking peoples—Religion. 3. Swahili-speaking peoples—Kinship.
4. Minazini (Tanzania)—Religious life and customs. 5. Minazini
(Tanzania)—Social life and customs. I. Title.
DT443.3.S92C36   1997
305.896′392—dc20   96-25693
                                                                  CIP

ISBN 0–415–13723–3 (hc.)
ISBN 0–415–13724–1 (pbk.)

For Mohammed, Mwahadia and Subira

Contents

List of illustrations

PLATES

FIGURES

MAP

Dramatis personae and place names

Mohammed: Main character, informant, writer of diary. Husband of Mwahadia. Born around 1935.

Mwahadia: Mohammed's wife, and mother of all his children. Divorced in 1976. Re-married in 1986.

Kombo: one of Mohammed's older brothers who helped him financially until his death around 1980.

Seleman: eldest son of Mohammed and Mwahadia. Worked in hotels until his death in 1990.

Asha: eldest daughter of Mohammed and Mwahadia. Has been married and divorced several times. Was living with Mohammed in 1994.

Subira: second daughter of Mohammed and Mwahadia. Has been married and divorced several times. Was living in District Capital in 1994.

Waziri: second son of Mohammed and Mwahadia. Died in a ship-wreck at the age of 19.

Amina: third daughter of Mohammed and Mwahadia. Lived in Zanzibar with her husband, and died there in her 30s around 1992.

Miza: fourth daughter of Mohammed and Mwahadia. Married and divorced. In 1994 was living with Mohammed.

Juma: third son of Mohammed and Mwahadia. He was living with Mwahadia in 1994.

Habiba: fifth and youngest daughter of Mohammed and Mwahadia. Married and living with her husband and baby son in 1994.

Pwani, Kisiwa, Karibu, Kisiki, Mashariki: places on Mafia Island mentioned regularly. They are all villages near to Minazini which have been given pseudonyms.

Baleni, Kirongwe, Utende: other villages on Mafia.

Kilindoni: district capital of Mafia.

Acknowledgements

Where material has been gathered over such a long period, there are so many people who have made contributions that it would be impossible to mention them all. I owe long-standing intellectual debts to Philip Gulliver, who originally supervised my PhD research in the 1960s, and to the late Wilfred Whiteley, who supervised my work while I was in Tanzania and encouraged me to collect material on spirit possession. Many years ago, Ioan Lewis examined my PhD thesis, and made useful comments: since then he has repeatedly asked me when I intend to publish something on spirit possession, and I thank him for the reminders, as well as the stimulation of his own work. I have also derived much from the work of fellow coastal scholars: Janet Bujra, Françoise Le Guennec-Coppens, David Parkin, Farouk Topan and other members of the on-going Franco-British Swahili Workshop, as well as from that of John Middleton.

Papers and lectures which relate to this book were given in a number of places, including the Association of Social Anthropologists Conference and the Franco-British Swahili Workshop, both in 1989; at the Kitty Lundy Memorial Lecture at Atkinson College, York University Toronto and at the Department of Anthropology, University of Illinois, Chicago, both in 1994; I am grateful for comments from participants at these events.

Several colleagues and friends gave me useful advice when I began to consider the topic of personal narratives: I am particularly grateful to three historians: Leonore Davidoff, Angela John and Pat Thane. I wish I had been able to spend more time following up all of their leads.

Several people in Tanzania have given very practical help over the years: on Mafia Island, Mr and Mrs Sachitanand, and Mr and Mrs Thampi were generous with their hospitality, while Henry Stanley provided endless help on numerous occasions. In London, Karen

Catling has assisted in the production of this book by scanning old
typescripts and inputting their contents into the computer, as well
as being a source of much support at a time when I was engaged in
several projects at once. Catherine Brain typed the bibliography.

Funding for my various field trips to Tanzania has come from the
Goldsmiths' Company, the University of London, the Nuffield
Foundation (on several occasions) and Goldsmiths' College. I have
received Personal Research Fellowships from the Economic and
Social Research Council and from the Nuffield and Leverhulme
Foundations to enable me to devote time to writing. I am grateful to
all of them.

The Tanzania National Research Council has given me permission
to carry out fieldwork on Mafia Island several times and I thank them
for this privilege. I have also been fortunate in the local scholars
with whom I worked in Tanzania: Simon Mesaki of the Department
of Sociology, University of Dar es Salaam in 1985, and Marjorie
Mbilinyi, of the Tanzania Gender Networking Group, in 1994; the
latter's own work on personal narratives has also been a source of
inspiration.

Several friends and colleagues read this book in manuscript form,
no light task in these hard-pressed times, and made useful comments:
Patricia Jeffrey, Brian Morris and Farouk Topan; the last also
checked some of the Swahili. Lionel Caplan read numerous drafts
and, as always, provided much moral support. I thank them all.

Finally, and most importantly, I owe debts which can never be
repaid to the people of Mafia Island, especially 'Minazini' village
where I have come to feel particularly at home. Above all, my thanks
to 'Mohammed', 'Mwahadia' and 'Subira' for explaining so much,
and for sharing their lives with me. *Tukijaliwa, tutaonana tena.*

Pat Caplan
London, April 1996

Prologue
A special prayer

In the summer of 1994, I returned for the fourth time since the mid-1960s to a village on Mafia Island, Tanzania. The main purpose of my visit was to discuss with one of its inhabitants, 'Mohammed', the book I was writing and which focused upon him and the numerous texts he had given me over the years.[1]

GREETINGS

Mohammed wanted to record himself giving me formal greetings, so we had to pretend that we were meeting again for the first time since my last visit.

M. I will greet you and you reply.
P. Alright.
M. Peace be with you (*Asalaam aleikum*).
P. And with you (*Aleikum is salaam*).
M. Patricia Caplan,[2] welcome (*Ahlan wa sahlan*). My lord, my benefactor, how are you? (*Saidi yangu, mfadhili yangu, ke fahalik?*)
P. Well (*Taib*).[3]
M. How are things in London?
P. Everything in London is fine.
M. And are our children well?
P. They are all fine.
M. And is Mr Caplan well?
P. He's fine too.
M. And are all our elders quite well?
P. They are indeed.
M. What other news is there from London, Patricia?
P. There is no other news, everything is fine. And are you well?
M. I am fine.

P. And our children and grandchildren?

M. All of them are well.

P. And our other relatives? What news is there from Minazini?

M. I have a lot to tell you and talk to you about. It must be about nine years since you left here, Patricia. There have been deaths, and ceremonies (*mashughuli*) and troubles (*mashida*). I have been afflicted by many deaths, first our son Waziri, then our son Seleman, and our daughter Amina also died recently. Many, many things have happened. I have been seized by our ancestral spirit, and so has our daughter Subira. You will know about all those things when we talk.

We did talk, at great length, and usually in private. Mohammed often came to my house, especially in the late afternoon or the evening, and demanded to be admitted by knocking with his stick on the front door, as well as giving the verbal signal which is usual in Swahili: '*Hodi*' (Can I come in?).

I explained to him that one of the major tasks of my current visit was to collect material for a book about him, and that I wanted to tape-record his life story. Mohammed was fascinated and agreed to cooperate, but stipulated that we needed greater privacy for this work. My village house was far from soundproof, and its verandah was used by a wide variety of people, many of whom frequently chose to pay me a visit. So we decided to go to the south of the island, where I had some friends living in a large plantation with a substantial house. We spent several days together there, taping his life story, and discussing the proposed book.

DISCUSSING THE BOOK

P. You know that if this book comes out, it is sold in shops?

M. Over there?

P. Over there, anywhere – England, France, America, even East Africa. So this book that I am writing is not my work alone, it is also yours [indicating his first diary]. But I have also worked on it because I have translated it, and furthermore, the other thing I have still to do is add explanations. Because people who read it and who do not know East Africa will be a bit surprised. For example, you have written here 'having a spirit' (*mwenye mzimu*) and people will wonder what that means. So I will have to explain it to them. [For such reasons] I thought that this book will be half mine and half yours. So you could have your name there if you wanted to, but if you decided not to [to protect his privacy], that's all right. As to the profits – if God grants me to finish the book, to send it to the publisher, and if they publish it and it gets sold in bookshops, then I will divide this money with you. But this will not happen today or tomorrow. It is a lot of work, it might take a year or more.

What happens is this – each year they pay out [royalties]. But if you have written a book, you don't get all the money yourself. Suppose a book is sold for 1,000 shillings,[4] you get only 100 shillings because the book sellers and the publishers take the rest. So if you are lucky you get 100 shillings [for each one]. They see how many copies they have sold. Suppose they sell 100 copies, that means they have sold them for 1 lakh, but I only get 10,000 shillings, and of that, half I think should be for you and half for me.

M. You know me, you understand me. So if you write my name, and if you get 1,000 shillings, you will know how much to give me, won't you? If it is [only] 500 shillings or 600 shillings you will know. I won't be able to know that. But it doesn't have to be this month or this year. All of these things you know about. So what I say to you is this, I do not know about these things, but I do know about your affection (*mapenzi na mahaba*).

P. Yes, you and I have known each other a long time. Do you trust me?

M. Yes, I do. If you had not been [that kind of person] I would not have told you [about these things]. But because you have told me this, we have started differently. I can tell you that in the village of Minazini, here in Mafia, there isn't anyone who received you right from the beginning as I did.

P. Yes I remember the first day when you came with Ali [my cook and his friend].

M. And I have no doubt that Ali told you that I am his friend.

P. Yes, indeed he did.

M. But the heart (*kiini*) of the matter is that I have remembered you and you have remembered me, all of our lives, up to the time recently when I was called, together with your [village] brother,[5] to get the letters which you had sent us. And the word got around that Patricia had sent letters to Mohammed and to her brother and it is they who are the ones [who are special] in spite of the fact that you also have fathers and mothers here, brothers and sisters, aunts and uncles, grandparents. They are the ones she talks to in confidence (*pembeni*), isn't that right? Isn't that true?

P. Yes, completely. Now I want to ask you another question. If we write this book, I would like it to contain pictures. And on this trip I have taken many photos of you, so what do you feel about having some included?

M. [laughs] So what will people say about it? Will they think I have written the book?

P. They will be pleased.

M. But will they say I've written it?

P. If you want your name on the cover, fine. If you don't, then in the Preface I can say that I was helped in this work by so and so. But if you don't want that either, then I can use another name for you.

M. You will know what's best (*utaelewa wewe*) and you will know [who it is who has helped you].

P. But even if we use another name for you and someone from here reads it, they will know it is you because of the photos [if I include some of him]. I mean I can't say that copies of the book won't come here to East Africa.

M. No doubt. When people go on the pilgrimage to Mecca, they buy things there and bring them back here. So things do get around. In that way, it could happen that someone from Minazini might buy that book and say, 'Ah, this is Patricia and Mohammed', mightn't they? And a lot of people know me, not just in Minazini, but in Mafia, even in Dar es Salaam.

P. The way I see it is this – we are born and we die. If we are lucky, we leave some property in this world when we go. One is children [he says the word at the same moment as I do] and perhaps other property as well. If I write a book, when I die, it will still be here, and people can continue to read it. It becomes part of knowledge (*elimu*). Students in universities in England, America, France or other countries can still read the book. And with our book, it can be the same, so that even if we die, you and I, people will still know our names. What do you say?

M. [laughs] Fine, but what I think is what I already told you. You write your name [only], and you alone will know who is the man you have behind you (*ugongoni kwako*). So it is your decision (*wazo lako*).

But when your children come here,[6] you should give them a good account of me: 'This man is such, and he has his children, and the end of all human beings is death. So if you come here, don't neglect to ask for him. And if you get a letter from Mohammed of Minazini, Mafia, this is the man himself.' And if they see my picture they will know it is me.

Since Mohammed did not want his name in the book, I decided not to include photographs of him either.

A SPECIAL PRAYER

Early in my stay, Mohammed came with a suggestion. He told me that the son of his half-sister by the same mother is a Koran school teacher (*mwalimu*) and is much respected. He first studied in the village, then in Zanzibar, and now he continues his studies every Wednesday with a Sheikh in a neighbouring village. He performs marriages, prays over corpses after washing them, gives sermons and runs Koranic readings (*hitima*). 'Wherever he goes, he is called to lead (*mbele*), and he is called upon very often. This man does special prayers (*kuombea dua*) for people.'

Mohammed suggested that he should ask this relative to say a special prayer for me. 'You don't have to, only if you want to. Let him ask that your work prosper and that you be above everyone (*juu ya watu wote*).' I told him that the former, not the latter, was my primary wish, but agreed that we can do the prayer as I had not witnessed it before. The fee (*ada*) was 1,500 shillings (500 shillings above the usual), plus the cost of incense (20 shillings) and tea (100 shillings).

From my notebook:

> On July 10th, Mohammed comes to collect me in the evening after I have had supper at a friend's house. We walk up to his house in the darkness along the narrow winding path, with Mohammed stabbing at things which get in his way with his stick and indicating where the path becomes tricky – 'Mind the roots here.'
>
> On arrival I sit on the verandah. The *mwalimu* is already there. On the other side of the unfenced courtyard sit the other members of Mohammed's household eating supper – his two divorced daughters and their children. The man says that it would be good to do this inside so we go into a room where a new mat is spread. We sit in the flickering light of a little wick lamp (*kibatali*).
>
> On the way Mohammed had asked me if I had anything else that I wanted to add other than 'above all others'. I said that I was less interested in that than in good health and prosperity for my children, and safe journeys. Mohammed did explain some of this to the *mwalimu* at the beginning, but the emphasis of both of them, rather to my embarrassment, is very much on 'Let her be above all others.'
>
> The *mwalimu* begins by explaining that in the Koran God tells people that they should pray; he lights the incense bit by bit and begins praying, using a book from which he reads in Arabic and then explains things to us and makes specific requests in Swahili. Mohammed listens intently and I notice that he knows many of the words and prays along quietly.
>
> The prayer takes about 20 minutes. At the end we put our hands over our faces in the usual fashion. Then we retire outside to the verandah again. Mohammed calls for tea which is brought and which I decline on the grounds of potential insomnia. The *mwalimu* says it has the same effect on him. Mohammed walks me back to my house. He is sure now that our work will be successful and that my career will benefit from it.

1 Introduction
Anthropology and personal narratives

ANTHROPOLOGIST AND INFORMANT

> There are no conventional words for the relationship between the anthropologist and the 'key informant'.
>
> (Prell 1989: 244)

This book is a personal narrative which presents the life history and world-view of a Swahili man, a peasant from Mafia Island, Tanzania. As far as possible, this is done through his own words, but I have also used other voices, including those of his wife and children, as well as my own.

I have been carrying out field-work in one of the villages – 'Minazini' – of Mafia Island for almost thirty years, with stays of eighteen months in 1965–7, and shorter visits of two to three months in 1976, 1985 and 1994. My interests have shifted from kinship and land tenure in the 1960s (Caplan 1975) to gender relations in the 1970s and beyond, encompassing food, health and fertility in the 1980s and 1990s.[1] In addition, throughout this period, I have gathered a considerable amount of data on spirit possession and its rituals. In much of this work, Mohammed has been an important informant, as have members of his family, and during my most recent visit, in the summer of 1994, as the Prologue suggests, we spent a good deal of time discussing this book.

As I have returned to the village each decade, subtle changes have taken place in individual inhabitants who, like the ethnographer, have been passing through the life cycle with all its attendant joys and sorrows. Each time we meet, we are slightly different people, even though we continue to recognise each other. Furthermore, the village itself, part of a wider society and economy, has also been changing, and although such changes are not at first sight very dramatic, it is apparent that there has been an increase in the poverty of the majority of villagers, including the main characters in this book, as a result of wider social and economic forces (see Caplan 1992b). Also noteworthy, to myself at least, have been the changes in the discipline of anthropology from the time of my first foray in the 1960s as a postgraduate student, when it was still firmly embedded in structural functionalism, to its fragmentation into numerous strands in the late 1960s and early 1970s with the influence of structuralism, feminism and Marxism. More recently, even those who would not wish to be labelled as postmodernists have found themselves influenced by some of its currents, and obliged to think more carefully not only about how and what they do and why, but also what difference *who* they are makes to what they see and experience.

In all of this situation of flux – in persons, places and questions – there have remained areas of continuity provided by friendship and, in some instances, adoptive kinship between myself as ethnographer and certain people of Minazini. This has enabled each new encounter to possess a greater depth than previous ones – we now share something of a common history, and many of our conversations are on the lines of, 'Do you remember when?' This commonality is powerfully realised in the fact that my family and I appear in the photo albums which are beginning to be owned by a few people in the village, even as the villagers appear in mine. Many villagers are also actors in the film of the village which I helped make for the BBC in 1976,[2] and which has to be ritually screened each time I return. On my last visit, I also found a further dimension of communication; my village younger brother, who is relatively well-educated and can read English, had returned to live in the village after a long absence and for the first time I was able to discuss both my published work and work in progress with someone from Minazini itself.

Furthermore, while relationships with villagers are reaffirmed and renewed only on the occasion of my visits, in the interim there are letters which go back and forth; unfortunately, there have been virtually no reciprocal visits (a great contrast to my field-work in India where numerous informants have visited London and stayed with my family). Finally, relationships with villagers are also rethought and remembered in the process of writing ethnography.

I first met Mohammed because he was a friend of a man named Ali whom I employed as a cook[3] during my first period of field-work. Mohammed and Ali had spent time together working on the dhows which ply up and down the East Coast of Africa. Ali was from the south of the island and a stranger in Minazini. He was very happy to discover that an old friend lived there, and encouraged Mohammed to visit our house. In my own diary, the first mention of Mohammed includes a note that he had stayed for a long time and that, by the second visit, he had borrowed a shilling, the first of many such 'loans'. In fact it would be naive to pretend that Mohammed's willingness to act as informant did not have a pecuniary motive. He is a poor man, with a large family, and, as will become plain, most of his projects have failed to come to fruition.

It was not until half way through that first period of field-work, however, that I realised just how knowledgeable an informant Mohammed was. At that stage, I left the village for several weeks to travel on the mainland. As I was worrried about missing several events, I asked a number of men in the village who could write (there were hardly any literate women at that time) to keep diaries for me. Several did so, but Mohammed's was the longest and fullest.

The diary proved so useful that I asked him to continue writing it even when I was back in the village, and later when I moved to carry out research in another village. In the second village, Mohammed, often accompanied by his wife Mwahadia, would visit me for several days at a time, and we would work on his diary, as well as going through notes from other informants to clarify certain points.

Strangely enough, although I found the information which it contained useful at the time, I did not think of the diary material as being *sui generis*; it was all just part of my 'field-notes', and awareness of the significance of different kinds of texts struck me only later. Indeed, when I went back to the village in 1976, I did not even ask him to keep a diary again, in spite of the fact that, in the interim, he had been my most regular correspondent. It was only in the 1980s, when I went through all my old field-notes during a year's sabbatical spent working on a new monograph, that I even remembered the existence of the diary as such, and extracted it from other material in my notebooks.

As I have stated elsewhere (Caplan 1992a), it is perhaps remarkable that Mohammed and I developed such a close relationship, given not only the difference in our backgrounds, but also in our genders. In my own 1966–7 diary, I wrote on one occasion, 'Mohammed makes me laugh.' My relationship with him has several unique qualities about it. To begin with, we have never attempted to put it onto a fictive or adoptive kinship plane, as has been the case for other villagers. Yet our relationship is a close one. Mohammed is the only person in the village who calls me by my name, with no embellishment, in contrast to others who use kinship terms, if appropriate, or preface my name with 'Mama' (lit. 'mother', but also 'woman', now extended to translate 'Mrs'). In the village, relationships between non-related males and females often involve gifts of money and kind usually passing from male to female in return for sexual favours. In our case, however, there was never a hint of sexuality and the flow of goods was in the opposite direction: he provided me with information, and received in return gifts, money or loans. This must sometimes have made him uncomfortable, and at the end of my first stay, Mohammed tried to redress the balance by giving me a coconut tree for which he wrote out a document in *Kiarabu* (Swahili in Arabic script), and I of acceptance in *Kizungu* (Swahili in Roman script).[4]

ANTHROPOLOGY AND PERSONAL NARRATIVES: MONOLOGUE OR DIALOGUE?

In focusing upon an individual in this way, I can of course make no claims to originality. There is a respectable lineage of anthropological life histories,[5] and in contemplating the literature which this genre has already produced, we are faced with a number of questions. One is that of voice – is it that of the subject alone, or should it include others, such as members of his or her family? Second, what of the ethnographer and his or her presence – should this appear in the text and if so in what form? Possibilities include dialogue between anthropologist and informant, or the anthropologist's framing of the informant's text. Whatever method is chosen, ultimately, the anthropologist has the job of editing the final manuscript, and presenting it in a way which is intelligible to a wide range of readers. As will be seen, different anthropologists have used different styles in presenting life histories.[6]

One of the earliest examples of a life history presented by an anthropologist is Paul Radin's *Crashing Thunder* (1926). Radin himself maintained that the only acceptable form of ethnology was the life history, self-told, but for a long period of time relatively few anthropologists followed his example of allowing informants to speak for themselves.

One notable exception, albeit twenty years later, was Marcel Griaule's work with the Dogon elder Ogotemmeli (*Dieu d'Eaux: Entretiens avec Ogotemmeli* (1948) (later published in English as *Conversations with Ogotemmeli* in 1965), in which Griaule recorded thirty-three days of conversation with a key informant who provided an outline of Dogon cosmology. Although this is not a life history, it is worth mentioning at this point because the text is dialogical: we hear the words of both Griaule himself as well as those of Ogotemmeli.[7]

Although between the 1930s and 1960s several distinguished anthropologists, such as Dollard, Kluckhohn and Langness, noted that the potential of the life history is great (Watson 1976: 95), the genre remained a marginal technique until relatively recently. A few American anthropologists did publish life histories prior to the 1950s (see, for example, Dyk's *Son of Old Hat* (1938)), but no British anthropologists did.

In the 1950s and 1960s a small number of important life histories appeared; again, most were by American anthropologists, such as Sidney Mintz's *Worker in the Cane* (1960), Theodora Kroeber's *Ishi in Two Worlds* (1961) and *Ishi – Last of His Tribe* (1973 [1964]). Casagrande also published an edited collection of what he called 'portraits' of twenty anthropological informants (1960), one of which was of Victor Turner's informant, Muchona the Hornet. From the British side there also appeared Mary Smith's *Baba of Karo: A Woman of the Nigerian Hausa* (1981 [1954]).

Mintz's work is the life history of a Puerto Rican sugar cane worker who was his close friend. Mintz is aware that the format of interviews was based largely on his questions and Taso's answers and in the introduction notes that, as a result, the text varies from long uninterrupted passages of Taso's words, to short dialogues between himself and Taso (1960: 6, 8).

Theodora Kroeber wrote two books about Ishi, a 'wild' American Yahi Indian who was 'found' in 1911, and thereafter spent the rest of his life in the company of white people, including anthropologists who made him a subject of research. Kroeber describes her first book (1961) as a biography, but it contains few of Ishi's own words. The second book (1973 [1964]) is written as a novel, but although much of the material must have come from Ishi himself, he is referred to in the third, not the first person.

In Mary Smith's book (1981 [1954]) there are three voices: that of the author herself, that of Baba, an elderly Hausa woman talking about her life in response to Smith's questions, and that of the anthropologist M.G. Smith (the author's husband), who wrote the introduction and explanations. For some time, this book did not receive much recognition, perhaps because it was seen as the work of an anthropologist's wife, rather than of a *bona fide* anthropologist, perhaps because British anthropology at the time was uncomfortable with the genre. Several decades later, it was 'rediscovered', and in a Foreword to a later edition of the book, Hilda Kuper notes the importance of such a text which can confront 'the human condition . . . the existential reality' (Kuper 1981: 9).

In none of these works, however, does the anthropologist him- or herself appear other than fleetingly, and we learn little about them or their relationships with their subjects. Life histories or 'personal narratives' from the 1970s onwards, however, such as the work of Dumont, Freeman and Crapanzano discussed below, have tended to be much more self-conscious about the role of the ethnographer in their construction. Rabinow, writing of the ethnographic enterprise in general, notes that:

> The data we collect is doubly mediated, first by our own presence and then by the second order reflection we demand from our informants.
>
> (1977: 119)

As a result, 'a system of shared symbols must be developed if this process of object formation is to continue' (1977: 153).

Dumont, too, recognises the dialogue which is established in the doing of ethnography; in *The Headman and I* (1978) he asks 'Who or what was I for the Panare?' and notes the importance of understanding 'how they gaze at me' (1978: 3). Here, then, there is a suggestion that informants too have agency, and actively construct the encounter.

In his life history of Muli, an Indian transvestite (*Untouchable*, 1978, 1979) James Freeman suggests, following Schechner (1977), that taking a life history is rather like being a theatre director, and that it is important to understand this liminal phase of the creative process (1979: 399–400). He introduces a third possible actor, the assistant/ interpreter, maintaining that the book is the creation of three people – Muli, Freeman, and his assistant Hari, and acknowledges that the last played a crucial role. However, several other studies which record that translators, assistants or stenographers were present at interviews do not attribute a significant role to this third party (e.g. Griaule 1965 [1948], Lewis 1976 [1959], Crapanzano 1980).

Crapanzano describes his book, *Tuhami: Portrait of a Moroccan* (1980), as the life history of a Moroccan tilemaker married to a female jinn (*jinniyya*) named A'isha Qandisha. Crapanzano is not only concerned to reproduce some of Tuhami's words, many of which focus upon his sexuality and his relationship with the spirit, but also to discuss the encounter between the anthropologist and the informant:

> The life history, like the autobiography, presents the subject from his own perspective. It differs from autobiography in that it is an immediate response to a demand posed by an Other and carries

within it the expectations of that Other. It is, as it were, doubly edited: during the encounter itself and during the literary (re)-encounter.

(1980: 8)

Indeed, more of the book is taken up with Crapanzano's musings upon Tuhami and his relationship with him, than by Tuhami's own words. Crapanzano maintains that as the interlocutor he was an active participant in Tuhami's life history, even though he rarely appears directly in what the latter has to say, and anthropologist and informant do not appear to have met outside of the interview situation. Towards the end of the book, Crapanzano writes of himself as having become a 'curer': 'Tuhami and I negotiated our exchange into a therapeutic one' (1980: 133), and thus their encounter became 'an articulatory pivot around which he could spin out his fantasies in order to create himself as he desired' (1980: 140). Crapanzano also suggests that the ethnographer's presence inevitably produces a change of consciousness in the informant and, indeed, in the ethnographer himself (1980: 11). Such work presages the debate on authorial authority which was to be the hallmark of much of the anthropology of the latter part of the 1980s and early 1990s.

Similar concerns had, however, already been raised by feminists (see Caplan 1988, Mascia-Lees *et al.* 1989, Bell 1993), and it is not surprising that the 1980s also saw the publication of a large number of life histories by and about women, of which perhaps the most often cited is Marjorie Shostak's *Nisa: The Life and Words of a !Kung Woman* (1981). Shostak describes the book as 'my work but her story' (1981: 350). In a later article (1989), she notes that there are actually three distinct voices in the book: that of Nisa, that of the 'professional anthropologist' who writes the framing explanatory sections which introduce each chapter, and 'my own' which appears in the introduction and epilogue. Here Shostak explains what motivated this work: 'I hoped I would learn from the !Kung what it meant to be human' (1989: 238). Her further concerns as an American feminist seeking to understand what it meant to be a woman in another society are also clearly articulated, although this agenda was later to be criticised by some (e.g. Clifford 1986).

In writing the book about Nisa, Shostak decided to leave out her own questions and promptings (a decision for which she was taken to task by Crapanzano (1984), but this is a convention which has been followed in a number of life histories of women published during the 1980s. One such is Burgos-Debray's editing of *I, Rigoberta Menchu:*

An Indian Woman in Guatemala (1984), which is the life story of a politically active 23-year-old Quiche Indian recorded during the latter's stay in Paris. Burgos-Debray notes in the introduction that she decided to utilise a monological form and delete all her own questions: 'By doing so I became what I really was: Rigoberta's listener' (1984: xx). Another book which utilises a similar format is Mayra Atiya's *Khul Khaal: Five Egyptian Women Tell Their Stories* (1988). Atiya, an Egyptian woman brought up abroad, and not an anthropologist, gives as her reason for doing the work her desire to know more about the world from which her family had originated. She herself taped, transcribed and translated the accounts, but she says almost nothing about her relationship to the women; furthermore, their lives are not framed by her, but in an introduction written by an American anthropologist (Andrea Rugh) who has herself carried out field-work in Cairo.

A third book from this period which also uses a monological format is Mirza and Strobel's *Three Swahili Women: Life Stories from Mombasa, Kenya* (1989). The authors see life histories as very much part of a historical project: 'The explicitly historical use of personal narratives contrasts with the more common anthropological perspective of classical texts documenting the lives of African women' (Mirza and Strobel 1989: 2). Unusually, this book gives the real names (and photographs) of the subjects, who present very little of their personal lives or emotions, but rather talk about their public lives, especially the associations to which they belong. Mirza and Strobel are obviously acutely aware that their book will be read not only by a Western audience (for whom copious footnotes are provided at the end) but that it could, and indeed *should* be read by a local audience. At the end, Mirza took the transcripts back to Mombasa to gain the approval of the women before publication. Uniquely, the book was published in both English and Swahili (*Wanawake Watatu wa Kiswahili: Hadithi Kutoka Mombasa, Kenya* (1991)). The Swahili version is much shorter than the English version because of the omission of both the footnotes and much of the discussion in the introduction which considers theories of personal narratives and oral history; these, presumably, were thought unnecessary for a Swahili audience.

However, other writers of this period have explicitly decided upon a dialogical mode, such as Kevin Dwyer in his *Moroccan Dialogues: Anthropology in Question* (1982). Dwyer maintains that dialogue is essential in order to represent the presence of the anthropologist, and its important effects. He suggests that without this clear acknowledgement, anthropologists risk a 'contemplative stance': 'perpetuating dominance, and refusing to explore the subjectivity of the Self or to allow the challenges of the Other' (1982: 269). Dwyer argues that the text should be distorted as little as possible by 'cutting into bits and pieces', and that much of the work of interpretation of it should be done by the reader, whose participation he describes as 'crucial' (1982: 281).

Fatima Mernissi's book, *Le Maroc Raconté par ses Femmes* (1984), later published in English as *Doing Daily Battle: Interviews with Moroccan Women* (1988) also retains her own voice in interviews with eleven women who talk about their lives. In the introduction, Mernissi notes that she broke the first rule which had been taught her in universities in both France and America: 'I identified with the interviewee' (1984: 31). Mernissi's discussion of the role of the interviewer arises not only out of her epistemological and methodological problems, but also out of her feminist commitment: 'I left a space free for the personality of the interviewee to expand herself – that is why I renounced the control so beloved of researchers' (1984: 31, my translation).

In much recent writing of this genre, the term 'personal narratives' has been adopted in place of 'life histories' or 'biographies'. As the members of the Personal Narratives Group note, this genre can take many forms: diaries, journals, letters, life histories, biographies, autobiographies. What such diverse texts have in common is that:

> They recount a process of the construction of the self, the evolution of subjectivity . . . they also provide a vital entry point in interaction between the individual and society.
>
> (1989: 6)

Thus 'personal narratives' is a broad term, and allows us to subsume within it a range of literature which not only encompasses the narrative or story of a life, but which is 'personal' and focuses upon individuals.

Furthermore, such work need not concentrate upon a single individual - several anthropologists have chosen to utilise whole families as their subject, notably Oscar Lewis in his series of studies of poverty in Mexico and Puerto Rico during the 1940s and 1950s: *Five Families* (1976 [1959]), *La Vida* (1965), *A Death in the Sanchez Family* (1972 [1969]) and *The Children of Sanchez* (1983 [1961]). He looks at the family through the eyes of each of its members, focusing both on the everyday and on a special event or crisis which is related from differing perspectives. Lewis himself argued that, at that period, anthropologists had a new function to serve as reporters on peasants, the crucial feature of whose lives is their poverty, and that the life history is a suitable vehicle. In her introduction to a new edition of *Five Families*, Margaret Mead describes such work as a form of 'passionate ethnography' (1975: vii).

Recently, other anthropologists have also focused on families. Munson, for example, has written of the lives of several generations of a Moroccan family in *The House of Si Abd Allah* (1984), utilising the voices of two of its members: a male pedlar in Tangier, and his female cousin living in the United States. Like Crapanzano's Tuhami, the former has a close relationship with a *jnun*, but much of the focus of the book is Islam and its role in shaping interpretation. Trawick, too, has presented a study of Tamil culture through the life of one particular family with whom she lived in India. It features her conversations with its members, particularly her 'guru' and head of the family, Themozhiyar, who came and spent some time working with her in the USA (*Notes on Love in a Tamil Family*, 1990).

Another recent example of this genre is by Richard Werbner, who describes his book *Tears of the Dead* (1991), as the 'social biography' of an African family, arguing that there is a great lack of this kind of work in the literature on African family life. His work seeks to place life history and memory in a broad historical context, covering the memories of several generations of one Kalanga family, including the period of the war for independence in Zimbabwe and its even more violent aftermath, during which many of them lost their lives. Werbner uses a number of voices, which give different accounts of the history of the family, and he suggests that: 'Only through knowledge of the sensitive, sometimes petty, personal discourse among family members can we understand the moral argument resonating in each life history and between all life histories' (1991: 3).

WHY WRITE A PERSONAL NARRATIVE?

A fundamental question is why one should write a personal narrative at all, as opposed to any other form of anthropology. For some, as we have seen, the purpose of publishing such personal narratives may be less the story of an individual or family, than the utilisation of aspects of lives to illustrate wider social processes: Mintz is interested in historical change (1960), Lewis in the 'culture of poverty' (1976 [1959]), Munson in the role of Islam in shaping the way Moroccan Muslims interpret such phenomena as imperialism, nationalism, dependence and modernisation (1984: 3), Mernissi in how women survive, both in terms of earning their daily living in adverse circumstances and in terms of creating their own discourse which runs counter to that of

male hegemony (1984), and so forth. In similar vein, but geographi-
cally closer to the subjects of this book, is Mbilinyi's work with a
Tanzanian woman Kalindile which also focuses upon labour processes
and politics (1989). A second recent exploration of Tanzanian
women's lives through the vehicle of personal narratives is Ngaiza and
Koda's *Unsung Heroines: Women's Life Histories from Tanzania*
(1991: 10) which focuses on 'women's life struggles for social and
economic justice . . . the perspective of the struggling woman as an
oppressed and exploited member of society'. Here the personal
narrative also becomes an account of 'little heroes' or heroines, whose
lives might otherwise pass unrecognised by the wider world. Prell,
writing of Myerhoff's work on personal narratives, sees it as a 'witness
to invisible lives, lives seen and made important by the anthropologist'
(Prell 1989: 252).

Indeed, the subjects of personal narratives have frequently been
presented by their authors/editors as heroic, struggling against the
odds, coping with difficulties in life, manifesting admirable qualities
in spite of often problematic circumstances. Personal narratives
which portray their subjects in such a way include, for example,
Mintz's depiction of Taso (1960), or Myerhoff's of a Paiute shaman
(*Peyote Hunt*, 1974) and her informant Shmuel in *Number Our Days*
(1979).

Marks, reflecting on the writing of her book *Not Either an
Experimental Doll*, notes that: 'by intervening between the subject
and the reader in the presentation of the self, we grapple with the
central problem of human agency' (1989: 40). For this reason, she
suggests, we are much more comfortable dealing with successful than
unsuccessful people. Shostak, too, confesses that she was tempted to
leave out some of Nisa's less appealing traits and highlight only those
that ennobled her (1989).

Indeed, it is somewhat rarer to find writers presenting portraits of
'anti-heroes', although there are several notable examples. In his
study of a bisexual Untouchable in India, Freeman maintains that
'Muli was a failure, a deviant, neither a friend nor a person I admired'
(1979: 34). Crapanzano's portraits of two of his Moroccan male informants – Mohammed (Crapanzano 1977) and Tuhami (1980) are also
unflattering, while Munson describes his informant Al Haji
Mohammed as a failure in his career and marital life, widely viewed
as irresponsible and unstable, *jnun-* (spirit-) possessed (1984: 14).
Such pronouncements by anthropologists about their informants
raise a number of awkward questions.

Recent debates on authorial authority (e.g. Clifford and Marcus

1986) strike into the very heart of anthropology and its life-blood, ethnography, provoking issues about ethics, ideology and epistemology, and questioning the rationale for the existence of the discipline. In many respects, attempts to use experimental genres such as personal narratives do not solve such problems – they may even exacerbate them. Utilising the voice of an informant may risk accusations of false credentialism (see Bell and Nelson 1989). It also raises other issues: how representative is the informant? How do we deal with ownership and authorship, including such practical but crucial questions as whose name appears on the cover and who gets the royalties? What are the ethics of delving into the depths of someone's life and psyche? Can confidentiality and privacy be preserved?

As many have pointed out, it is false to suggest that by adopting such a genre, we overcome other problems fundamental to anthropology. One of these is the translation of meaning. Does the use of a personal narrative allow us more fully to represent 'the native's point of view' (see Geertz 1977)? Does it reduce the difference in power between the author and the subject (which is frequently also one of a privileged northerner and an underprivileged southerner)? We cannot assume a positive response to either of these questions. Yet, on the other hand, writing a personal narrative is perhaps worth a try because the prize is very great: that of some degree of transcendence of difference, of reaffirmation of common humanity. This sounds rather grandiose, but it can be thought of at the simplest level – the successful 'human interest' story in a newspaper or soap opera on television works when it enables the reader/viewer to identify with the subject, to find commonalities in their lives and their predicaments; in short, to empathise, even though differences between them may be profound. Some anthropologists have tackled these issues head-on: Shostak maintains that 'the most important ethical message regarding life histories is not a restriction but an obligation' (1989: 239), in other words, she sees it as necessary for such work to be written. Wolf, cutting through what she sees as diversionary debates, maintains: 'I do not speak for them but *about* them, even though I occasionally use their voices to tell my story' (1992: 11). She views knowledge as emancipatory, therefore ethnographers should not be silenced by suspicion of 'spurious polyvocality' (1992: 122).

TEXT AND GENRE: THE PRESENT WORK

In this book I seek to recognise and embrace the atypical specific nature of life history (Ngaiza and Koda 1991), as well as hoping that it reflects what many have termed the 'human condition' (Kuper 1981, Shostak 1989). This is done through telling the story of Mohammed's life and presenting something of his view of the world through his own words, those of members of his family, as well as through my own observations of him over this period.

A number of authors make the point that in writing experimental ethnographies and personal narratives, the conditions of their production are significant. This biographical study differs in several respects from many others in the anthropological literature. For one thing, Mohammed wrote, and thus selected topics himself, as well as responding to my questions on a variety of issues. It is true, of course, that he would not have kept the diary except at my behest. But as he became interested in the project, he came to regard it as 'our work', and it fitted well into his own interest in other people's doings.

It is also probably significant that the texts which we produced were unmediated. Because I had studied Swahili as part of my undergraduate degree, I was already reasonably fluent when I first began field-work. Thus I never used an interpreter, and, during my conversations with Mohammed, no other person was present apart from his wife Mwahadia on some occasions.

A third and final difference between this study and other anthropological personal narratives concerns the temporal depth of the texts, covering as they do a period of three decades, during which time a great many changes occurred in the lives of the informants and the anthropologist. During this time, Mohammed and Mwahadia gave birth to a large number of children, some of whom died in infancy, then they separated and eventually divorced; several of their children had children of their own both in and out of wedlock, and three of their adult children died. Mwahadia eventually re-married after a long period of living alone, but Mohammed remained single, although he continued to have sporadic affairs. During the period of the 1960s to the 1980s, Mohammed made an inadequate and intermittent living as a farmer, a sailor and a trader in raffia, but as his misfortunes mounted, he disposed of more and more of his only capital, coconut trees, until by the time of my visit in 1994, he had virtually none left. During the same period, he manifested great interest in spirit cults, communicating with his ancestral spirit in his dreams, but he never became possessed. It was only in 1990 that he finally joined a spirit possession cult, and by the time of my 1994 visit, was regularly possessed by his ancestral spirit, and had accepted responsibility for making offerings at the spirit's shrine.

From the four periods of fieldwork conducted on Mafia between the 1960s and the 1990s, there has accumulated a variety of texts. From the first and longest period of research, there are some twenty-eight spiral-bound handwritten notebooks which contain records of interviews, genealogies, censuses, reports of meetings, rituals, and texts dictated by informants. Mohammed and his family appear frequently in all of this data – as informants, as actors, and in some cases as commentators. Second, there are recordings of various rituals, particularly those connected with spirit possession, which Mohammed, among others, helped me to transcribe and understand. Third, for most of that first period of field-work, I too kept a daily diary, and in this Mohammed, Mwahadia and their children appear quite often, particularly as our relationship became closer.

In addition, Mohammed's own diary is scattered throughout my notebooks. The diary was written in Swahili, but in Arabic script (*Kiarabu*) which was difficult for me to read.[8] Mohammed would read out his entries which I would transliterate into Roman script (*Kizungu*). But as we worked, he often augmented his entries, or else I would ask questions and he would respond. On other occasions, he would be reminded of particular events and would recount them, and I would take notes.

The document which has now been extracted from various note-books and translated as the 'diary' thus contains an eclectic mix of material. In the first instance, there is the text of the diary as he wrote it. Mohammed's original entries themselves consist occasionally of personal matters, but more often of village gossip which he picked up on the shop verandahs where, like many village men, he would spend hours. Mohammed also regularly attended spirit possession rituals with their accompanying divination sessions at which the most personal aspects of people's lives are laid bare (see Chapter 9). In addition to his written entries, there are his often lengthy oral comments about what he had written, as well as stories or anecdotes which he remembered when we were transcribing the diary.

Another category of text produced by Mohammed himself is the letters which he wrote in the late 1960s when I had returned to Britain, with various of his sons acting as his amanuenses. They contain information about his family – birth and death of children, health of his wife Mwahadia, news from the village such as the state of the weather and crops, enquiries about my health, and often, hints about his state of poverty. Unfortunately, I did not keep copies of my own letters to him.

When I returned to the field for the second time in 1976, Mohammed and Mwahadia's marriage was breaking up, and each came to tell me their tale, while their daughter Subira, a teenager by this time, also came to talk to me about her feelings on the separation of her parents; I kept notes on all these conversations. In addition, since I had come on that occasion to make a film for the BBC, both Mohammed and Mwahadia were interviewed several times on camera, and there are transcriptions and translations of all of their interviews.[9] I became much closer to Mwahadia during this period, perhaps because I was by then married and with children, and in her eyes, had finally become an adult.

My third visit was in 1985, when Subira also acted as informant on spirit possession rituals which we attended together.[10] From this period, there are extensive notes on interviews with both Subira and Mohammed on spirit possession and with the two of them and Mwahadia on other matters.

Curiously, given his willingness to appear on camera in 1976, Mohammed had never wanted to be interviewed on tape, but in 1994, on the occasion of my fourth visit, he changed his mind, and most of our conversations were tape-recorded. A major part of these recordings was of Mohammed's life history, which he dictated over an intensive period of several days when we left the village to stay in the south of the island in order to work in private. In addition, he kept a diary for about a month of my two-month stay, and we transcribed it together, with frequent explanations from him, in the same way as we had done the 1966–7 diary. During that last visit, I again had lengthy conversations with both Mwahadia and Subira, on which I kept notes.

Thus some material concerning Mohammed is written or spoken by himself, some given by members of his family and some is jointly created by the two of us. In this way, authorship is multiple, although a large part of the text emanates from Mohammed himself.

In thinking about how to organise this disparate material, I considered a variety of schemata based on chronology, voice, and topic. In the end, I decided that none of these would work on its own, and my final ordering of the material incorporates all of them. In the first part of this book, consisting of a single chapter, Mohammed relates the story of his life, with occasional promptings from me, in a text which is largely monological, especially in the latter part when he speaks of the death of his eldest son. This text, which was recorded in 1994, is a chronological narrative of someone looking back over his life.

The second part of the book, entitled 'Mohammed as Ethnographer', utilises passages from Mohammed's diary of the 1960s which

I have arranged by topic. Here Mohammed is the observer, and my role is to provide explanations of what he writes about. This section of the book is thus very much a joint construction between the two of us. Two chapters (3 and 4) focus on everyday life in the village. In Chapter 3 he writes of making a living: agriculture, land rights, fishing, trading, the cultivation of cash crops and the weather; in the following chapter he is concerned with marriages, births, circumcisions and deaths, with their attendant rituals of Koranic readings (*hitima*) and *maulid*, feasts (*karamu*) and dances (*ngoma*). He does not omit, indeed he takes pains to include, quarrels over adultery and divorce, the wayward behaviour of children and parental curses, even mention of cases of incest.

The third part of the book, consisting of Chapters 5–7 and entitled 'Three Encounters', is a record of each of my three visits between the 1960s and the 1980s, and follows the lives of the main protagonists – Mohammed, his wife Mwahadia and their daughter Subira – utilising my notes or recordings of conversations and meetings with them. In each chapter, there is a section on each of the three main characters. In many instances, more than one version of the same event is given in different voices. The focus shifts slightly in each episode: in the first, it is on Mohammed, in the second on Mwahadia, and in the third on Subira.

Part IV of the book, entitled 'The Search for Knowledge', is concerned with ways of dealing with affliction. The first two chapters return to Mohammed's diary and consider the various ways in which he writes and speaks of misfortune: who or what causes it, what can be done to prevent it, and how to deal with it when it happens. Chapter 8 considers a variety of explanations for and treatment of affliction, as well as ways of preventing misfortune, while Chapter 9 is particularly concerned with spirits and spirit possession. In the final chapter of this section of the book, I write of my fourth encounter in 1994 with Mohammed, Mwahadia and Subira, and consider why, in the early 1990s, he became possessed by his ancestral spirit.

The book is framed by a Prologue and an Epilogue, both of which are in the form of a dialogue between anthropologist and informant. The Prologue seeks to do two things: to say something about the relationship between Mohammed and myself, and also to introduce the subject of Islamic belief and practice, which is an important back-drop to what follows. As will be seen, the Epilogue is also about the relationship between anthropologist and informant, but in addition shows spirit beliefs in practice. Taken together, the two illustrate what we may view either as one of the creative tensions in Swahili culture, that is between Islam and the propitiation of spirits, or as alternative ways of trying to ensure success in life. A theme which is common to both is Mohammed's desire that my work should go well; on other occasions, he would refer rather to 'our work', and he knew full well the important role he was playing here.

There are many variables to be handled in all of this material: different periods of time, different types of text with different authors, and varying content. For this reason, it is difficult to be as purist as some postmodern writers propose, i.e. to present the texts with little or no editing, because they would be incomprehensible and unreadable. On the other hand, to present them as seamless narratives would be to do violence to their heterogeneity. After much reflection, I have decided to attempt a middle way – to write a seamed narrative in which the ethnographer sews the seams and is seen to do so, but in which the people who are its sources – their voices and the occasions on which they speak – are made explicit.

Part I

A life history

Introduction

This first part of the book consists of Mohammed's life history as he gave it to me on tape in 1994. As already mentioned, he had previously been unwilling to be taped, but this time he agreed, only stipulating that we should leave the village to work in greater privacy.

Mohammed tells his story in more or less chronological order. He first talks about his early life, including his Koran school education and his circumcision. He then moves on to describe how he got married in spite of parental opposition, and how he and his wife made a living. He relates the birth of many children and the deaths of several of them: a daughter as a baby, a son as a youth, another daughter as a married woman and mother, and, most tragic of all in his eyes, his eldest son Seleman as an adult. In the first part of the chapter dealing with his early life, the text is dialogical, in that I prompted him with questions. However, some topics, such as his circumcision and his marriage, needed few questions from me, and during the final section, where he recounts the moving story of the death of his son and his own dramatic flight to Dar es Salaam to attend the funeral, I could only listen intently, and not speak.

Much of this text, then, is monological and it falls closer to the category of 'autobiography' than any other part of the book. It has needed very little editing: in the early part of the chapter, I have rearranged some sequences so that they follow on better. There are also a number of footnotes which either give further explanations, or forward references to later parts of the book where the issues are discussed in greater detail. The text is as faithful a rendition of his words as possible, although where the meaning might not be clear to the reader, I have added additional words in square brackets. Where text has been omitted, I have indicated by a series of dots.

2 Mohammed's story

FAMILY: 'I WILL TELL YOU WHAT YOU WANT TO KNOW'

M. So I will tell you what you want to know, and if it is not what you want you will tell me, won't you?

P. Yes, I will. I would like to go back a bit and ask you about your parents and your brothers and sisters. What sort of work did they do?

M. He cultivated fields of rice, cassava and millet jointly with mother. The work which she did on her own was to grow sweet potatoes, and cut raffia and dry it, plait it into strips, then sew them into mats and sell them. Father's work was to fish with a canoe, both with traps and lines. When the tide was low he would put out his fish traps (*madema*).

P. Was this to sell or just for the family to eat?

M. Both to sell and to eat. But fish then were not like now. Today you pay 70 shillings for a bit of fish which you would have got for 5 cents in those days, and fish for which you pay 100 shillings nowadays, was only l0 cents in those days. So his income from that was very small.

P. Did he fish on his own or with someone else?

M. When he used the canoe, it was with someone else. It wasn't his canoe, he was like a sailor on someone else's canoe. But if he said to someone, 'Let's go fishing', they would divide the catch, or if they sold it, they shared the money. They might get 50 cents each, or 30 cents.

And father had two problems – one was *mshipa* (aches and pains),[1] the other was that he had one swollen leg (*ugonjwa wa matende*, elephantiasis),[2] which was very heavy. My father was tall and dark (*mweusi*). He was the darkest of his four siblings, the others were rather browner (*wekundu*) such as Mwatika, the one who didn't have any children. On my father's side, they were four siblings, two males and two females.

P. Do you remember your grandparents?

M. Yes, I knew them. My mother's mother also had swollen legs, she walked like this [demonstrates], that is my maternal grandmother. She was called Mwasiti. My father's mother was called Mwahamisa.

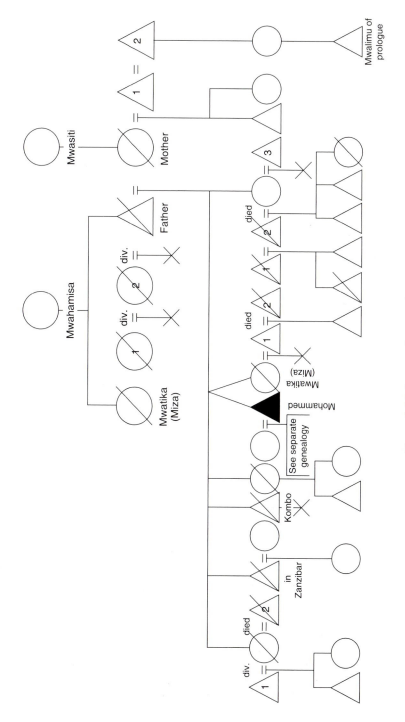

Figure 1 Mohammed's genealogy

P. And were all these people from Minazini?

M. Yes, except that my grandmother on my father's side, after being divorced, did not marry again but lived with her daughter Mwatika in a neighbouring village. My daughter Miza is called after that woman Mwatika, her father's sister, who was also nicknamed[3] Miza. And the mother of my grandmother was also called Miza.[4] My daughter's father's sister [i.e. his own sister] died before she was born, so I called my daughter after her [see genealogy].

P. How many children were you altogether?

M. I'll tell you, but don't forget that I haven't finished telling you about the kind of life that we led.

P. Yes, we can continue that. But first tell me about your siblings.

M. Do you mean from the same father and mother?

P. Let's start with them.

M. First I'll tell you about the children my mother had by her first husband. . . . She married a man from the Mrima coast of the mainland, [although] his home place (*bandari*, literally 'harbour') was Pemba Island. He came here, he arrived [disembarked] in Pwani [a neighbouring village]. But that man was not my father. She had a son by him and a daughter. I don't know whether their marriage ended in his death or in their divorce. I do know that their daughter married a man right here in Minazini and had one daughter by him. . . .

So then, my mother married another husband, and whether he died or divorced her I don't know, but she only had one child by him who was the mother of that man [who read the prayer for me – see Prologue]. She had other children as well, but perhaps that's enough of that branch. . . . So let's get back to my mother.

That man [second husband] divorced her, and she married again [this was Mohammed's father]. And she had our eldest sister, who married a man in Kirongwe by whom she had two children, but he divorced her, after which she married a man who lived where we had the *ziara* (Sufi ritual)[5] the other day but she did not have children by him before he died.

And then my [first] older brother was born. He lives in Zanzibar but you met him when he came here, and he also hosted you in Zanzibar when you went there [in 1966] – you sent me a letter to tell me so.

P. Did he ever marry?

M. Yes, he married the daughter of our father's younger brother and they had one daughter who is still alive. . . .

The third child of my parents was Kombo but although he got married he had bad luck and did not have any children.

Then mother had another girl and she in turn had two children; one died but the other is still alive and had a daughter who married here in Minazini.

Then my mother got pregnant again and bore twins, myself and my sister Miza. I was the first to come out, she came out after me. For that reason, the elders say that I am the older one.

P. Did your twin sister marry?

M. Yes, she married but did not have any children by her first husband. Then she married someone else from central Mafia and she had a son by him but he died. And it was there that she got problems with her eyes.

P. Yes, I remember her, she was blind when I knew her [in 1965–7].

M. And then my youngest sister Rabia was born. She married a man from Kisiwa village, and had one son by him, but the boy died when he was in Standard 2 [at school]. Then she had another child who now lives in Kisiwa. Later she married a man in Pwani village. She had by him a boy who still lives there, then another who lives in Minazini. Then she had a girl who died, after which her husband also died. She married again, this time in Minazini.

P. Did your mother have any other children?

M. No, she was the last one (*kifunga mimba*, lit. 'the closing of the womb').

P. So that you were seven children who had the same parents (*baba mmoja, mama mmoja*, lit. 'one father, one mother'). And did your father have other wives?

M. He married two other women. The first one, I wasn't born then – I only heard about it. He did not have children by her. He married again, I forget the woman's first name, and did not have children by her either and he divorced her. So my father had seven [live] children by one woman, and my mother had ten children by three husbands.

P. That's a lot.

M. And out of all those, everyone except two have now died. Myself and my youngest sister.

P. And when you are one of twins, what does that mean, actually?

M. All-powerful God decrees that either two seeds (lit. 'descendants', *dhuria*) enter [the womb] at the same time, or that one enters after the other. And what people say is that the older one is the one who comes out first.

P. So do twins resemble each other?

M. It happens, but it's a matter of chance. My sister and I were born of the same pregnancy, but she was a woman and I a man – so are we likely to resemble each other (*kulingana*)?

P. I don't know.

M. Isn't she a woman, and me a man, and aren't our bodies different? Sometimes you get twins of the same sex, like SK and AK, who have the same features. But other twins, [even of the same sex] like MJ and SJ look a bit different. The twins [my wife and I] had, one of whom was your *somo* (namesake),[6] were not identical, they had different features. Similarly your [other] *somo* and his brother, how do you see them?

P. They look different.

M. But even when they have the same face, one might be tall and the other short.

P. My sister has identical twins and I can't tell the difference between them. Even at school the teachers have problems.

M. Yes, [I heard a story that] the wife of a man who was a twin knew that she had a brother-in-law. But one time when they were all in Zanzibar, she actually thought that her husband's twin brother was her husband!

CHILDHOOD: 'THE ORIGIN OF MY LIFE AS I UNDERSTAND IT'

M. Are you ready? Then, Patricia, I will give you the origin of my life as I understand it. In those days, when I was still a child, I was busy with my work of fishing. Not with a canoe, or traps, it was just pastimes (*nyemo*) with my companions. You dig for sandworms, that is the bait (*chambo*),

Plate 1 'It was pastimes with my friends': boys playing on beach

and you put them on the end of the line, and off you go to the beach when the tide is low (*maji kukutu*). We would sit on the rocks, six or seven of us, and fish, using the sandworms as bait. The fish comes to eat the bait, and it gets caught, you pull it in, and you tie it to the stick which you have taken with you. And when you are fishing, it is a matter of luck. You might get fifteen fish, you might get twenty, you might only get five or three, or nothing at all. So that was what I used to do with my friends.

And that was how we went on until it was time for us to get married. So I got married, and carried on fishing as before.

P.   Let's go back a bit. You told me that you studied at Koran school?

M.   Yes, I studied with my father's younger brother. Neither my father nor mother sent me – I myself wanted to do it (*mapenzi yangu mwenyewe*). I went to Koran school with three of my friends but as it happened, I was better than they were. They were still reading the first chapter (*juzu*) when I was already on the third.

P.   How long did you study in Koran school?

M.   For three years. I was already grown up when I left, and had my ambitions (*tamaa*) and could make proper choices. And I could participate in dances, of which there were many – *mkwaju, kidatu, zuiya*,[7] the dances which young people like. So I managed to read four chapters [of the Koran] and then I left. I was called by an Arab man [who lived in the

Plate 2 'I managed to read three chapters': boy at Koran school copying out an excerpt from the holy book onto a board (*ubao*)

village] to work for him as a servant (*'boi'*). And I also worked as a sailor – I used to go back and forth to Zanzibar. The first trip was for a man called Saidi. But when I came back, one of my companions said 'Leave off travelling; get off this boat.'

P. Why was that?

M. Because you have a lot of difficulties when you travel like that. You go from here to Kwale Island, to Dar es Salaam, to Zanzibar [see Map, p. 33]. So I left that work. In any case, we didn't get on (*Kiswahili chetu mbalimbali*, lit. 'our Swahili was different'), so we said goodbye to each other. Then there was a small dhow (*mashua*) called *Shauri Gani* which belonged to two men, it was jointly owned by them. I went on one trip with them to the Rufiji Delta to buy bananas, but after that I stopped working on boats for a long time and did not accept offers to sail. [Later he started sailing again.] Then there was a big dhow (*jahazi*) of Chole Mjini [in the south of Mafia], it was the one which I told you about with the captain who gave me such trouble (see p. 41). So I stopped travelling in that [as well], and went to another one called Kubalii and the captain was called Saidi. [One time] we set off with only a small load, although that boat could take sixty bags of coconuts. We only had four sandbags as ballast and we really needed ten to keep the boat straight so we set off for Pwani to load some more bags. Anyway, it was a day when there was a very strong south wind (*kusi*), like today, and extremely cold. There were three of us. Well, the wind was really howling, and [we had only] those few bags

Plate 3 Dhow at anchor

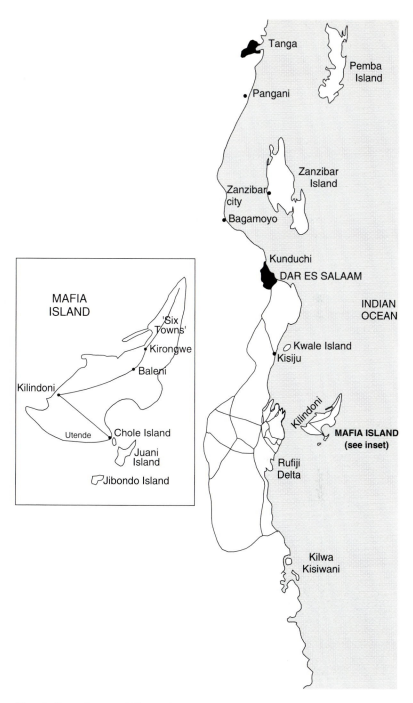

Map 1 Coastal area of Tanzania

of sand. I had with me a black pair of trousers and a loin-cloth (*shuka*), and I was wearing my underpants. Well, my *shuka* and my trousers were blown away! And then on that 21st day of the [lunar] month at 6 a.m. we were shipwrecked. The tide was coming in, and we swam after the boat – I was here and my companions were there [indicates] and we managed to get back into the boat and get it to the beach.

Another time we left [on a voyage] at 10 p.m. and we were shipwrecked; we didn't know where we were and one of my companions didn't make it to the beach, although he tried to swim.

P.   But you knew how to swim?

M.   You mean in those days when I was with my friends? Yes, I used to swim. I used to push with my legs and hold my head like this [he demonstrates and laughs]. If you swim in a river at spring tide (*bamvua*) you swim like this and you can swim under water with your eyes open.

CIRCUMCISION: 'THE THING THAT I WANTED'

P.   There is something else I have remembered I wanted to ask you. Do you remember the day when you entered the *jando* (circumcision ritual or lodge)?

M.   Yes, I was well aware by then (*fahamu yangu*, i.e. no longer a child).

P.   What was it like? Did they tell you beforehand, or were you taken by surprise?

M.   At the wedding of my twin sister they cooked porridge, buns (*mandazi*), rice cakes (*vitumbua*) and, I think, beans. Then afterwards, at around 2 p.m., they slaughtered the cow and cooked rice. And that feast was a joint feast [for the wedding] together with the circumcision ritual.

P.   And were you done [circumcised] on your own?

M.   There was another one, the son of my brother, but both of us were big, I bigger than him.

P.   Do you have any idea how old you were?

M.   Perhaps 15, or maybe 12.

P.   Were you already pubescent (*baleghe*)?

M.   Yes, I was.

P.   Really? Why did they wait so long? Or was that when they used to do it in those days?

M.   Oh, I wasn't the only one [to be circumcised so late].

P.   And were you secluded (*kualikwa*)[8] afterwards?

M.   Yes.

P.   And were you taught songs and so on?

M.   No, our *jando* was just in our house.

P.   And were you afraid?

Plate 4 'The thing that I wanted': child being carried to be circumcised

M. Should I be afraid of the thing that I wanted? The young women wanted me because I was already grown up. But I couldn't approach them (lit. 'say anything to them') because of my [uncircumcised] state.[9] I hadn't been circumcised. I hadn't been to the *jando*. For that reason I felt ashamed. I didn't want to be teased.

P. So, what was it like that day? Was it very painful?

M. Extremely. Give me a pencil – now, hold one end of it. I lay on top of one of my grandfathers, the father of my mother's half brother. My legs were stretched out like this on the bed, and the circumcisor (*fundi*, lit. 'expert') who had been called was sweating, his name was Ahmed, he was from Minazini, he was my classificatory father's younger brother, and he was related to me through his mother as well. He himself had wanted to do this, he had asked my father that I should be his initiate (*mwali*). They agreed. There was another old man who had married my grandmother and who lived there in our place, in the house where my deceased brother used to live. He was related to my father through their mother. He held me from the front and he put my hands like this. He held me like this [demonstrates] and that other man put his hands here. Yet in spite of all these people [restraining him], I was almost too much for them. And I could have broken away from them, but I kept quiet, I did not cry. I just kept saying '*Mtume, Mtume*' (Prophet).

　Here, take hold of the pencil again. This is my body [his penis], the other people were around me, and the circumciser caught hold of it. He cut a part of it, he let go, then he cut another part. He measures carefully, because it has to be the same [all round] and he knows that he can injure me if he cuts too much. So he measures carefully, and follows the cuts he has made on the top and bottom. He takes his knife and he cuts this side, then the other side.

P.   So does he cut you four times?

M.   He cuts like this, until it is clear (*peupe*), and cuts again [demonstrates on pencil] and then with his fingers he does like this [demonstrates]. He cuts again, he is careful because he knows that if he cuts there it will be very dangerous, and he throws it [the foreskin] away. And then blood begins to flow.

P.   Is there a lot of blood?

M.   A fair amount, not too much. [Your attendant] is told, 'Take him', and you are taken and put in a place like that and nowadays you are given tea, but in those days you were given a green coconut [to drink], into which they put medicine: 'Give it to him and let him drink it.' And in the same way, they go on with the rest, even if there are ten of them. Because they want you to urinate.

P.   They want you to do that quickly? And what about smearing medicine on?

M.   Yes, you are given that, and it is dressed (*kubandikwa*).

P.   And are these local medicines which are used?

M.   Yes, local ones.

So, for three days you are in what is called '*mogo ya kuiba*'.[10] At the first or second cock-crow, they take some cream of coconut (*tui*) and it is used to smear on the wound where the cut is, and then they put cotton on it. And when the time comes for the wound to be washed, all the bad stuff comes away with the cotton. And you are given water with which to clean it. Some people get salt water. In the old days, some children were even taken to the beach to be washed in the sea, but these days it's rare for sea water to be used.

And when it's all ready, they will have cooked sweet potatoes, or cassava, and when you've finished [washing the wound], they put some more medicine on it, and some more cotton. And then, if you're big, you just take care not to knock yourself. That goes on for seven days. So if you were circumcised on a Monday, then on the seventh day, that is the following Sunday, there is the first proper [i.e. public] *mogo* ceremony [which is actually the second *mogo*]. People come from all the different towns like Karibu and Kisiwa. They say to each other 'There is the *mogo* of our brother, let us go', and they come. Have you followed me so far? Have you heard [what I've said]? So you are bathed, and the swelling goes down, and more medicine is put on it, until you see that your body is quite clean, and the wound has healed.

Then they say that the children are ready to be brought out, so let us fix the day. It's usually around the fifteenth day. So they fix a day to have a meeting to arrange to bring the children out. And how do they plan? They say after the third *mogo* we should put rice out to dry, then we pound it on the next day, then we sleep over and the following day we hold the feast. And that's the end. So they slaughter a cow and cook rice. They cook gruel (*uji*) in the early morning, and serve the feast at around 1 p.m. The children are brought out and each parent takes his or her child. Then the whole thing is finished.

P. Did you get new clothes?

M. At that time, the Arab [the man for whom he worked] was still alive. He lived then where his grandson lives now. He used to laugh a lot. He had a beard. He said to me, 'Mohammed, I hear you are going into the circumcision lodge this year?' I said, 'Yes.' He said, 'Three days before you are due to come out, I want to be informed; if it is a Wednesday, let me know on the Monday.' He prepared a beautiful loin cloth (*shuka*), like a *kikoi* (a white one with a coloured border) and so I got that, as well as other clothes my parents had made for me – a vest, a shirt and a gown (*kanzu*). So there was none of that business of going round to other relatives like mother's brother or father's brother [to ask for help with the mandatory set of new clothes]; we didn't do that.

I stayed in that circumcision lodge for seven days, then another seven, then another, a total of twenty-one days, isn't it? And I came out on the twenty-third day.

P. And did you see your parents during the time you were inside?

M. I did not see them. But the circumciser gave [my mother] permission saying that if there were no men around, then you, sister-in-law, can take the food to the children. But [he told her], you mustn't go into the seclusion hut. You just put out your hand, and they will take it from you. During that time, all we wore were loin-cloths around our hips.

P. And you were happy that day when you came out?

M. My happiness began that day when I was cut. I had become like my friends. That very month, we danced *kidatu*, *zuiya*, *mkwaju*, aha! The girls were drawn to me, and I to them. And there wasn't a week in that month when I didn't meet with them, the girls, and then there was no stopping me (*moja kwa moja*) after that! First this one, then that one, then another, that was what it was like. My blood was hot, I was still young.

Plate 5 'All the dances young people like': youths at a dance wearing
a variety of hats

MARRIAGE: 'I MARRIED THE ONE WHOM I WANTED'

M. But I was late in getting married. Several of my younger brothers had
already got married before me. Because I married the person I wanted
myself. I wanted her myself, that Mwahadia.

P. Yes, you told me before. But you said your father didn't want her?

M. No, it was my mother [who didn't approve]. But to my father I said
that is the one I want. And if I die . . . anyone in the world [who dies]
gets a grave to himself, his father's grave is separate, his mother's grave
is separate.[11] Only if a woman who is pregnant dies are she and her child
buried in the same grave. So I married her.

But [prior to this] I said to my mother, 'The one whom I wanted to
marry you are refusing to marry me to her, so for this reason I am going
away.' And so I went off to Zanzibar and I stayed there for about two
months picking cloves, then I came back. I even got [the things for] the
trousseau (*sanduku*) ready there. And then I came back here.

While I was there I had been sent a letter, which said that there was a
certain woman [i.e. Mwahadia] I should come and marry. Her period of
seclusion [*edda* – after widowhood or divorce] had finished, and people
were arranging a marriage for her that she didn't want. [The letter said]
'Come.' But the man who had been given the letter did not give it to
me. I met him in Zanzibar City and he said he had a letter for me. He kept

saying that he would bring it to me, he would bring it, [right up to the time] I came back here, but I never did receive the letter.

When I came back here, I went to say a final farewell to my mother. And I told her that on my trip to Zanzibar I had made some friends and that one of my friends wanted us to go together to Pemba to pick cloves. At that time, the price of a *pishi* (measure of cloves) was 1 shilling. So if we picked 30 *pishi*, we would each get 15 shillings. And he had told my [classificatory] brother that we should do this as a team, and split each day's wages. So we had agreed on that. I told my mother: 'I have got friends there. But I am not going to tell you their names, nor the place in which they live. And when I go, I won't even tell which dhow I'm going on, nor from which village I'm leaving. Nor will I even write you a letter to say that I'm in such and such a place. Because, mother, you don't care for me and so for this reason, I am going away again, because the one I wanted [to marry] you didn't want.'

So my mother talked to herself all night and all day, and she said to herself: 'Mohammed will be lost to me.' Meanwhile, my older brother was getting engaged in Pwani village. So [that day] I went to the meadow land where my [classificatory] father said to me, 'Mohammed'. 'Yes?' 'Don't feel you have to go off (*kutoroka*). Nor that you have to lose yourself. Your father has gone to Pwani to arrange the betrothal of your brother. He is sleeping there tonight. When he gets back tomorrow, your father's younger brother will arrange your betrothal. It will be to that fiancée whom you want, that is who it will be.' So that was the end of the matter.

P.   They agreed?

M.   Yes. And they all came to the wedding.

P.   Was it a big wedding with lots of celebrations?

M.   It was a moderate affair.[12]

MARRIED LIFE AND MAKING A LIVING: 'IN THOSE DAYS FOOD WAS CHEAP'

P.   So what is a man's work, and what are his rights if he is married?

M.   The answer is that he has to take care of the woman, and make sure that she obeys his authority. For example, a woman says to her husband that she wants to go home to visit her family. She asks her husband [and he says] 'Go' or 'Don't go.' Suppose she doesn't take any notice of the fact that you have said she shouldn't go. 'I want to go to my place! I absolutely have the right to go (*ni kitu sheria hasa*) – my mother is sick.' [The husband says] 'Don't go.' [She replies] 'I will go.' Her husband replies, 'Even if your mother is dead a woman does not have the right to go.' Because even if her father dies, or her mother or her sister, if her husband is not there [to ask his permission], the *sheria* (law)[13] forbids her to go. She should not go until he comes back home and she says, '*Bwana*, I have got news that so and so is dead' [and he either says] 'Go to the funeral' or 'Don't go, I will go myself.'

P.   But what exactly is the man's job?

M.   A man has the right to do many kinds of work. First of all, if she is married, a woman doesn't have any work at all on her own account; all the work she does is done for the man. She washes his clothes and says 'Ready', she prepares food, she gets a coconut and grates it, and cooks [the rice] and makes the curry. And he gets on with his own things, or he rests. And when the food is served, he might expect her to go and eat on her own, or he might say: 'Let us eat together.' Afterwards when the food has been eaten, she should wash the dishes, and fetch water, and warm it for the bath, and put it in the bathroom and tell her husband: 'The water is ready for your bath.' And at bedtime she should make the bed for him to sleep on.[14]

P.   But what rights (*haki*) do women have?

M.   To do what her husband tells her. Those jobs should be done by women, otherwise it's wrong (*kosa*).

P.   So are you saying that women do not have any rights?

M.   Do you mean in regard to work?

P.   No, I mean doesn't the law say that clothes, food and so on is the responsibility of the husband? So suppose he doesn't do that? What can the woman do?

M.   She has the right to go and make a report [to the elders or to the Village Development Committee] 'Today my husband didn't fulfil his usual responsibilities.' Her husband may reply: 'She didn't fetch water for me today, she didn't cook for me today, she didn't give me drinking water, she didn't put water in the bathroom for me to bath, she didn't make the bed for me to sleep on. I don't know why her behaviour is like this to me, her husband.' And at this point, it needs someone who knows the law, who is well-versed in it, not someone like me who isn't. It could be that I might say something which is not what the law says because I don't know it.

At that time [when he got married], there was another Arab who lived in Minazini and he used to buy up coconuts. So I used to do two things [for him] – one was to husk them (*kufua*), the other was to carry them to his place where we would put them into sacks. In those days, in the evening [at the end of the day's work] each one got his dues – it was 50 cents for 50 coconuts, or 1 shilling for 100, 2 shillings for 200. But in those days food was cheap: for 1 shilling you could buy rice or millet for the day, your fish for the curry, your cigarettes, and you'd still have some money left over. Not like things are today. At that time, if you bought paddy for 1 shilling you'd get three measures, no, five.

And then I would cultivate, together with my wife. We used to get between three and seven sacks of rice [each year], and a sack of millet or even one and a half sacks. There was one year we got seven and a half bags [of rice] in the bush field (*konde*) and two and a half bags of sesame (*ufuta*), and we also got millet, I can't remember exactly how much. And in the meadow field (*dawe*)[15] we also got rice, another two sacks. The total was nine and a half bags of rice.

At that time, we were also bringing up the child of my deceased younger brother[16] so I started thinking about what work I could do to earn some cash. I started cutting raffia palm fronds (*ukindu*) and bringing them to the house. My wife would dry them. I would go again and get two more loads – one I would bring home, one leave in the bush. Sometimes I would get three loads in one day. And the next day, she would come with me, and she too would cut raffia. We would take what we could carry, and some might be left again.

So I would consult with my friends, other young men like me who were also cutting raffia and we would decide to rent a *mashua* and take our raffia to Zanzibar. Or a captain would say to us, 'Come on, let's go to Zanzibar.' But in those days there was no decent price for raffia. For three or six or eight loads, you'd only get 30 shillings for each. Anyway, I'd go there and sell it, and buy clothes for myself and for her and eight or ten days later, I'd be back. I did that once, and then a second time. I started doing it several times a year, when I wasn't cultivating.

One time I made an effort [to get a load together] and I went on a trip aboard a dhow called *Kicheko*. I think it was the time when you were here [during the 1960s]. And I went to Dar es Salaam. But the then Village Chairman, now deceased, told me: 'Mohammed, because of those things that are being done in that dhow, you [had better] get out of it.' It was to do with a *mazingera* spell[17] and because the captain was a man who 'ate' [other people's] money but still did not get rich enough [to satisfy himself]. So the owner put another captain there instead who paid all the people properly. But when that first captain left, he put a spell on [the boat] because of being sacked; he wanted that he should be the one to do the work [of being captain]. So I only went on one trip [in that boat] because of the *mazingera* witchcraft.

PARENTHOOD: 'HAVING CHILDREN IS LIKE PLANTING A COCONUT TREE'

M. And God granted to us that we had children.

P. So what in your opinion is the meaning of having children and what is the benefit (*faida*) of it?

M. Tell me again?

P. Yesterday we talked about having children, you said children were wealth, that they were of great benefit. Now I ask you, when you started having children, were you pleased?

M. I was pleased.

P. Why was that?

M. You mean the kernel (*kiini*) of it? How a child gets born?

P. I mean what is the benefit of having children, according to your customs?

M. I will tell you how children get born, isn't that what you want? You marry a girl – I marry so and so. She becomes my wife and I her husband. And this has been since the time of our ancestors. And that woman is my property, to use her at any time. And that woman at any time can say [to her husband] '*Bwana*, let's make love (*fanya jambo la starehe*), I feel a great desire.' And that urge will not leave her unless she has been penetrated. So the man's penis is held by the woman for a short time when they are together.

As far as birth is concerned, it happens after seven months or nine months, which is the proper time for a child to be born, either a male or female child. And you realise that you have got a child. And they [the relatives] rejoice, saying, 'Our child has had a child.' And my siblings' children will say, 'Our mother's brother has had a male child', or 'Our mother's brother has had a female child.' So everyone on your father's side rejoices, and on your mother's side as well, that so and so has had a child.

Having a child is like planting a coconut tree. When you have planted it, it [eventually] starts bearing nuts. And you can either use the green coconuts, or get the ripe coconuts and make food, or else sell them and use the money to buy food, to get cash. Isn't that what happens?

P. Yes.

M. And that child, once it gets a bit bigger, you can send it on errands, 'Go and fetch me some water.' The child goes. And when it brings it you give thanks, 'Praise be to God, who has given me a child.' Or perhaps you are not able to go somewhere because of your health, you tell your child to take you. And if it's a boy, he can carry you. And when he's big, he can look after himself by going to the beach, and getting something to sell. Or he can go and work with coconuts and get me money to buy food. [You'll say to him] '*Baba* (lit. 'father'), go and get me some cigarettes. Buy me a couple of cigarettes.' Or if it's a woman and she smokes she'll say [to her child] 'Go and buy me two or three cigarettes', or if she chews

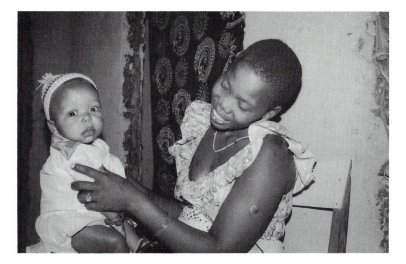

Plate 6 'And God granted that we had children': young mother with her baby son

tobacco, 'Go and buy me some tobacco.' And at such a time you'll say, 'God be praised and look after my child. Today s/he has given me this, tomorrow let them give me that.' So that is what birth is about, that is the profit of giving birth.

CHILDREN AND GRANDCHILDREN: 'MY RELATIVES ARE MY WEALTH, MY RELATIVES ARE MY CHILDREN'

M. My first child was a girl who was born dead. Then the next was Seleman. He went to primary school in Minazini, and then in Kirongwe, but he failed his Standard 7 [to enter secondary school]. However, he had a friend in Kirongwe who first helped him to get work in a hotel . . . , and so started him on his career. Seleman had a friend from Arusha when he first worked there but they both changed their jobs and went to Arusha together. [While he was there], one evening at about 5 p.m. he saw some kind of animal, and ran away fast, until he reached the hotel exhausted and fell down, injuring his knee. God granted that the animal stayed back and then it went away.

It was Seleman's job to sell things and his accounts were always OK but his friend's were short because he was stealing. Seleman wanted to get out of this situation and so he claimed that his parents were sick and he had to go home. But actually he went to Dar and got a job at a hotel

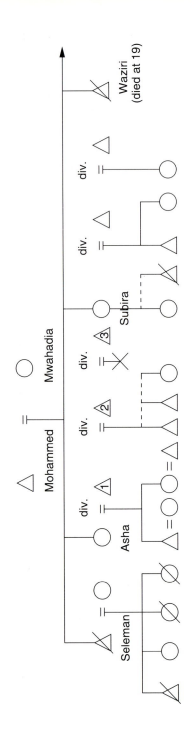
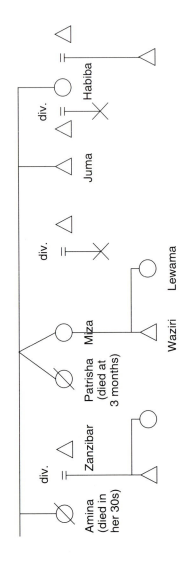

Figure 2 Mohammed's and Mwahadia's children and grandchildren, 1994

where he worked until he died. [I show him a photograph of Seleman and his family which I took in Dar in 1985.]

That is Tatu, the youngest. She was eaten by witchcraft (*uchawi*). Witches (*wanga*) came and took her away in her sleep. She never spoke and she died at the age of 5. Her father took her to many hospitals, but she did not get better. He also used local medicine (*dawa ya kienyeji*). Although she used to walk on her own, she never started speaking. . . .

Seleman's first child was a boy called after his father's brother, but he was born sick. His mother was bewitched in pregnancy and he died at 3 months. Their second child . . . is now about 11 and lives with her mother. . . . Seleman and his wife then had another child – a girl – who died at the age of 2 after the death of her father, but before that of Tatu.[18]

Our next child was Asha who has been married several times. She first married in Pwani village and had two children, a boy and a girl. Both are now married and live in Dar, and the girl has a child of her own. Then she [Asha] got divorced and re-married in the south of the island, where she had a boy. That marriage did not last, and she was divorced again. Her third husband was a Minazini man. She got sick and thought it was because her co-wife had sent a spirit (*shaitani*) after her. She came home and had some treatment from shamans (*waganga*) who told her to go back to her husband and she was given some medicine to put in her clothes. But she did not want to go back to her husband. She said, 'My heart is heavy [at the prospect].' So she got divorced. Then she 'went about' (*kutembea*) and got pregnant and had two more children, a boy called after me, then a girl called after my deceased twin sister. And she hasn't married [again] to this day. No one has come along to seek her hand. She and her children live with me.

The third child was Subira. Before she was married she first had a child on her own called Pingu who lives with Mwahadia (see Chapter 6). Then she married in Kirongwe village and had two more children – a boy and a girl. Then she got divorced and got a child on her own, but the child was born dead. She married again in Baleni village and had a daughter who is now being brought up by her father's mother's sister. [The Baleni marriage also did not last.] Subira now lives in Kilindoni, but she came here the other day to visit. Sometimes the child she had with the Kirongwe husband comes and stays with her and her eldest child [by that marriage] is also there [in Kirongwe]. She has no husband and depends on herself (*anajitegemea*).

Next we had Waziri who died at sea [in the early 1980s]. He had studied up to Standard 7 in Minazini. He was taking coconuts to Dar es Salaam to sell and his brother had fixed a job for him there. He and all the other people in that *mashua* died. It was a very heavy monsoon (*masika*) and they were travelling at night, having been advised not to go during the day because of the wind. There had been a quarrel between the owner of the ship and someone else and the latter had sent a spirit to chase the boat, and the owner died as well. At the time when Waziri died, there were nine of them in the boat, and not one of them was saved. They had been warned not to set off because of the wind.

I looked for them everywhere, but their bodies were never recovered. The vessel turned up nine days later in Zanzibar. So finally we did the third-day Koranic reading (*hitima ya tatu*) and then we did the forty-day ceremony (*arobaini*) for them.[19]

The next child was Amina. She also studied up to Standard 7, then she had a child by herself; she got pregnant in Kirongwe where she was at school. Then she married her father's sister's son who was a soldier in Zanzibar. She had two children by him, one of each sex. He had another wife. She got divorced and came home. She would go back to Zanzibar to see her children, and the second time she went she had stomach problems and died in hospital. I did not attend her funeral but her mother went.

Mwahadia's sixth and seventh pregnancies were miscarriages. Then you [PC] came and Mwahadia said she would give her next daughter to you. She got pregnant and had girl twins, but the one with your name died at 3 months. The other is Miza. She studied up to Standard 7 but it

Plate 7 Hoisting the sail of a *mashua* prior to sailing

doesn't seem to have done her much good. She has had two children by herself [i.e. without being married]. Her first child is called Waziri, her second Lawama. Then she married a relative of the man who had married her sister Subira. She got divorced – they had no children. Then she went off to Dar with a girlfriend of hers from Pwani. She stayed with a relative there and used to make raffia covers for trays (*makawa*). She stayed for four months then returned. Now she and her two children live with me.

The ninth child and third son is Juma. He lives in a hut near to his mother. He studied up to Standard 7 but he was only there in name, he didn't really attend much.

The youngest child is Habiba. She also studied up to Standard 7 and she did better, she has some education. Then she got engaged. Her fiancé wanted her, but his father did not. He slept with her but did not marry her. So she married a man from another village whom she wanted but he divorced her because of the quarrels caused by her first boyfriend. The ex-fiancé still wanted to marry her but his father still refused. Meanwhile she had a child by him. They went to the Sheikh and he said he could not marry them without my consent. But I said that while I had no objection myself, I would not give my consent unless the boy's father agreed as well because otherwise if one of them were to get sick, it would all fall on me, whether to hire a vehicle, or go to the shamans.[20] So they went to the Magistrate in Kirongwe and he said they could get married. He gave them a letter to the Sheikh and told them to go and get married. No one was there except one relative.

The very last pregnancy [of Mwahadia] was a premature birth, a girl, who was born dead (see Chapter 6).

P. I have another question which is also to do with birth. You mentioned that some of your daughters have had children on their own: Subira, Asha and Miza. Three of them.

M. And Habiba the fourth. And even the one who died, Amina, also had a child [outside of marriage], which is still alive, but in Zanzibar, and is already big.

P. Does that happen often?

M. Since olden times. Especially in Kirongwe and the south, many men have lovers.

P. And what do you say? How do you see such things?

M. It is shameful (*fedheha*), shameful and disgraceful (*aibu*) for them to do such things. To sleep with a man who is not her husband, that God should grant her to do such a thing and to have a child which depends on her alone, which is hers alone. To have only a mother, not a father. But these things don't happen only to me [i.e. to his children] – it is common these days. I am not the only one to feel shame.

Plate 8 'My relatives are my wealth, my relatives are my children': old woman with great-grandchild

P. Yes, I know. Even the children of Sheikhs. Supppose that your daughter comes to you and says, or perhaps she can't say but you know anyway, that she is pregnant, and she hasn't got a husband, what do you say to her?

M. I don't say anything. She is the one who knows that it happened.

P. But won't you see her stomach?

M. And by that time, hasn't she already been caught (*kunaswa*)? What can I do to her?

P. You can't do anything. But you have grandchildren who have fathers, and some who don't. Is there any difference for you?

M. All of them are my property, my children. I don't dislike this one or that, they are all the same to me. My relatives are my wealth, my relatives are my children [and their children].

Then I divorced Mwahadia. I gave her her formal divorce (*kipande*), and she stayed thirteen years without marrying again. [Altogether] I divorced her three times – the first two times I recalled her, when our son Seleman tried to reconcile us (see Chapter 6). [Since divorcing her finally] I got engaged once but it didn't work out, the one I wanted didn't want me.

ASHA'S ILLNESS: 'OUR CHILD IS BEING EATEN'

P. You told me before that when Seleman died, you sold a cow. Were those cows your property or shared?

M. It was just one cow. Our daughter Asha was ill, at that time she was the wife of someone here in the village. She got sick, Asha, and it was the cultivation season. Around that time, Seleman had come to Mafia with his wife and child. So we told him about her trouble. And we decided to bring her back from her husband's place. Seleman himself carried her, and he had a friend to help him.

After taking her back home [to her father's house], Seleman said, 'Let's go to a diviner.' And so AS was called, together with two other shamans all of whom had possessory spirits[21]. . . . So they came along to my house at night to divine for her. They all came to look at her, and they made themselves possessed. When they were possessed, they said, 'Our child is being eaten, but we do not know why. We do not know the people (*makongwe*) who have done this. This creature (*kiumbe*, i.e. the patient)[22] met with a spirit (*jini*) [by chance], it was not sent to her. The jinn, which was on its travels, met up with her on the path.' They said that in her goings around she had met up with a spirit whose area it was. It was not as if she had been sent a spirit, it was just that they happened to meet and the bad smell (*vumba*) of the spirit got her. So we said, 'You know what to do, shaman (*utaratibu wewe mganga*)' [and he replied] 'We say that she should be treated (*agange*).' So they said they would treat her with their own spirits.

[And we asked] 'Yes, and what will we have to pay? An offering tray (*chano*)?' But they did not agree that it should be only a tray, [they said that] it had to be a cow, because it would be a big struggle (*vita vikubwa*), since they were trying to get rid of this spirit. So the family agreed to pay a cow when she was well enough to get out of bed. We agreed, and they agreed. But who was the one who contributed the most? It was Seleman.

The second day the shaman Kombo and his colleagues lit their incense burner (*kiteso*) and said to the spirits: 'This child of Mohammed has been taken hold of by a spirit (*jini*), now we entrust the curing to you, fight with it and send it away. If she gets better, you will get a cow or you will get money to the value of a cow.' So they treated her, but it was mostly Kombo who did so. He would come in the morning, he would come in the afternoon; if she had a trouble, he would come, he would fetch her medicine and tell us to grind it, and he would put it on her. Until all-merciful God brought blessing and she got better.

P.   But that business of selling the cow, was it you or she who sold it?

M.   I am coming to that. So she got better and we said that it was time for her to go to her husband. She refused. 'I won't go back to him.' 'Why won't you go?' 'My heart is heavy' (*Roho yangu nzito*, lit. 'my soul is heavy'). I can't do it (*nimeshindwa*). I won't go, my heart is heavy.' So can I say to her, 'You must go'? Suppose something were to happen? Whose responsibility would that be?

So she said she wouldn't go. We informed the husband. 'Do you hear what your wife says?' [He replied] 'I cannot do anything because she has said her heart is heavy, and if anything happens, whose fault would it be? So I am defeated. Even if I invoke the law (*sheria*)[23] and make her go back, if something bad were to happen, it would be as if I had caused it. So for that reason I will divorce her.'

By this time, as I said, she was better, and those people [the shamans] wanted their cow. And it was up to me and Mwahadia and Seleman to find that cow. But it was especially the responsibility of myself and Mwahadia [as her parents]. We had to get money to buy it.

P.   And where did you get this money?

M.   Wait a bit. So Seleman had come with money from Dar to buy a cow to get her treated. We did not know that he had brought it until he came and said 'Well, folks, we have to fulfil our promise. The girl is better. We have to give our cow.'

I said to Seleman: 'I don't have 5 cents. And her mother is in the same state.' But Seleman said, 'I have money which I brought with me with the purpose of buying a cow for our ancestral spirit.'[24]

I said, 'OK but we will divide [the cost] into three parts: one mine, one your mother's and one yours, so that we find a way of paying you back the money. You will give the money and we will support you (*kuunga mkono*). 'Her mother said, 'I am not ready' [i.e. she could not contribute]. I told Seleman: 'In the morning let's go to the cow pen.' And [I told him] 'This young cow (*mbuguma*) I am selling for 2,500 shillings , and 1,250 shillings is yours, 1,250 shillings is mine. So this animal will be jointly owned [by the two of us], and this will be a way of paying you back for the money which you have paid out to treat your sister. And when it gets a calf it will be ours jointly. It will go on like this for the rest of my life, and I will tell your brothers and sisters this. If I die, they will know that this cow is jointly owned by Seleman and myself, and what the reason is for giving part to him.' And it [that cow] did have one calf while we owned it jointly.

SELEMAN'S ILLNESS AND DEATH: 'ALL-MERCIFUL GOD ALLOWED ME TO BE IN TIME TO BURY HIM'

Later, Seleman himself became ill and because of this he came [again] to Mafia, because he had been told that the ancestry of his father had caught hold of him – that is our ancestral spirit – and that he should take an offering tray [to placate it]. He bought the appropriate things – dates, raisins, cinnamon, and so on [see Chapter 10] – and brought them here. He asked me how many chickens were needed. I said two would be enough. So we bought the chickens. Then we had to plan a day. What day should it be? We decided on a Wednesday.

Seleman said that because of his health he would not be able to go himself, and that we elders should go. So we went [to the spirit shrine] and got them to intercede (*kuwasalisha*) and came back.

And then it was the end of the month's leave that he had been given from work. And he said to us, 'Parents, my [financial] state is poor, I am ill, and you know the state of my children and so I will take one of our [jointly owned] cows and sell it, so that I get some money to use.'

I asked him which one he would sell. Would he sell the cow or its calf? He said he would sell the calf. So he sold the calf for just 2,000 shillings. It had just been weaned. So he sold it, but the young fellow who bought it wasn't able to come up with the money [immediately], so Seleman said to me that the money should be sent to him in Dar. He would send someone for it and it would reach him. And that is what happened. Someone took the money and later we got his letter saying that he had received it.

P. And you also told me that you had been to Dar es Salaam subsequently, three or four times.

M. . . . I went three times when he was ill.

P. And you said you had to sell some of your coconut trees?

M. That's right, I sold them with Mwahadia when he was ill. . . . I had no one to help me, and of the deceased Seleman and Waziri, Waziri was the first to die, but Seleman was the one who used to help – food, money, that was how it was. So I thought it was better to sell trees or a donkey when my son was ill. If I had no money what was I to do?

P. Oh, you had to sell.

M. Who would give money to me? I had to sell what was mine, so that I could go and see my sick child, so I sold my property, but it turned out that he died and all-merciful God allowed me to be in time to bury him. Did you know that he spent two months (sixty days) in hospital? and had sixty injections – isn't that two months?

P. Poor thing.

M. One time when I went with Mwahadia she sold some coconuts and so did I. So I went to Dar for several days, and then I had to come back. Doesn't all of that cost? And then I sold some more to go back again – that time I went by boat. Everything costs – going and coming and eating there. Morning, afternoon and evening – it all costs. And it's not as if there they just say, 'Give me 500 shillings *bwana*' [they ask for much more for everything]. Nor do I have a father or mother there whom I can ask for money. [And Dar] It's not my place. There isn't anyone there to help me (*kuunga mkono*).

THE DEATH OF SELEMAN AND MOHAMMED'S JOURNEY TO DAR ES SALAAM

But soon after [Seleman had returned to Dar], we got a phone call saying that Seleman Mohammed had died. It was on a Thursday, and he was to be buried on the next day, Friday, after the midday prayer. We in Minazini didn't know about this but people here [in Kilindoni] [had heard and they] got together to write a letter and sent it. [Someone said] 'Friends (*Jamaa*)!' 'Yes? (*Naam*)'. 'Our brother who was related to us has died, our friend.' And there was one girl called Mwachum in Kilindoni. She used to work in the same hotel as Seleman . . . and it was none other than he who had got her that job. [She said] 'Let us club together and go to Dar to bury our brother Seleman, whom we all knew was a quiet man, a gentle man (*mpole, mtaratibu*), we know how we used to be with him.' But each of them said they didn't have the means to go. 'So let us go to the Area Commissioner to get a motor car, and let us go to the airport – tomorrow's plane leaves at 7 a.m. Let us send word to his father. It is possible that he can get to Dar to bury his child. It would be a good thing to do (*jambo la maana*).' So they went and got permission and were told that they could have a vehicle if they put petrol in it themselves. Then they went to the plane company ticket clerk: 'We have been bereaved. Our brother in Dar has died. We got a phone call that he died, and that his funeral is tomorrow. For this reason, we have already got a car, and now we ask, whether there is a place for his father on the plane tomorrow so that he can go and bury his child? Perhaps two places, so that the mother can go too.' He replied that there was only one place left. They said, 'That is enough, his father can go.'

So then someone had to come to fetch me, because I still didn't know about this. They asked each other, 'Do you know where his place is?' 'I don't know', 'I don't know.' 'Then let us send his sister's son to give him the news, perhaps he doesn't even know about it yet.'

So when the news came, Patricia, I didn't have 5 cents on me. So I thought I will sell our joint property [the cow] and use my half. It was 4.30 in the morning, and I went around asking for money. I went to one of the shop-keepers: 'Please, *bwana*, lend me 3,000 shillings. I want to go to Dar to bury my child Seleman.' He said, 'I do not have such money. And I doubt if today you will find anyone to lend it to you, given the way you and his mother are, to go to Dar and bury your son.' He said that I would have to sell him something. So I said that I had a cow which I would sell him, that black one called Akiba Yangu (lit. my treasure). I said I wanted 5,000 shillings, and we bargained and bargained until we settled on 4,400 shillings.

P.   And was this a big one or a small one?

M.   It was that young cow (*mbuguma*) which had already had one calf.

P.   So he got it very cheaply?

M.   Very cheaply. I was hoping for at least 6,000 shillings. But I was caught – if I stuck out for the price I wanted, there would be a delay. So I agreed to the 4,400 shillings and sold it to him.

P.   You didn't have much alternative.

M.   That's right. So then I was ready. I called my daughter Habiba and I said to her: 'You are a witness, I have sold this cow for 4,400 shillings , and half is mine and half belongs to your deceased brother. Now I am leaving. Here is 1,200 shillings which you and your mother will use. When your mother comes, tell her that your brother has died, and that I have gone in a vehicle to catch the plane to go and bury him. And that I have sold our cow, the one he and I owned jointly. And this 1,200 shillings is because people will gather here tomorrow, and it will help you to buy sugar and food because people will want to sleep over here.'

[She replied] 'Very well.' So I gave her the money with HS as witness and also another man who forgave me the witness fees, and a third man, who was also a witness. And I went off with the remaining 3,000 shillings .

So off we went, we kept going until the vehicle in which we were travelling got stuck. And I thought, 'God isn't going to grant that I get to Kilindoni in time to catch the plane.' We got stuck, once, then again; it was weather like we are having now, with rain. The pot holes [in the road] were full of water. So at 6 a.m. we reached that corner where you and I turned off the other day to go to AK's house. There tea was made for us very quickly and I was told 'Have a bath, uncle (*mjomba*).' 'I can't have a bath, I won't be in time. I want to be there at 7 a.m., not leaving here only at that time. If the plane comes, it will leave without me.'

But God delayed the plane. It did not come. The phone lines got busy. They said it would come in at 8 a.m. 'Alright, we have time to go and have tea.' [But I replied] 'I won't leave here, I don't want to leave the airfield.' So I stayed there and 8 a.m. came and the plane still hadn't come. So they phoned again and were told that it would come at 9 a.m. Another phone call – this time they said the plane would come at 10 a.m. 10 a.m. came, and I began to think that there was no hope for me [to be on time for the funeral]. Ten o'clock came and went, and then at about ten past the hour they said, 'The plane is on its way, it's already taken off.' Then suddenly, the small children were shouting, 'There's the plane, there's the plane', and it landed.

When it had landed, the passengers got out with their bags. And this was the first time I had flown. The man said to me, 'Uncle, are you ready? Get into the plane with your bag.' They weighed the stuff. I already had my ticket. 'Are you ready to get into the plane?'

So we got into the plane. And in the plane on one side three people sit together, and on the other side two, isn't that right? I sat by myself and looked through the window. I saw all the small islands and the sea. And you can see roads as thin as a knife edge below. I told someone it was my first flight and he helped me to fasten my seat belt. There are two pilots and as I sat right at the front I could see them and what they were doing.

P. Were you frightened?

M. No I liked it. And I timed it, it took exactly 35 minutes. So it was my first flight. There was a young man sitting behind me who happened to be someone who worked at the airport. Sitting behind him was another young man who had, I think, seven children, and that day he was travelling with three of them. He had left his wife and some of the other children to travel on another day. I had already explained to him that this was my first time in a plane and I did not know what to do. He said that he had previously telephoned Dar to say that he was coming and to ask for a car to meet him at the airport. So he said that he would help me, and so did a young man from Dongo Jekundu, who lives near that white house. He said to me: 'Elder brother, do not worry. I am going to Dar to buy goods (*buznes*) to bring here. And once we arrive, we can get the car to Kariakoo [market]. Do you have people you know there?'

And I said to him: 'The people who sell coconuts in Kariakoo are youngsters from Mafia – from Minazini, Pwani, Kilindoni. I would certainly have people there whom I know.'

So he said, 'Right, then when we arrive, we will go by car and I will drop you there.' And that was what he did.

THE FUNERAL: 'I COULD NOT SEE IN FRONT OF ME'

When we arrived [at Kariakoo market], immediately my [classificatory] son was there: he is my son through his mother, as well as my grandson and my son again through his father.[25] When we had greeted each other he said to me:

'Father, you have arrived?'

I said, 'Yes, I have arrived this very day.'

'How did you come?'

'I came by plane.'

'What is the reason for your coming?'

'I got a phone call to say that your younger brother has died and that his funeral is at 1.00 p.m. today.'

And he said, 'That is also the reason why I have come, to attend the funeral of my younger brother. So, father, do not worry. We are going on the same journey. But I do beg you, father, come and have some tea'; since we were right outside a tea-shop.

And I said to him: 'My son, I do not have the breath [i.e. appetite] to drink tea. I can't.'

'Father, come and have some tea. *Mzee* (old man – a term of respect), do have some tea. Bear up, come and have some tea.'

So we went into the tea-shop and he ordered some bread, and I had just poured some tea into my saucer when I heard a radio announcement[26] which said that the son of Mohammed, from Minazini, who lived in Dar es Salaam and who worked at such and such a hotel, died on Thursday. And his funeral is today at Magomeni.

At that moment, Patricia, I tell you, I could not finish my tea. I put down my saucer. The announcement was being relayed right there in the tea-shop. I did not see the person who was making the announcement but I saw the speaker. So I couldn't drink that tea. But that young man said, 'Come on, bear up, drink your tea, please, *mzee wangu*.'

So I managed a cup and two slices of bread, that was all. 'Have some more, father', but I said it was enough. So we left there and went to the taxi stand, and we took one straight to Magomeni.

We got out at Magomeni, and we continued on foot to the funeral of Seleman Mohammed. They were reading the call to prayer (*adhan*) for noonday, and had started to pray for the deceased, the person they were going to bury. So as we went on, past the mosque, just a short distance, about as far as from here to that coconut tree [pointing], the corpse was being brought. And there were people coming in front of it. So because those people did not know that I was the father (*baba mzazi* lit. 'the father who bore him') of that young man (*mtoto*, lit. child), I said, 'Who is the deceased?' I said it to the people who were coming ahead of the corpse. And they replied: 'He was our brother Seleman Mohammed who lived in Kunduchi and who died. And his corpse was taken to Muhimbili hospital to be washed, and after being washed, it was brought here. And today is his funeral after the noon prayer.'

At that moment, Patricia, I went forward to receive the bier.[27] God helped me at that moment. When I had received the bier I almost dropped it because my manners (*adabu*), my self-respect (*heshima*), my intelligence (*akili*) all went. But I received it, I hardly knew what I was doing, until someone took it from me, and helped me. I felt myself being held by one arm, and then by the other. I could not see in front of me. Only later did I see that there were two people, one on either side of me. One was MT from Kirongwe, my [classificatory] grandson.

He was a friend of Seleman's, someone whom he had helped to get work at the hotel, and later when Seleman was in Dar, he had sent for this man, and they had shared a house there, until Seleman got his own plot and built a house for himself. And that young man also got a plot of land himself and built a house together with the son of my [classificatory] older brother. So [this man] got work, and he got a plot of land because of the help of the deceased Seleman.

So we went back there, and there were a lot of people, but I could not see in front of me. All I was aware of was being jostled by this one and then that one. Finally we reached the house, with the mosque over there [indicating]. Then I heard a voice saying, 'Don't let him see the bier again.' I heard that voice. So they finished praying for the deceased and then the corpse was taken for some way. So I went forward slowly with those people, and I heard the voice of someone I knew, and there were others whom I didn't know, but who were his [Seleman's] friends and neighbours. So we continued on until we arrived, and I could see that the bier was far ahead, and we arrived at a place where there was a mango tree and a coconut tree, and that place is called Mtaa Sungura. And to the north there was a school, and to the south there was a clinic and there were graves there, together with his grave. So we went up to the grave, which had not yet been finished.

There was one youngster called Abbas, my [classificatory] child, whose father's elder brother was related to my father's elder brother, in other words he is my [classificatory] son, the son of my [classificatory] older brother [and he said to me] 'Father (*baba*).' 'Yes (*Naam*).' 'Now, *mzee wangu* (lit. 'my elder), it is ready, it is time to go into the grave to bury our brother.'[28] And I replied to him: 'Here, my brothers, in Dar es Salaam, I don't know things. So as you have decided among yourselves, since your brother has died, to wash his corpse, and to pray for him, and to take on the authority to dig his grave, and you took on all the responsibility while I was still in Mafia, and it was only by luck that I arrived here in time, so if you want me to help you, I am ready.'

'Father, go into the grave.'

'I will get into the grave. And let Seleman Mohammed be put into the grave. And let my [classificatory] son from Baleni, Mafia, get into the grave as well.'

Then someone said that there was another man who was Seleman's brother-in-law because the deceased's mother-in-law and his father had the same father and mother. So he begged to be allowed to be one of those who do the actual burying, and he was given permission. So they discussed the matter, then they got into the grave. But then [it turned out in the end] that he was afraid to get into the grave, so he wanted to ask someone else to do it [instead], some other brother, I don't know how he was related. For this reason I put another brother in to bury [the corpse]. Alright. So we buried him (*tukamstiri*, lit. 'covered him'), and it was finished. Then we read the post-burial prayer (*tarakani*) and when we had finished doing that then someone, I think it was my classificatory son, said 'Gentlemen, all of us who have gathered here to bury our brother are invited to the place where the funeral took place. Today is Friday. Tomorrow, after the evening prayer, there will be a [Koranic] reading.'

'Very well, *bwana*.'

So we left there, little by little, and I still had those people supporting me on each arm, and I told them to leave me; we went on back to the place where the funeral had taken place, where we found people eating beans and doughnuts. I was taken by the hand inside and we entered a room like this one, and I was followed in by one of my grandchildren, the child of my daughter Asha, who I told you is in Dar. They brought in the money from the funeral collection – I think it was 60,000 shillings or more. Later another 2,000 shillings appeared.

So, let us get on with things. One of the brothers was given the job of the distribution of meat (*arafa*) and went to discuss matters in the court-yard [with the women] and with those brothers and sisters from Mafia who were living or married in Dar and had come [to the funeral]. So at about 4 p.m. I was called: 'You are called by your daughter-in-law, that is the wife of the deceased.'

I went across the courtyard and went into a hut and there I found a plate of beans together with doughnuts. 'Please sit down there.' There was one of my [classificatory] children, the child of my cross-cousin, a woman who was in Dar that day. So I asked her how he [her father] was and then she invited me to drink. I said I had already had something to drink. So she said, 'Try and eat something.' I ate a little, but I couldn't manage any more, so I had water brought and I washed my hands. And I left and went back to the place where I had been put at first. Then my brothers, my children and my grandchildren called me to receive the incense money (*ubani*) – it was 500 shillings from one, l00 shillings from another, and that [giving of money] went on until the next day.

And on the Saturday evening they cooked bread and coffee, and it was taken to the mosque to be distributed after the reading. When we had finished we were given permission to leave. Everyone went to their own place. On the Sunday, we had to rent a vehicle to take us to Kunduchi [where Seleman had lived], because the funeral (*matanga*, the wake) had finished. So we went off to Kunduchi and we stayed there for about eleven days, during which time there was a lot of rain.

On the eleventh day I was to leave. The Mafia people wanted me to go on the plane because the route through Kisiju[29] would be difficult because of the rain. But a young fellow turned up and he said, 'Don't go on the plane; a vehicle is due any minute which will give us a report of how things are at Kisiju, and whether the road is passable or not.' By good fortune, we waited, and the people who came in the vehicle said that the road was fine. So we went off to Kisiju. When we arrived at Kisiju, there was a boat which had come from Kilindoni, the captain of which is called Mgenje. So we slept there and left at dawn and by 10 a.m. we were in Kilindoni. There I got the Minazini lorry, and by 5 p.m. I was back home.

Part II

Mohammed as ethnographer

Introduction

The document from which this second section of the book is drawn is the diary which was kept by Mohammed from August 1966 to February 1967 and which runs to just over a hundred pages of typescript (approximately 50,000 words). As already noted in Chapter 1, it was not all written down by him: some of his entries were augmented at the time of transcription, and other items were included because he was reminded of them when we worked together over his own text. What all of this material has in common is that Mohammed himself chose to present it, although sometimes, of course, I asked for further explanations.

The diary thus represents very much his view of life in the village; someone else would have kept a rather different diary, if they had done so at all. Indeed, as already noted, when the idea of asking people to keep a daily record of happenings in the village occurred to me, I did ask four men if they would do so when I was going to be away for more than a month. All agreed, and all presented me with something on my return. Some of the entries overlapped – the same weddings and funerals, for example – but the emphases were quite different. One of the temporary diary-keepers, for instance, never wrote anything about spirit possession. Much later, in 1994, he told me that he had never in his life attended a spirit possession ritual, because his father, a Koranic teacher, considered such rituals to be counter to the teachings of Islam. Mohammed, on the other hand, almost never makes mention in his diary of political events – there is an occasional reference to a village meeting or an election, but many such are not even reported; they simply did not interest him. Mohammed's main interests are personal relationships – marriages, divorce, adultery, quarrels – and spirit possession, which is often linked to conflict, as well as to illness and other misfortunes. He is also interested in aspects of village life in which he himself has participated: dhows and their journeys, the cultivation of both subsistence and cash crops, and life cycle and calendrical rituals.

I begin this section, then, by reproducing verbatim the first week of the diary, in order to give some idea of its flavour. As will be discussed later, Mohammed reported issues as they came to his attention, rather than in strictly chronological order:

MOHAMMED'S DIARY: THE FIRST WEEK

Saturday, 16th day of the 6th month (*Mfunguo Sita, mwezi 26*)
MS of Pwani village committed adultery with the wife of UH, who then divorced his wife but later recalled her.

Tuesday, 29th day of 6th month
Minazini: Death of child of MM. Funeral at house of his brother.

Death of child of M. whose mother is the now-divorced daughter of HA. Funeral in Kisiwa village.

A *maulid ya Jamwiya* [religious reading about the birth of the Prophet Mohammed] was held at Dawe Simba near Kilindoni at night.

Saturday, 26th day of 6th month
Bt. W, the wife of MK, committed adultery with HH. The latter ran off to B's house [for help because he feared the husband's wrath]. However while B was trying to persuade K (his brother-in-law) not to fight with MK, the latter kicked B in the groin. [Nonetheless] the wife was not divorced, nor was HH accused [of committing adultery].

Thursday, 2nd day of 7th month
The dhow of AJ went to Kisiju. CM [the wife's brother of the dhow owner] went to sell fish.

Friday, 3rd day of 7th month
A *ziara* [annual ritual of the *tarika* or Sufi mystical order] was held in Karibu village with a meal of beef curry and rice (not pilao).

There was a meeting at the TANU office. Every cell leader was told to urge his people to cultivate a field of cassava and clear their coconut fields, or there would be serious trouble.[1]

Wednesday, the 1st day of the 7th month
TA divorced his wife Bt. M.

Sunday, 4th day of 7th month
The dhow of HB from Pwani village went to Kisiju.

That night, MHK found his wife with another man. He beat the man and knocked him down. The woman and man have been having an affair for some time, but the husband did not know for sure.

The first week of his diary is not untypical, beginning as it does with a reported case of adultery, and indeed, three such cases are mentioned in the course of a single week. The last incident was noted in brief in Mohammed's diary, but later elaborated at some length during the transcription (see Caplan 1992a). Mohammed reports on the deaths of two small children, also a very common occurrence (see Caplan 1989). Two journeys of local dhows are mentioned, a topic in which he would have been interested both because of his own intermittent work as a sailor, and his occasional trading trips by dhow. Two annual rituals are reported: a *maulid* (religious reading about the birth of the Prophet) and the *ziara* (annual ritual) of a *tarika* (branch of a Sufi order), both of which took place in other areas of Mafia but which might well have been attended by Minazini villagers.

When considering how best to present Mohammed's diary, I contemplated a number of different strategies. One was to replicate as much of the diary in as unedited a form as possible. However, I discarded this idea both because of the style in which the diary is written, as well as because of the complexity of its content which would have required a large amount of commentary or footnotes in order to render it intelligible. Instead, I have selected several major themes in the diary and woven these together with linking passages and explanations as necessary.

Another difficult decision to make was how to deal with Mohammed's style of writing. This involved considerations of his use of time in terms of tenses and chronology, his use of the person, of direct and indirect speech, and of singular and plural.

As is apparent from the first week of the diary, Mohammed does not write in totally chronological order, but rather in the order in which matters come to his attention, as can be seen from the first week's entries given above. Furthermore, at various points in the transcription, Mohammed would be reminded of other events or stories, which may have happened recently or a long time ago, and would retail these, often in the present tense, thus rendering time an even less linear matter. In the chapters which follow, I have tried to give some indication of time, but I have to confess that sometimes in Mohammed's flow of speech, it was not always easy to distinguish whether something had happened the day before, the year before or 'long ago' (*zamani*).

Mohammed often uses the present tense, especially when elaborating an entry verbally, or relating a story. This adds considerable immediacy to his telling of a tale, but where it might be confusing for those unfamiliar with the context, I have changed the tense. In writing this book, I have myself had considerable difficulties in being consistent in the use of tenses – I often use the present tense, as did Mohammed, to convey greater immediacy. It is not, of course, meant to be read as an 'ethnographic present' in the conventional anthropological sense.

Another stylistic point is that Mohammed frequently utilises direct speech; he might, for example, tell a story in the form of a dialogue. This can be confusing, and where necessary, I have inserted the name of the speaker.

There are relatively few personal entries in the diary, and when these occur, Mohammed usually writes about himself in the third person, although when augmenting an entry, or telling a story in which he is an actor, he often switches between first and third person. His use of the third person is interesting; it is perhaps a way of putting matters concerning himself and his family on a par with other entries in the diary. He categorises them as events in the village, and, as such, part of his work as an ethnographer in writing the diary; for that reason, I have left his diary entries about himself in the third person.

Mohammed kept his diary at my behest, and was well aware that he was writing it for me. Indeed, the way in which he presents material here contrasts sharply with several other kinds of text which he produced. For example, when recording interviews for the BBC film *Face Values* ten years later, he was cognisant of the fact that he was talking to an audience which had little knowledge of life on Mafia, and was careful to explain matters in much greater detail. In contrast, the text of the diary takes it for granted that it will be read by someone who is very familiar with the village and its inhabitants, as well as with many of the practices mentioned. Many entries consist of only a few words, but these nonetheless contain a great deal of information. In order to convey this to an outside audience, I have sometimes found it necessary to elaborate entries slightly and to add a certain amount of commentary.

There are thus three kinds of text: the written entries in the diary, the verbal addenda relating to these given at the time of transcription, and additional stories of which he was reminded. Sometimes further detail was given by Mohammed alone, sometimes it was in the form of a conversation between us. I have tried to indicate the status of each item of text (diary, elaboration, story, conversation), but I have to confess that for some pieces of text, I am not totally certain of their exact status, since in the 1960s, I categorised them all merely as 'notes'.

I have also decided to choose a limited number out of the many themes which can be identified in the diary (one index constructed has over eighty such), and draw these together, so as to present them as far as possible from Mohammed's viewpoint. In Chapter 3, then, the main theme is wresting a living from the land and the sea, not always an easy task in this area. Mohammed writes of subsistence crops, and the religious and magical measures needed to ensure their growth, of cash crops, fishing and trading, which link Mafians to wider markets, particularly to other parts of the East African coast and its islands.

Chapter 4 considers the life cycle and social relationships. Attempts are made to control the life cycle through rituals, particularly around birth, circumcision, puberty, marriage and death, and thus to construct an ordered social existence for people and their relationships of kinship and affinity. Nonetheless quarrels erupt even between people who are supposed to be nearest and dearest to each other, such as parents and children, or husbands and wives. Such conflicts bring about suffering, and may result in a variety of emotions – anger, jealousy, bitterness – which can in turn lead to actions such as cursing, divorce, violence, or various forms of witchcraft accusation. Some of these themes are picked up later in Chapters 8 and 9, which consider ways of dealing with various kinds of misfortune, particularly illness, and the role of spirit possession in coping with affliction.

3 Making a living
The land and the sea

INTRODUCTION: SPACE AND TIME

Like other dwellers on the coast of East Africa,[1] people in Minazini village make their living from the cultivation of both subsistence and cash crops, and from fishing and trading. A consideration of these topics involves concepts of kinship and descent, beliefs in spirits, and ways of thinking about space and time. Mohammed's world begins with Minazini village, itself categorised into different areas: the residential land of the village, with its coconut trees and fertile rice meadows, is surrounded on three sides by bush-land, the abode of land spirits, and cultivated on a system of shifting cultivation. To the west of the village lie the beach and sea.

Mohammed also has close links with all of the neighbouring villages on Mafia. These are all nucleated villages (what Middleton 1992 calls 'country towns') unlike the sprawling villages elsewhere in the island. Mohammed, like most men in Minazini, visits the district capital, Kilindoni, fairly regularly. Like most other male villagers, he has often visited the mainland and Dar es Salaam, and he has also been to Zanzibar and Pemba, both for trading and to seek casual work. Journeys to these areas would usually be in a small dhow (*mashua*), occasionally in a large one (*jahazi*).

Time is also an important factor in considering cultivation and fishing. Cultivation operates according to an annual cycle of seasons, beginning with the Swahili New Year, which is based on a solar calendar. The first day of this solar year is marked by a ritual which Mohammed reports in his diary:

> New Year's Day (*Kuoga Mwaka*)[2] took place on the beach. The adult women and young boys went, they made loaves and cut them into pieces and ate them on the beach. When they came back to the village, they danced at HA's house.

Plate 9 Women and children emerging from the sea to picnic on the beach on New Year's Day

To some extent, the seasons, called by the names of the prevailing winds, govern the movement of sailing vessels as well. But vessels are also subject to the movement of tides, which are linked to the Islamic lunar calendar. This enables people to know each day what time the moon will rise, whether it is a waxing or waning moon, and what time the tides will be high or low, while the conjunction of lunar and solar calendars determines whether there will be a neap or spring tide. In keeping his diary, Mohammed used the lunar calendar.

THE LAND AND LAND TENURE: SUBSISTENCE CROPS

The cultivation season starts in earnest in January, and the main crop, rice, is harvested in June. As Mohammed began his diary in August 1966 and completed it just as I was leaving the island at the end of February 1967, it only deals with the first half of the main agricultural season.

The cultivation season opens with people marking out the boundaries of their rice fields. Rights to bush land are obtained through membership of cognatic descent groups, as Mohammed explained when we were transcribing an account of a dispute over rights to a particular field:

All the members of the descent groups go along when the fields are divided up, because those fields belonged to our ancestors. Or [if I wish] I can go and get land through my affine. Perhaps the section (*vuvu*) which is to be cultivated only takes five people, and seven of us wish to go. So even if we don't cultivate big fields, two of us won't get land there that year if we plant [the usual] six measures (*pishi*) of seed each. Thus those who missed out will go and ask for land through someone else, perhaps through their mother's brother, or a friend, or in the place where they were brought up.

However, it may turn out that that year, we may cultivate two or three sections [in which case there will be room for everyone], or perhaps we don't get anything at all. Then you will go to your mother's side, and if there isn't any land there, you will go to a friend, or to your mother's brother, and you will ask (*kuuga*).

Another year, those who missed out five years earlier will get first choice, and other people will have to go looking elsewhere. If you yourself have space in your section you will probably be approached by other people. Or maybe some bush will be left over, which happens often.

Sometimes, however, there are disputes over who gets which section of land, as the following account of a quarrel mentioned in Mohammed's diary between Mohammed's wife's father, AJ, who had wanted land for Mohammed and Mwahadia, and another man, SJ, reveals:

There is a [bush] field which my wife's father AJ wanted to cultivate (it is in his ancestral section) but another man SJ had got it and put his older sister there together with his son to cultivate jointly (*kwa sesa*). Now AJ and SJ are each saying it is their field.

AJ says that he went to take land in that section with the intention of putting his son [-in-law] Mohammed there. But that SJ came in and . . . said, 'My elder sister didn't get [any land]' and so he went to enter the land which AJ had already cut.

Mohammed added:

At the beginning of the cultivation season, Mwahadia went to her father and said they [she and Mohammed] hadn't yet got a field. [He replied] 'You are not the farmer (*mkulima*).' So Mohammed went himself and AJ agreed that Mohammed should get a field. When they [the villagers] were discussing the allocation of land (*kupakana*), AJ said, 'I have taken a certain field and I will put my son[-in-law] Mohammed into it.' But SJ wanted it, and before the time [for that field] to be 'cut', he started cultivating it himself.

AJ asked, 'Who has taken this field when I wanted it?' They replied, 'Ah, is the field being cultivated? Go and you will see the cut bush (*mchenge*).' AJ said, 'We have our rights (*haki zetu*) there, I will go and take it myself. . . . Why is he cultivating? I had taken it and he came along.'

So Bwana AJ saw that he had no alternative but to accuse him [SJ] [before the Village Development Committee, henceforth VDC].

Unfortunately for AJ, the land laws in Tanzania had recently changed in the 1960s, and all land had been declared government land; any Tanzanian citizen was given the right to cultivate 'unused' land. Mohammed continued his account:

AJ went to accuse him [SJ] before the VDC. They judged that by the laws of today, they were not able to tell him [SJ] that he should not cultivate, nor could they tell someone he should cultivate [in a certain place]. Because it is [now all] government land. Those matters [obtaining land through descent group membership] are from before, the time of ignorance (*upotevu*), that AJ should cultivate here and SJ should cultivate there. AJ wanted a letter [from the VDC] to go to [the court in] Kilindoni, but he did not get it. So SJ continued cultivating.

A little while later, Mohammed's diary contained the following entry:

The field which was contested was divided between SJ and AJ. The elders were SA [the Village Chairman] and HK who went to the field and divided it equally. It was a bush section (*vuvu*) of one descent group (*ukoo*).

As is frequently the case, Mohammed does not tell this story in a strictly chronological fashion – he starts with the bare facts recorded in his diary, then goes back further in time to explain the case. This dispute hinges on two factors: one is whether or not Mwahadia's father had actually marked out the bush which he wanted to cultivate by making cuts on the trees. Although it would appear that he had not done so, he maintained that he had claimed the field during the discussions in the village which precede the marking out of the fields. SJ, however, had pre-empted him by marking it out himself by cutting the trees. Second, the land tenure system in this part of Mafia Island, which allocated land according to membership of cognatic descent groups, now had no formal legal status, and the VDC refused either to remove SJ from the land he was occupying, or give AJ a letter so that he could pursue the case in court. Mohammed himself seems to have been philosophical about it, noting that there were other sections of land to which he could have had acccess, but AJ, as an elder, plainly felt that he should have had first call on this particular piece of land. Eventually, the VDC suggested a compromise, and divided the field.

Once agreement has been reached about who is cultivating where, the next stage is to clear the bush, a job which is always done by men. Occasionally, a man might 'sell' his cleared field, as in the following entry in Mohammed's diary:

> MJ is selling his cleared bush (*uchange*) because he has got another field in another area. *Uchange* is a field in which the bush has been cut but not yet fired. He is not selling the land, but his labour (*nguvu*, lit. 'strength'). No one has yet bought the field.

Later:

> No buyers came forward so MJ is still there.

Mohammed added:

> Anyone can buy *uchange*, but they only get cultivation rights for a year, not for longer.

Mohammed notes that that year (1966), he himself 'cut' a particularly large field:

> Mohammed planted beans and rice. The name of his field is 'they insulted me' (*wanitukana*) because [a man called] Mushibe cultivated this field alone one time, but the next time round, it took two people to cultivate it. Mushibe maintained that no one but himself would be able to cultivate such a large field. People had mocked Mohammed saying that he couldn't cultivate a field of eight *pishi* [i.e. a field which needed eight measures of seed] without help.

Women or men who are not capable of 'cutting' a bush field alone will organise help, as in the following two cases in the diary:

1 There was a cultivation party (*ukulima*) held by Bt. N in her bush field. She prepared food for her male friends, relatives and grandchildren to help her cut her field.
2 MS was helped by all three of his sister's sons to cultivate bush-land. There was no cooking because it is now Ramadhan.

Following the cutting down of the trees and scrub which have grown up in the period since the fields in a particular area were last cultivated (at least five, usually seven years of fallow in the 1960s), the felled woodland is fired. Some of the bush land surrounding the village is under the guardianship of particular land spirits (see Chapter 9), and for these fields, offerings must be made at specific points in the cultivation cycle, including the firing of the cut bush.

> The people of one descent group slaughtered a white cow 'for the boundary' (*ng'ombe ya kipako*) and took a little blood and meat to the spirit shrine (*panga*), then they divided the meat into big pieces and everyone who was going to cultivate there got a share.

My notes record that going to the spirit shrine in this way was seen as dangerous, and there is a further record in my own diary:

> Mohammed came here specially to warn me that if I go to the killing of the cow, then I should not follow the *waganga* (*shamans*) when they take the blood [to the shrine]. This is because anyone who is given this blood may also be given [himself or herself] to the spirit since when the sacrifice of the cow is made, a human is also needed.

Furthermore, failure to wait until the offering had been made to the spirit before firing the land could have serious consequences. Mohammed records that one of his elders, a shaman, gave him the following advice:

> If you go and cultivate in that area of bush-land, don't set fire until one of the shamans of that spirit does so, because they will entrust the field to the spirit. One man did this the other year, and he began to be very sick, he defecated blood, until the shaman AJ treated him.

Later he records in his diary:

> The fields were fired in the bush-land on the ridge by every single person cultivating there.

Mohammed added:

> Before this could be done, incense had to be burned (*kutia buhuri*) to inform the spirit that this was about to happen to its land.

If a field is not protected by a spirit, other measures may be taken, as Mohammed records in his diary:

> In the area named Mchane they read a *hitima* to protect it (*kitu kingo*). This is done for a field area which has no spirit (*iblissi*). The intention is to protect all fields in Mchane even if not everyone [who is cultivating there] turns up. They could have gone round in two groups reading chapters from the Koran (*majuzi*) and the call to prayer (*adhan*) and

eating loaves (*mikate*). But this was not done, they just sat in one spot and read [the Koran]. No food or money [was given to the participants].

Here the use of various Islamic formulae are mentioned as a way of protecting a field which has no guardian spirit. A third method is the use of charms, which Mohammed himself used in 1966, when he cultivated a field which was not under the protection of a spirit:

Mohammed asked his elder [who is the shaman of his ancestral spirit] to protect his field because it is on the path. He has also promised protective medicine (*dawa ya kuchanjia*). Mohammed must first get l5 shillings, seven times three beans [i.e. twenty-one][3] and a new pot. The beans must be cooked together with herbs (*dawa ya miti*) and swallowed whole one at a time. Then the shaman says: 'Go your way, believe in God and the Prophet.' This medicine is called an 'inoculation' (*chanjio* or *kago*).

In this entry, all three methods of protecting a field are mentioned. Mohammed goes on to record that if there is no spirit to guard a field, people plant medicine in the ground as a precaution (*zindiko*):

Gather the leaves of two trees, pound them, put into a cloth and fasten it up, wet them, finally squeeze this over the seed. Then leave the cloth in the basket of seed. You can then mix the treated seed with all your other seed.

Or if you have [already] planted all your seed, you go and dig some roots of the *mgo* tree when your rice has started to sprout. Before starting to dig you hold the leaves and say, 'If anyone wants to get my field, let him not get it', then you dig up a root and put it in your shirt or trouser pocket or another safe place. Then you cut the root into five pieces.

You go to another tree called *mgiza* and say, 'Hey, you *mgiza* tree, if anyone looks at you, s/he sees only darkness, because you are a black tree. So I take you to go and do my field. If anyone with evil intentions passes my field, may s/he not see it.' Then you dig up the root and cut it into five pieces like the other.

Then you go to the *kuku mweupe* tree, which is a thorny tree like the *mgo*, and say, 'No one can penetrate you, so I take you to do my field, and let no one see my field. If s/he sees it, may s/he see it as if it were you, that it is impenetrable.' Then you dig up the root and cut it into five pieces.

The fourth and last tree is called *mjimvu* – it has no thorns, but a lot of leaves (*unavaa sana*). You say, 'No one can penetrate you without being caught. Now I take you to go and do my field. If anyone sees it, let him see it as if it were impenetrable like an *mjimvu* tree.' Again you cut the root into five pieces.

You dig a hole at each corner and one in the middle of the field, and put one piece of each tree in each, saying 'I bury you (mentioning the names of all trees), I entrust [this field] to you. If anyone comes for a bad reason (*dhami*), let it not be open to him or her (*asilifungue*), I have "closed" it (*nimefunga*) specially.'

The cloth which is used to hold this medicine (*dawa*) for the seed is kept until the whole seed is planted because it also helps to keep away an insect called *nyevule* (edible grasshopper – this resembles a locust) which eats ripening rice, or rather the 'inoculation' (*kingo*) of the medicine keeps it away.

So both these types of medicines are utilised but only if there is no spirit; if there is, you do not do anything, otherwise it would be an insult, like saying: 'You are no guardian.'

Even with all these precautions, however, the firing does not always proceed smoothly, as Mohammed records in his diary several times:

1 I [Mohammed] received a report that in setting fire to their field, MA and MJ's fires had spread and that all the fields around there caught fire.
2 AS was accused by HU of causing a fire in his coconut field. AS set fire to his bush field next to HU's coconut field. The latter is now claiming damages.
3 MH set fire to the bush left after the first firing (*biwe*) and it spread over the whole of the marsh (*tanda*).

Mindful of the problems already experienced by some, Mohammed himself took precautions when he fired his own field in 1966:

Five people went at his [Mohammed's] request to see that no one else's field was damaged; some were members of the VDC, others came along to fight the fire if need be. This was done because of the quarrel between AS and HU [case 2 above].

That incident (case 2 above) resulted in a case before the Village Development Committee:

AS was fined 30 shillings because he set fire to HU's field. It was settled out of court (*kirafiki*). In fact the VDC had fined him 45 shillings.

Mohammed added:

AS began by denying to the VDC that he had ever set fire to the field. But because HU was so rude and unmannerly to the members of the

Committee, and had no proof of damages, he was the one who got thoroughly told off. For example he claimed that money had been burned in the fire; in fact he hadn't lived in the house concerned for two years so it was unlikely that he kept money there. It was fairly obvious that he had grossly exaggerated the damage caused by the fire.

AS, however, still denying that he had caused the fire, refused to pay the 45 shillings fine imposed by the VDC and offered only 30 shillings as an out-of-court settlement, a move which alarmed his sister:

> AS's sister came to him and said: 'If a *Halbadiri* is read, we'll all die and our children too, because it is true that you did set fire to that field.' So AS gave in and paid up the 45 shillings.

A *halbadiri* reading is sometimes used either to protest innocence ('May God punish me if I am lying'), or to force someone suspected of lying to tell the truth ('May God punish him if what he has sworn is not true').

A few days later Mohammed himself was involved in helping to stop a fire spreading:

> Bt. O [a single woman] set fire to her field and it spread to other fields and burned the fence of her neighbour MS and the coconut trees of various people. But no one claimed damages from her. The people who helped to put out the fire included Mohammed and Mwahadia, and AS and his wife. Bt. O herself lost her basket of plaited raffia strips in the blaze.

This case seems to have been recognised as an accident; furthermore, the woman herself suffered the loss of her supply of plaited raffia strips, which probably represented several months' work, and would have been the major source of her cash income for the year.

Once the land has been fired, planting begins, with the first seeds usually being beans (*kunde*):

1 SM planted beans in his Mchane field.

Mohammed added:

If it rains, you plant beans first and then rice as soon as possible. If there is no rain you plant rice first, together with sesame if you intend to grow it.

2 JH spent the day planting rice on the ridge.

Mohammed added:

Some people have a special day for planting, e.g. a Thursday. If they can't plant properly on that day, they just plant two or three holes.
P. How does someone know which day?

M. They remember past years – if it was a bad year, he or she won't begin again on the same day.

P. What if you get a good harvest from a Thursday the first year, and a bad one from planting on the same day the following year?

M. Then you will choose.

Much planting is done in reciprocal work parties (*wiazi*) usually composed of relatives or affines:

1 All the people in [the area called] Mlimani are planting, they are working in parties of five or six.
2 Three women cleared grass and planted rice cooperatively (*kwa sesa*) in Mlimani.
3 Bt. H had a work party (*wiazi*) and food was cooked.
4 Bt. O had a *wiazi* in her field at [the area called] Mchane.

Mohammed himself does not seem to have been much involved in helping other people in their cultivation, and there is only a single mention of such an event in his diary:

AR came to help Mohammed in his field for half a day. He [Mohammed] will go to his field [AR's] in turn.

However, there are several entries in his diary which indicate that his wife had attended cultivation or planting parties:

1 Mwahadia went to help her husband's brother's wife to clear grass from her meadow land.
2 Bt. A had her planting party (*upanzi*). Only Mwahadia went.
3 Mwahadia went to help Bt. M with planting.

Mwahadia was subsequently able to call several work parties of her own:

Mwahadia had two *wiazi* and planted one and a half measures of seed.

By January planting is in full swing, and in some areas, the rice is beginning to sprout. However, there may be problems as Mohammed notes:

Six years ago Mohammed exchanged two measures of one kind of seed for three measures of another kind with Mzee J. But all this seed got eaten by pigs. Later he [Mohammed] heard that if you buy from or exchange seed with this man, you'll get nothing. In fact, the latter had bewitched (*kuroga*) that seed expressly so that the pigs should eat it. That man has an evil eye (*jicho baya*, see Chapter 8), and does not want other people to prosper. He behaves like this towards everyone, not just Mohammed.

In order to help prevent eventualities of this kind, additional precautions may be needed, for example the 'encirclement' of a field through a Koranic ritual:

> An encircling (*kuzingua*) of the fields was held in Mlimani, and then people ate dates together.

P. But isn't there a spirit there [to protect the field]?
M. It is alright to do this provided that you inform the spirit first. But they do not use other kinds of protective medicine (*zindiko*), of course [as this would be an insult to the spirit].

Circling the fields, like circling the village (*kuzingua mji*) once a year, is considered an Islamic rite invoking God's special protection, and many people see no contradiction in using this as well as spirit protection for their crops.

Towards the end of the month of January, people begin to move out to live in their fields, so that they can protect the ripening crop from pests such as monkeys, birds and wild pigs, and there are numerous mentions in Mohammed's diary of people leaving the village to take up residence in their fields for the remainder of the cultivation season.

People who are cultivating in fields which are guarded by a spirit have to be careful of their behaviour, as Mohammed recalls:

One year I was sleeping outside my house [in the field] and I felt someone shaking me [and asking]: 'Who are you sleeping here?' Then he [Mohammed] knew that the field spirit didn't want him [to sleep] there [but inside the house]. Next morning he was to leave on a journey, but he felt so heavy and sleepy. He knew it was the spirits [who had caused this].

That same year, he had an even closer encounter with the field spirit:

> Mohammed said he wouldn't give any contributions to the field spirit because he had got nothing from the field [the previous time]. As a result [of his refusal to contribute] he had not been invited to the ritual which is held to inform the spirit that the fields will be fired (*mavugo ya pori*). But in his sleep he saw the spirit – an old man with elephantiasis and charms (*hirizi*) sewn all over him – and his troops (*jeshi*).
>
> He saw people coming, first a man whom he knew, then a youth with his mouth covered in sores who said [to Mohammed] 'What do you say?'
> 'I did not get any rice.'

Then came the old man described above, wearing a red coat, and he said, 'Did you say you got nothing? Let us go then', and he went off with the rest leaving Mohammed. He knew that this was the spirit and his troops (*jeshi lake*). He never paid any dues, but he had no more trouble.

Although cultivation of rice is seasonal, cassava is cultivated all year round, much encouraged by government agricultural officers because of its resistance to drought. This strategy was proving relatively successful in the 1960s and there are several entries in Mohammed's diary concerning good yields:

JA pulled up four bags of cassava from his field. NA got four sacks, JH got two and a half, TH and MA got one each.

People from . . . all of the neighbouring villages came to buy cassava here.

AA sold two bags of cassava for 40 shillings. One bag was bought by MA, one by the Sheikh. Cassava has now gone up from 15 shillings per bag.

But even this hardy crop can run into problems:

Pigs have been destroying crops in the main cassava area. Mohammed's cassava was eaten by pigs and monkeys which broke through the fence, and not a bit was left.

Four men were cutting cassava into slices to dry it, each one in his own field in [the area known as] Bagoni. [But it rained and so] it got drenched and spoiled.

Crops can also be lost to pests against which the villagers themselves have little defence, other than sling shots:

In Mlimani, the monkeys and crows are scratching up the rice. The men all go before dawn [to guard it] and stay until after dark.

Very occasionally, help from the government would be forthcoming:

Five people came to Pwani village to hunt the animals which were eating the crops there, such as pigs, bush babies (*komba*), monkeys, civet cats, etc. Their weapons were guns.

Later:

Sixty-three monkeys have been shot in the last three days by the people of Pwani and the hunters. The hunters shot 110 monkeys in Minazini.

These entries indicate that cultivation is a hazardous business – obtaining land in the first place can be a fraught affair leading to disputes, crops can be destroyed by weather, too much or too little rain, or rain coming at the wrong time, and by pests. In order to mitigate such eventualities, a range of measures is adopted: invoking the protection of God and/or the spirits, and using protective 'medicine'.

THE LAND AND LAND TENURE 2: CASH CROPS

Villagers not only cultivate crops such as rice and cassava primarily for subsistence, they also grow coconuts and cashew nuts as cash crops:

> Many people are clearing their coconut fields because the Area Commissioner [the chief government official of the district] is in Minazini. Starting from Monday onwards, top priority has been given to clearing the coconut fields.

During the 1960s, coconuts were supposed to be marketed as copra (the dried flesh of the nut) to the government-backed cooperative in Kirongwe. From Minazini, the journey was usually made with donkeys carrying the copra, but from the neighbouring village, Pwani, the nuts would often go by sea:

> MM's *mashua* went to Kirongwe carrying copra from Pwani.
> AJ's *mashua* went to Kirongwe with copra from Pwani.

However, the cooperative had frequent problems attracting people to sell since it offered low prices and sometimes even lacked cash with which to pay farmers, and so not infrequently, the nuts were sold elsewhere:

> The *mashua* 'Sheli' from Shahwizi went to Zanzibar from Kisiwa village with 1,500 coconuts

Some villagers also own cashewnut trees which flourish on the very sandy soil found mainly in the south of the village. They too were supposed to be sold to the cooperative and indeed, usually were, since the price offered at that time was good:

> In the whole of Mafia, the cashews are ready. The price is 73 shillings per 100 kg in Kirongwe. Some people are drinking *uraka* [an alcoholic drink made from the fruit of the tree] and children are selling nuts [as snacks in the village].

Where harvests are exceptionally good, Mohammed notes this fact in his diary:

SN sold 100 kg of cashew nuts for 73 shillings but he still has more.

Later:

SN sold a second lot of cashew nuts – another 100 kilos.

HT sold three sacks of cashew nuts and still has more.

Later:

HT has had a total harvest to date of five sacks of cashew nuts.

Mohammed notes that growers received an extra payment that year:

The Chairman of the Cooperative Society came to Pwani and Minazini and told a meeting that receipts for cashew nuts and sesame should be produced for an extra payment.

A few years later, I was to find on a return visit that prices of cashew nuts had dropped to such an extent that some people were actually grubbing up their trees. Thus villagers are very much at the mercy of national and indeed international price fluctuations for their cash crops. However, in contrast to subsistence crops, there is no mention in Mohammed's diary of people seeking to protect their cash crops through supernatural means.

THE SEA: FISHING AND TRADING

Fishing is carried out by a number of men in the village by a variety of means: lines (*mishipi*), traps (*madema, wando*), nets (*nyavu*); fishermen work either from the shore, or else use dug-out canoes with outriggers (*ngalawa*) or small dhows (*mashua* or *vidau*). In his account of his life, Mohammed recorded how he used to do a lot of fishing when he was young (see Chapter 2), and although he was no longer doing so when he wrote the diary, he was still interested in the topic. When people were particularly successful in catching a number of large fish, which they could sell to fish traders to dry or smoke and then take to markets in Dar es Salaam, Mohammed would often record such instances in his diary:

1 A shark was caught in a nylon net and sold for 150 shillings [a considerable sum in the 1960s] in Pwani.
2 In the fishing trap belonging to AH of Pwani, two *bêches de mer* were found and the meat was sold.

It will be noted that fishing on a larger scale, using nylon nets or *wando* traps, often involves more than one person, and people come from as far afield as the mainland to fish in the Mafia waters:

> Five sharks were caught by fishermen from Kuruti on the Mrima coast and sold to the people of Pwani village.
>
> [On the same day] AO, a man from Kuruti in the Mrima, caught a shark in his nylon net and sold it in Kisiwa village for 100 shillings. AB bought it on credit.

There are frequent references in the diary to journeys by dhow to sell fish in the capital:

> The *mashua* of AJ, Pwani, went to Kisiju to take fish to sell in Dar es Salaam.
>
> [On the same day] The *mashua* of AJ, Minazini, went to Kisiju with passengers SA, CM, and MH to sell fish.

But fishing is an activity which is not without its dangers:

1 AA was injured by a *katwa* (stingray) on the beach
2 SH was also injured by a *katwa* in Pwani.
3 OA, a man from Kwale Island, had dived into the water while fishing. He looked up and saw four sharks swimming above him!
4 The little dhow of Dongo Jekundu [a southern village] was returning some fishermen to land when the sail split and they were carried away. Some Minazini men took AJ's *mashua* and went and caught it and towed it back to shore.

Fishing and sailing are thus often hazardous enterprises, as has already been shown. As with misfortunes in agriculture, explanations are sometimes sought in terms of human malevolence, such as the *mazingera* spell mentioned in Chapter 2.

Mashua also travel to the mainland and to Zanzibar for trade in other goods, as Mohammed frequently mentions:

1 The Pwani *mashua* called Hayakuwa belonging to HB went to Kisiju carrying MA with mats, and JA with hens and dried fish.
2 The *mashua* of KM from Kisiwa village was rented by youths from Karibu village to go to Zanzibar. They paid 300 shillings and took their own food. They carried fifty-seven bundles of raffia. The captain was AN from Kisiwa.
3 The *mashua* of HB (from Pwani village) went to Zanzibar with IM, MF, HR, taking raffia and mats. Mohammed's elder brother also returned to Zanzibar [where he lives] on it.

Other references mention the sale of cattle and cow hides. Such trading trips link the people of Minazini to those of other nearby villages, whose vessels they frequently use (there was only one

Plate 10 Fishermen with sting-ray

Plate 11 Loading a *mashua*

mashua in Minazini at the time of fieldwork). But they also link them to other parts of the coast – Kisiju, the nearest point on the mainland from where buses and lorries travel up to Dar es Salaam, and Zanzibar, some 100 miles away by sea. Mohammed's world, like that of most coastal dwellers, is thus a wide one, with the sea giving access to many other parts of the East African coast and its islands (see Map p. 33). At the time of this diary, entry to Zanzibar was actually restricted for inhabitants of mainland Tanzania and its islands, in spite of the recent union between Tanganyika and Zanzibar, but the dhows continued to travel, both officially and unofficially.

CONCLUSION

Making a living in Minazini village is not easy: cultivation is very hard work and fishing is a risky business. Crops may fail, fishermen be unsuccessful in obtaining catches, or worse, may be drowned at sea. But people are not passive in the face of adversity: here, as elsewhere, they seek to understand the reasons for such misfortunes, viewing them either as the result of human agency – the evil eye, bad intentions, or forms of witchcraft – or attributing them to 'bad luck' or the will of God (*amri ya Mungu*). They also try to prevent their occurrence through a variety of means: holding Islamic rituals, using protective magic, and calling on spirits, methods which are discussed at greater length in Chapters 8 and 9.

4 The life cycle
Relationships, conflict and emotions

This chapter first considers Mohammed's portrayal of the life cycle in his village: birth, circumcision/puberty, marriage and death with their attendant rites of passage. The second part then looks at two sets of relationships formed during the life cycle: those of parents and children, and husbands and wives. Such relationships are ideally those of love, trust, respect and affection, and some people do manage to live their lives more or less according to these ideals. But here, as elsewhere, others become embroiled in conflict even with their nearest and dearest, with many painful consequences.

MANAGING TIME: THE LIFE CYCLE

On Mafia Island, as on much of the East African coast, the life cycle from birth to death is punctuated by three major rites of passage: circumcision for boys and puberty rituals for girls, first marriage for both, and funerals. All such ceremonies (*mashughuli*) include several common aspects including both Koranic and customary (*mila*) elements (see Caplan 1982). They are generally spread over at least a night and a day, and involve a night vigil (*kesha*) which, in the case of all rituals except funerals, usually includes dancing. Such ceremonies also invariably involve the sharing of food by those participating, and in Mohammed's diary, he always notes carefully exactly what kind of food was served. One of the meals offered to guests for each of these ceremonies should be a feast (*karamu*), and, as Mohammed explains in Chapter 10, a feast means the slaughtering of an animal (preferably a cow, but sometimes, if money is scarce, a goat) and the cooking of rice either as a meat *pilao*, or as the accompaniment to a meat curry. Close kin are invited to the 'drying of the rice' (*uanikaji*) held a few days before the ceremony, and more kin to the rice pounding (*utwanzi*); kin also contribute some of the rice for a feast.

BIRTH

Mohammed does not mention all of the births which take place in Minazini, indeed, in some sections of his diary, there are more references to the deaths of children, which would have been more widely known, than births. But his diary does indicate the high levels of infant mortality, which cause such grief and lead parents and other relatives to seek the help of spirits.

1 Bt. M wife of HM, had a female child.
2 Death of the child of HF in Pwani.
3 Death of 1-day old child of AJ, funeral at his house.
4 Death in Kisiki village of child of MG.
5 Death in Kidika village of child of MO, funeral at house of HJ.
6 Mwatika Bt. A, wife of MA, had a baby girl in the night.

Later:

> The same Bt. A had a girl child which died the same day and the funeral took place.

On occasion he reveals that childbirth is hazardous for women:

1 Bt. I, the wife of AF, had to be taken to hospital to give birth. She was given five injections here, then carried to Kirongwe, where they got a vehicle and arrived just in time in Kilindoni. It is not true that she had the baby en route. It was a boy.
2 Bt. J wife of HM, died in childbirth and the child died too. On the third day after the deaths, they did the third day Koranic reading (*hitima ya tatu*) and slaughtered a cow to cook with rice.

There are no required rituals for children between birth and circumcision (for boys) and ear-piercing (for girls), but some parents do try to protect their children from harm by additional rituals:

> There has been a cooperative pounding of rice (*utwanzi*) at the house of AM to cook food for guests at a *maulid* reading. The occasion was the first cutting of the hair of his child. The parents had made a vow not to cut it until a *maulid* was read.

Here the vow is an Islamic one, with the first hair-cutting delayed beyond the usual period, during which time the child is thought of as under the special protection of God. At the end of this period, a *maulid* (reading in praise of the Prophet Mohammed)[1] is held.

CIRCUMCISION AND PUBERTY RITES

Mohammed frequently mentions the rituals of circumcision carried out for all boys, usually in small groups. Entries in his diary occur particularly often in the months of August and September, when rice is plentiful for the holding of feasts.

1 There was a Koranic reading (*hitima*), and a cow was slaughtered and cooked with rice. The next morning four children were circumcised at the house of HK, in Kisiki village.
2 There was a *maulid* reading at the house of TJ and rice and chicken were served. This was to bring his son out of the circumcision lodge (*jando*). He had been circumcised by Kitumbako [the chief 'expert' on Mafia at the time], but there had not been a feast at the time of the circumcision.
3 Six children from Pwani were circumcised in Kilindoni hospital.
4 At 4 p.m. in Pwani, they cooked rice with goat meat. People sleeping over played games (*vichekesho*) and cards. The next morning ten children were circumcised at the house of BJ. The chief expert was YJ, but four other experts were called as well.

Mohammed's diary entries on the subject of circumcision indicate a wide range of practices. Some children are circumcised by local experts, others are taken to hospital. Some groups of boys are as large as ten at a time, most are in smaller groups, and occasionally a single child is circumcised alone. Food is invariably cooked and offered to guests before the circumcision, and again when the boys come out of their period of seclusion – at least one of these meals should be a feast (*karamu*). The circumcision ritual normally incorporates an Islamic element – either a maulid or Koranic reading (*hitima*). A *hitima* for a circumcision must include mentioning the names of the ancestors (*kuarehemu wazee*) 'on all four sides' Mohammed told me. Celebrations for a circumcision may involve customary rituals (see Caplan 1976) – and may also include dancing and card playing, etc. Mohammed's diary includes numerous mentions of such rituals:

> They slaughtered and cooked a cow with rice, read a *hitima*, and people slept over. The next day they circumcised ten children, and cooked porridge, cassava, sweet potatoes and bananas. The parents danced *upatu* [where money is thrown into a tray which is divided between the experts] and *tunza* [where the money is given directly into the mouths of the experts and each man keeps what he gets].

Occasionally, Mohammed reports on the intermediary rituals which are held during the period of seclusion between the operation and the 'coming out'; these are known as *mogo*:

> The *mogo* of a circumcision lodge (*jando*) took place in Kisiki village.

Mohammed added:

> A *mogo* takes place on the seventh day after the circumcision when the boys are washed. If the boys were circumcised on a Saturday, then the first *mogo* will be the following Friday, the second one will be on the next Thursday, and the third on the following Wednesday, on which day guests will sleep over and the boys will come out on the following day, Thursday. Thus they can be secluded for almost three weeks. On each of these occasions the children are washed and the experts put medicine on their wounds, either herbal medicine (*dawa ya miti*) or hospital medicine [in the 1960s this was usually sulphathyasol powder]. Otherwise, the boys do not wash completely every day, they only wash their faces and clean their teeth.
>
> There is also actually a *mogo* on the third day, called the secret *mogo*, but people are only invited for the one on the seventh day, when they get something to eat. On that third day, the wounds are washed [for the first time], then the whole body. On the sixth day, cotton is soaked in coconut juice and is put around the wound. The following morning when water is put on the cotton, it comes away easily and brings the dirt with it. On the fourteenth day, another *mogo* is held and people are again invited – if all is well, the children can even come out on that day.

At the end of the period of seclusion, there is usually a feast to bring the children out of the *jando*:

> Jando, Kisiki village: Waziri cooked fish and rice, the [ritual] experts (*mafundi*) sang, men and women replied and put tips (*tunza*) in the mouths of the *mafundi*. Later they danced the *mkwaju* with rattles and a rubbing stick. All the parents gave tips (*fupo*) [to the circumcisers]. Mohammed enjoyed himself by dancing and looking – he could not give any *fupo* because he had given all his money to his girlfriend and their go-between.
>
> In the morning they cooked cassava, sweet potatoes, buns, porridge. They brought the children out [of seclusion] and each child wore a decoration of beads (*pambo la ushanga*). Four girls had their ears pierced, the *mafundi* sang again and the mothers (*wazazi wa kike*) gave more *tunza* to the *mafundi*.

The equivalent ceremony for girls occurs less often. All girls have their ears pierced, usually on the same occasion as the coming out of seclusion as their circumcised brothers, but this is considered a minor event, hardly worth reporting. Not all girls have their first menstruation ritualised to any great degree, and Mohammed, as a man, would not have been invited to such an event, or even known about it, especially if it was a customary (*mila*) ceremony (*unyago*, see Caplan 1976). In his diary, there are only two mentions of public events held to celebrate a girl's first menstruation:

1 A *maulid* was read by AS to mark the puberty of the daughter of KN of Minazini who lives with him. Then the girl was ritually washed. They cooked beans, bananas, sweet potatoes, buns and porridge.
2 An *unyago* was held in Pwani – it was a small affair.

In both instances, there would have been two common elements – a ritual washing of the girl, and the serving of food to guests. But in other respects, each of these events was quite different. In the first instance, an Islamic ritual – a *maulid* reading – marked the occasion, and would have been attended by guests of both sexes. The second was an *unyago*, a customary puberty ritual, which may be highly elaborated, but to which only women would have been invited. Mohammed would probably have known about it through his wife.

Some parents hold a special ceremony when their son or daughter completes their first proper fast for the month of Ramadhan, usually in early adolescence. Mohammed noted one such instance in his diary:

AJ and MA celebrated the ending of the first fast of their daughters with special food (*futari*) and each child got six *kanga* and a chemise. Other people were also invited.

Mohammed added:

This is called *kufunguzwa* (causing them to break their fast) – you do it if you can afford it.

MARRIAGE

The most important rite of passage from childhood to adulthood is first marriage for both men and women, which is arranged by parents and grandparents. Once a marriage has been agreed, a groom has to pay a formal visit to the bride's house to meet her relatives, especially his mother-in-law, so that he will be able to observe the proper distance from her in future.

NJ got engaged to the daughter of PW. He was called to be 'shown the house' (*kuonyesha nyumba*) of his prospective in-laws and paid *kilemba* (lit. 'turban', the customary dues to the father of bride) of 70 shillings. Rice and chicken were served.

Here Mohammed notes only the payment to the bride's father (*kilemba*) and does not mention the payment (*mkaja*, literally 'belt') to the bride's mother. It is possible that he did not know the amount, because such information might not reach male ears, but unlikely that the *mkaja* would not have been paid at that time. By 1994, *kilemba* had virtually died out, whereas *mkaja* was still considered an essential part of a marriage.

Such events, part of a complex process, are expensive, but both the bride's and groom's side can call upon other relatives:

1 AM, Mohammed's elder brother [who had been visiting from Zanzibar] gave 40 shillings towards the wedding of a child who is related to us. She lives with Bt. A [his sister] and is getting married soon. Since she is an orphan, her mother's brother and her classificatory fathers are arranging the marriage. Forty shillings is a small sum but he hadn't known about the affair when he came.

  19th and 20th days of 7th month:

  The wedding took place of the daughter of MS with HD from Kirongwe. It was the first marriage for both. It was held at the house of HK. At night they danced the *kalewa* (women's dance), and they cooked rice, together with cow meat. The couple moved that day [to the groom's place] by car.

2 The wedding took place of JA's daughter. People danced *mkwaju* (mixed sex dance), *kalewa* (women's dance) and sang *taarabu* (love songs). They cooked rice at night. Mohammed did not go because the bride's father and his own wife's father, who is also his classificatory father's brother, had quarrelled. None of the latter's children or classificatory children went.

In fact the quarrel which took place concerned another wedding, that of a divorced woman who was the sister of JA in the case above:

A man from Karibu village gave a *mahari* of 100 shillings to get engaged to Bt. A in Minazini. Her mother's brother was in charge of the negotiations. However, the woman's brother, JA, decided that he didn't want his sister to marry this man, even though everyone knew he was already sleeping at her house. So when another suitor came along, JA married his sister off to him, without consulting the mother's brother, who had not in fact informed him about the original betrothal.

Mohammed added:

> Strictly speaking, an adult woman [i.e. one who has already been married once] has the final word about her marriage, but according to our customs, once it has been done [i.e. the marriage arranged], that is that.

The wedding consists of a number of elements – the reading of the marriage contract (*ndoa*), which is performed by an Islamic teacher or Sheikh, the consummation (*kuingia ndani* lit. 'the going inside'), which happens directly afterwards, and the removal of the bride (*kuhama*) to her husband's home, which may be delayed for some time. After the consummation of a woman's first marriage, information is sought as to whether the bride was a virgin or not:

> A wedding took place at the house of FT. They cooked rice and fish afterwards, and danced the *mkwaju*. The consummation was at 10 p.m. The girl was not a virgin.

> **P.** How do you know?
> **M.** You ask [someone who attended] 'Was the wedding consummated (*kajibu harusi*)? And was she [the bride] 'big' (not a virgin) or 'small' (virgin)?' Or you can ask, 'Who was bigger, the man or the woman?' I got this information from a woman in Pwani who is my affine.

In another instance reported by Mohammed, the wedding was not consummated:

> HS and his wife were both bewitched (*wamerogwa*) when they got married. The husband was ready but the woman didn't want to be penetrated.

Mohammed added:

This girl was previously betrothed to another man and he is probably the witch [who has prevented the consummation].

Within a few days of marriage, the couple moves to the groom's home, with the bride being accompanied by female relatives who usually stay with her for a few days, as in the case of JA's daughter mentioned above, who had married a man from Kwale Island (see Map p. 33):

> The *mashua* from Kwale island took the bride, together with various women relatives, to Kwale [her husband's home].

Ties of affinity thus link Minazini village not only to the other villages on Mafia, but even further afield, to other parts of the coastal region.

DEATH AND BEING AN ANCESTOR

Deaths are invariably public knowledge, and burials, which usually take place within twenty-four hours, can be attended by anyone who chooses to go. Mohammed gave the following account of the funeral of a shaman who died in 1966, at which a man who was owed money by the deceased invoked his right to claim the money prior to the burial:

Waziri died at 8 p.m. The funeral was at his house. At the time when the bed [i.e. the bier] was being taken through the door, Ali said that the corpse should not be put onto the bed because he was owed 60 shillings and so they had a collection [to pay that debt] on the spot. And there was enough to pay for the shroud from the usual collection. They read a *hitima* [on the day of the death], and [then] the *hitima ya tatu* [on the third day]. They did not cook. Very many people came. Many people in the courtyard were possessed while doing *dhikiri* (Sufi chanting) and ran off [in their possessed state]. Very many women came – you would say that in Pwani there was not a single person [who did not come], in Kisiki, perhaps around fifty and in Karibu only twenty people would have been left [in the village].

Subsequent rituals, held on the third day and the fortieth day, are by invitation only and involve serving a lot of food, as in the following instances:

1 There was a Koranic reading for the third day at the house of SA in Karibuni, Minazini. They cooked rice with goat meat because of the death of his classificatory mother in Zanzibar.
2 A pounding of rice was held at the house of FI for the funeral feast of his deceased daughter.
3 People slept over at JK's house and cooked rice and fish. In the morning, they cooked rice and slaughtered a cow for the fortieth-day Koranic reading of Bt. J who had been the wife of HM in Pwani.
   Friday 14th day of 9th month:
4 [Later] There was a Koranic reading and rice and a cow were cooked for Bt. J of Pwani. But it was not the final feast (*karamu kabisa*).

P. Why not, since they had slaughtered a cow?
M. Because they had only read the third-day *hitima*, and had not yet put the headstone on the grave, nor the little stones which are placed there.[2]

The second and fourth cases above mention the feast which must be given for someone who has died. It is usually held along with the fortieth-day Koranic reading, but may be delayed until very much

Plate 12 Men at a funeral

later, especially if the necessary resources are not available, as was the case with the feast for Mohammed's daughter and sister mentioned in Chapter 10.

Where a death is that of a married man, his wife has to observe a period of ritual mourning and seclusion, known as *edda*. Mohammed makes mention of this in his diary, when the widow of a man who had died in Minazini was 'brought out' of her *edda*:

> Bt. A, who had been the wife of WH, was brought out of *edda* with the reading of a *hitima* and paying of money [in lieu of food] to the participants. Her co-wife was also brought out of *edda* at her own place.

Mohammed added:

During the *edda* period, a woman isn't supposed to look after herself. She wears a piece of the shroud cloth tied around her hair. Men who are closely related to her do not speak to her until the end of *edda* when there is a ritual called *anzo la humba*. I did not speak once to my wife's sister during the period of her *edda*. But now I speak to her as usual. If things aren't done properly in this way, it will harm her and make her ill, she will become sort of crazy (*wazimu*). Because *edda* is the law which was laid down by God.

The holding of the main funeral feast does not mean that there are no further rituals for those who have died. They become ancestors, and as such are entitled to be remembered in various ways, for example in the ritual of ancestral remembrance (*kuarehemu wazee*) held before a circumcision, and also during the seventh month of the lunar calendar when graves are swept, and people hold Koranic readings for their ancestors:

1 There was a Koranic reading to remember the ancestors at KH's house. He slaughtered a cow.
2 Kombo [Mohammed's brother] held a Koranic reading to remember his ancestors at his house. He did not cook food but gave 90 cents to each man who came.
3 Bt. A held a Koranic reading to remember her ancestors at her house and she cooked food [for the participants].
4 HM had a Koranic reading at the graves in our ward to honour his dead. He gave money to the participants.
5 MM and Bt. S read a *hitima* and cooked rice and fish for the participants. They had made a vow to remember the ancestors.

If ancestors are not remembered and honoured in this way, they might 'take hold' of a child and cause it to become sick (*kushikwa na maiti*) (see Chapter 9). In such cases, propitiatory readings have to be held.

Some people also hold readings for a particular ancestor, especially a parent, on the anniversary of the person's death; this is known as a *hitima ya mwanasha*:

SK read a *hitima ya mwanasha* for his father at his house, and cooked rice and fish.

Funeral rituals are followed by inheritance of property, which on Mafia follows Islamic law according to which men get twice as much as women. There is rarely any dispute about this, but Mohammed did record a case in his own family where the deceased had left different instructions:

My ancestor Daud laid down that his property should be inherited equally by both men and women, and whoever disagreed with this would suffer all their lives. Juma and Silima (the sons) disagreed, saying that it was not the law. Mwasiti and Fatuma (the daughters) said, 'Never mind, we have nothing to say' [i.e. they would not seek to have Daud's wishes carried out]. Juma and Silima both died, and that curse still haunts their children.

Mohammed added:

Juma was influenced by his son who was studying with a Sheikh in Kwale, and who told his father not to agree to Daud's instructions [presumably because they were not in accordance with Islamic law]. That son is now reaping the curse of his grandfather, and you can see how [miserable] Silima's son is, likewise even his children and grandchildren.

Here the men, who would have lost out by following Daud's instructions, invoked Islamic law, and the women, who would have benefited, decided not to make an issue of it. But according to Mohammed, the men and their descendants are haunted by the curse of the ancestor whose wishes were disregarded. In the case of Mohammed's own father, however, his wishes had been respected by the children:

> When Mohammed's father was alive, he told his children that he wanted men and women to inherit equally and he did not want them to sell. They followed his wishes. Thus they have only sold some of their mother's coconut field and prefer to rent out their trees [rather than sell them].

Ancestors are thus very much part of the lives of their descendants; they have to be remembered and propitiated through Koranic readings and the clearing of their graves and their wishes about inheritance of property respected. Failure to honour the dead in this way can provoke affliction, as is further discussed in Chapter 8.

FAMILY QUARRELS AND THEIR CONSEQUENCES

In his diary, Mohammed frequently refers to quarrels between relatives and affines, as well as to disputes between unrelated villagers. In the remainder of this chapter I consider two types of quarrel of which mention occurs most frequently: between parents and children, and between husbands and wives. Such information came from the kind of gossip that he might have picked up on the verandahs of village shops where men gather to talk. In some instances, where such events lead to accusations of witchcraft and involve spirits, he might well have heard about them at spirit possession rituals, which are always followed by divination sessions.

Parental curses

In the account of his life given in 1994, Mohammed talked about the benefits of having children (see Chapter 2). He made it plain that children should be obedient and helpful to their parents, and should care for them in old age. Such ideals are not always realised, and a parent, if very angry with an adult child, may withdraw his or her *radhi* (blessing or satisfaction before God). Such curses are used a number of times in Mohammed's diary to explain someone's state of poverty:

1 KH does not have his mother's blessing. She said to him: 'You will be as if you do not exist in this world.'
2 Fatuma does not have the blessing of her mother Bt. W.
3 DO has quarrelled with his mother; she caused him to 'drag himself along' by saying: 'The whole of your life which you live in the world, you will only know how to get things, but not how to keep them.'

Mohammed added:

All of these people are poor and appear to be unlucky (*hawana bahati*). DO's mother has now died, but the quarrels between the others have been going on openly.

P. What does 'withdrawal of blessing' (*kutoa radhi*) actually mean?

M. It is a kind of witchcraft (*kuapisa*). You do not have their blessing, and yet you are from their blood. She has carried you for nine months until she gets the pain of bearing you. It is that she has prayed a bad prayer to God [against you] – your mother is your Sherif.[3]

P. Suppose he or she is angry with you without reason or for insufficient reason?

M. You mean because she told you to divorce your wife or set fire to some-one's field [and you refused to carry out such unreasonable instructions]? How can God agree to such words?

P. So what are the reasons why parents withdraw their blessing?

M. Failure to help them in their field, if you steal often, if you seduce your mother's brother's wife or the wife of your elder brother or your own daughter, then your mother will throw you out, or if you sell coconuts to spend money on women, you'll get trouble on trouble.

After this conversation, Mohammed produced a number of other cases of parental curses:

1 MH does not have the blessing of his father, and the day on which this happened I was passing on the path [and heard it all]; it is not as if I heard it from other people. The father said: 'I do not bless you, you will be below [other] people.'
[Others intervened saying] 'That is not right.'
[But the father said] 'Leave him, he will move out of my place.'

2 Shomari does not have his father's blessing because the latter gave him 80 shillings to look after for him. When the father wanted it back, the son didn't give him a single shilling, saying: 'I do not have it.' [The father then replied] 'Alright, I do not bless you.'

3 Juma does not have his father's blessing because he had intercourse with his step-mother (*mkwewe*). Although he [Juma] said: 'From today onwards I won't fornicate with her again', and he swore not to do it any more, [still] his lot in the world is accursed (*laana juu ya laana*).

4 MS does not have his father's blessing because where the father goes, the child does not want to follow [i.e. he is disobedient].

5 AW of Ndagoni village [in central Mafia] does not have his father's blessing because when he was in Zanzibar, he used to get drunk and was locked up several times.

6 SM does not have his deceased mother's blessing, and you see how he is today. He is always in rags begging for a cigarette. He does not have his mother's blessing because [they quarrelled and he said to her] 'You are not my mother, nor do you have a passage (*daraja*, lit. bridge) through which you could have borne me.' The mother replied, 'Is that so? I don't have a birth canal? Then let your life be nothing until you die.'

Here the offending son insults his mother in the worst possible way by implying that she is not really his mother – she is physically incapable of having given birth to him.

In another mother–son quarrel, the former makes a request of her son to divorce his wife and he refuses:

JH married a wife who was already four months pregnant. She had a son, and her husband then divorced her, but afterwards he decided to recall her. His mother said: 'Don't recall her if you want to keep my blessing.' But JH recalled her nonetheless. His mother said: 'I withdraw my blessing from you, child. Your life will be as if you were not in the world.'

Mohammed stated earlier that for a parent to ask a child to divorce his or her spouse is unreasonable, but in this case, it was seen as reasonable because the woman was already pregnant at the time of marriage, presumably by someone else. However, the husband chose to put his wife before his mother, who then cursed him.

Mohammed's accounts in his diary of parents who have cursed their children should be set alongside his view (see Chapter 2) of what having children means: they represent wealth, and should be of service to their parents. This notion of filial duty is increased in the case of a mother, who, as Mohammed notes in the examples above, deserves the utmost respect for having carried the child in her womb and having gone through the pain of birth.[4] Where children fail in their duties to their parents, the latter feel pain and anger, and may be justified in calling on God to curse them.

Marital quarrels

Husbands and wives also have clear sets of duties to one another, as Mohammed has already mentioned in Chapter 2: a wife should seek her husband's permission before leaving the house, she should cook and serve food for him. Husbands should support their wives by giving them food and clothes. In actuality, on Mafia as elsewhere, marital relations are subject to constant negotiation. Some marriages are close and affectionate. On returning to the village on one occasion, I met a friend and greeted him, whereupon he told me news of a divorce. I teasingly asked him, 'Are *you* still married to the same wife then?' He replied very seriously: 'There will be no separating or divorcing until one of us dies (*Hakuna ya kuachana mpaka kufa mmoja*).' Another anecdote also springs to mind: a female friend of mine had toothache. A few days later, I met her husband who complained that he too had acute toothache. 'Oh, not *both* of you', I exclaimed, and he replied, 'You see, we love each other.' Later, his son told me that when this man was dying, he could not bear to be separated from his wife for an instant: 'He would call her name constantly.'

But weddings do not always mean that people live happily ever after. One of the commonest items in Mohammed's diary is reference to marital quarrels. They are enlightening on the subject of emotions – love, hate, jealousy, rage. Some lead to separation or divorce, some, albeit rarely, to displays of violence, some to accusations of witchcraft. They can be caused by a variety of matters, as the following cases recorded by Mohammed indicate:

> FM of Pwani divorced his wife because he didn't want her to go to her parents' place and she went there nonetheless.

A wife is supposed to seek her husband's permission before leaving the house (*kuagana naye*), which was part of the reason Mwahadia and Mohammed were to quarrel in 1976 (see Chapter 6).

> UH's wife Bt. M was not at home from 10 p.m. to 2 a.m. When she returned home her husband asked her where she had been and the wife replied: 'I have been where I pleased', whereupon he divorced her for the second time.

Here the woman has not only been away without permission, and at night, but she is quite unrepentant about it.

> WP divorced his wife because she refused to go and give the calves water. [On being divorced] she went first to her classificatory older brother, who took her to her sister's house. But he [the husband] recalled her the same day.

Here a no doubt exhausted wife refused to perform yet another chore, and her husband exercised his right to divorce her. However, the husband soon thought better of his action and took her back, which he can do twice before the divorce becomes final on the third pronouncement.

> MA told his wife Bt. M, 'Give me my marital rights (*haki yangu*).' The wife replied, 'I can't, I am tired.' He said, 'What kind of woman are you if you get tired?' Bt. M is still angry.

Mohammed made it clear (see Chapter 2) that, upon marriage, a man is supposed to have access to his wife's body whenever he pleases. In actuality, of course, this too is a matter for negotiation. The wife in this case was all the more furious because of her husband's slighting of her femininity, as well as his refusal to recognise the reality of her exhaustion.

Some husband–wife quarrels are over property, which under Islamic law is held separately, although couples on good terms do not always make a clear distinction about who owns what. In the event of an unhappy marriage, however, one or other may insist upon ensuring that each item of property is separately owned, and that the other has no rights to it, as in the following case:

> MA accused his wife before the Village Development Committee of eating one of his bags of rice. The VDC looked into it and decided that she should get one third of the value of their [joint] harvest.

Mohammed added:

Although this woman is his wife, her husband never goes there, claiming that he cannot enjoy himself [have sex] because there are big children living there. Only the other day, she had helped her husband pay off a debt. If she had had brothers or adult sons with any sense [to represent her before the VDC], she would not have had to pay this money.

Husbands and wives, even if they cultivate jointly, may decide, particularly if relations are not very good, to separate out the harvest.

In the above instance, a polygynously married man, who did not go as regularly as he should to the house of one of his wives, accused her of eating 'his' rice. Mohammed felt that the husband's behaviour was unreasonable: she had helped to grow the rice, and therefore had ownership rights in it. Furthermore under Islamic law a husband should be responsible for supporting his wife with food and clothes. Mohammed also felt that the final division was unfair – she should have received a half, rather than a third of the crop.

Although men have the right to divorce their wives without even having to give a reason, women cannot obtain divorces themselves. They may, however, complain loudly and sometimes publicly about their husbands' behaviour, as in the following case reported by Mohammed in his diary:

> Fatuma said [to her husband] 'I, my friend, am not yet properly married, because if I were [things would be different].' Her husband said: 'That is not reasonable. Forget about the past and don't remember it while you are with me.'

Mohammed explained further:

Fatuma said that formerly she got clothes such as *kanga* and *kaniki* (black work clothes) from her first husband, Mohammed's elder brother, who had divorced her when he went to live in Zanzibar. Then she married another man who also divorced her. Her third husband was also quite rich and she had all the clothes she wanted until he died. After her *edda* she married her current husband whose means didn't match up to those of some of her previous husbands, which was why she said contemptuously that it was as if he had never married her, whereupon her husband told her to forget the past.

Some women who are discontented with their marriages seek to provoke their husbands into giving them a divorce:

> Bt. W of Pwani village does not want to sleep with her husband because he is dirty and does not wash his clothes, or bath or clean his teeth.

In one instance recorded in his diary, an angry woman threatened her husband that she would poison him if he did not divorce her:

> [Subsequently], Juma [the husband in the case] saw a small bottle under their hen-house and took it to his cell-head (*balozi*) and accused her [of carrying out her threat]. [Before that] he had taken his wife's [sanitary] cloth, put water on it and squeezed out menstrual blood (*hidhi*) which he put in a bottle in an attempt to prove that she had tried to poison him.[5] But she saw him doing this and she shouted out. People came

running: 'Why are you shouting?' 'Ah extraordinary things are happening today!' Meanwhile, Juma threw the cloth away into a bush and she accused him in front of the Chairman. They were all called up [in front of the Village Development Council] and the law caught Juma. The wife was asked for her opinion. [She said] 'I shall forgive him, but this year don't let us go to [cultivate in] Z. [an outlying area of the village]; let us go to T., to the house of my father.'

In this instance, the cause of the quarrel between husband and wife is not recorded, but it seems to hinge on the decision about where to cultivate. Her threat to 'poison him' led to a counter-accusation that she had actually done so by using her menstrual blood, and evidence was fabricated by the husband to try and prove his allegations. The VDC, however, believed the story of the wife, who nonetheless, agreed to a reconciliation provided that they cultivated near to her family rather than his.

A variety of reasons have so far been given for marital quarrels; however, the commonest cause in Mohammed's diary is adultery, indeed, he reports no fewer than twenty-six such cases, some of which precipitated a divorce:

1 TJ found two *kanga* and some dress material in his house, and he has quarrelled with his wife Bt. N because he knows her lover AP gave them to her.
  later: Bt. T said she had seen AP with Bt. N and suspected them of having an affair. Mohammed thought it was indeed the case and that AP had given the woman the *kanga* and material which the husband had found and burned.
2 Pwani village. MM went to the beach [to fish], but when he got back [at night] he found his wife had been 'stolen' and he went to inform the elders: 'My wife is not there at home.' The elders remained at their house. When the woman returned, she went into the house and began to groan and she was asked what was the matter. 'My stomach hurts me, I have diarrhoea' [i.e. she was pretending that she had gone out for this reason].
  The elders said, 'You are a hypocrite (*mnafiki*). We have been here for a long time.' Then MM said, 'Elders, bear me witness. I divorce this woman for the first time.'

Mohammed added:

This woman has a lover and can't stand the husband who is very dirty in his person and doesn't bother about his clothes. Their elders are the same people since they [husband and wife] are cross-cousins.

A first divorce is not final, and indeed in this latter case, the following entry indicates a reconciliation after the quarrel:

> MM of Pwani recalled his wife. He had divorced her because she was seduced when he went fishing.

However, not all such cases end peaceably, as the following instance demonstrates:

> AJ committed adultery with the wife of HB in Kisiwa. The latter came to Minazini in the middle of the night and knocked at the door of AJ's house. AJ woke up, put on a *kanga*, let him in and gave him a chair, but then HB started beating him with a stick. They fought each other, even bit each other, and eventually HB ran off leaving his hat and shoes behind.

Mohammed added:

This affair has been going on for ages.

Later in his diary, Mohammed recalled a similar case:

> A long time ago, Hatibu from Kirongwe saw a man lying with his wife in his house, their heads on the same pillow and covered with a single cloth, a *kanga*. Hatibu went out and started digging a grave. The woman heard Hatibu digging. She went to his brother and said: 'Hatibu is digging inside his place. I am not sure what he has seen.' His elder brother called him: 'Hatibu, come quickly. Are you planning to kill someone?' 'No, I will not kill anyone. I do not want to do that.' The brother replied: 'Stop behaving like this, Hatibu.'

Mohammed added:

Hatibu had come back unexpectedly, since he was supposed to be at the house of his other wife. He did not wake the lovers up but went to dig a grave, giving the impression that he would come back and kill his wife's seducer. The brother then went and woke up the lover and threw him out.

In this case threatened violence was prevented by a relative, who thereby also saved the face of the wronged party.

However, husbands are not the only ones to become violent when cases of adultery are discovered; angry wives can also sometimes take drastic measures:

1 MM of Pwani committed adultery and was found out by his wife, who beat him with a stick for sleeping with someone else's wife.

2 JB was also beaten by his wife for sleeping with someone else's wife.
3 JM had an affair with Bt. M and his own wife found them in a deserted hut. Bt. M ran off. The wife tore her husband's shirt and yelled at him, while he just cried. Next morning, an older male relative took the wife back to her father, who provided another shirt for his son-in-law. Soon afterwards, the wife returned to her husband.

Many women do not accept that their husbands should have extra-marital affairs, and feel both sexual jealousy and anger at the diversion of scarce resources that such affairs often entail. But others, of course, may engage in their own affairs, as Mohammed reports:

If a woman wants to give a present to a lover, she makes up a basket containing bread, lime, buns, a betel-nut box (*kijalbe*), sugar, matches, cigarettes, cooked chicken, spices, fruit and says: 'I am giving a present to (*namhonga*) my man, my love.'

As several of the above cases suggest, another response to the discovery of an adulterous affair is for the elders to sort it out:

Pwani. Juma committed adultery at night with the wife of Hatibu his close relative; both had children in the same big circumcision lodge. The judgement was that he should receive four strokes [of a cane], because the elders were very upset and said it was an exceptionally disgraceful matter (*kitu aibu, fedheha*). When taxed with the offence, the man agreed that he had come [to commit adultery] and was beaten.

In this instance, the adultery of the man was deemed worse than that of the woman because of his close kinship with the wronged husband, and judgement and punishment were carried out by their elders. But in other cases of adultery, the elders may refuse to intervene:

Haji told his father and mother-in-law that his wife was committing adultery with Ali (a youth of Pwani), and they said, 'What do you want us to do about it?'

Mohammed added:

It is not respectful (*heshima*) to tell your in-laws [about such a matter] – he made a mistake that son-in-law.
But [in another case] Hatibu of Pwani also told his in-law that his wife was committing adultery with MJ and s/he replied: 'I will forbid it'.

In some instances, a cuckolded husband threatens to bring a formal complaint against the seducer of his wife:

Adultery. Pwani. At night, K caught someone in his house committing adultery; [as he ran away] he left his hat behind. The cuckolded husband went to his ten-house cell leader (*balozi*) and accused his mother's sister's son YM [of being the seducer]. The *balozi* said that YM should be judged, but the latter refused, saying that K had previously seduced *his* wife. Thus he was not judged.

Mohammed added:

They talk to one another even now. Whether each knows that the other is committing adultery with his wife I don't know.

In this instance, Mohammed suggests that the matter is quietly dropped because the suspected lover is well aware that the husband is also having an affair with his own wife. In another case, he suggests that such affairs can go on for long periods without breaking up the marriages of either party:

Bt. M committed adultery with MJ. The woman got pregnant and had a son. MJ said, 'Child (*mwana*), please let me marry you and the child will be mine.' But the woman replied, 'No, my love, my desire (*mahaba*) is that we just "play".' So they went on with their games, and the woman got 'caught' again (*kanasa tena*), this time she had a daughter. The man came again and asked her, 'What do you say now?' The woman replied, 'No, it is nothing at all; I am of the same mind, *bwana*.' [He said] 'As you please.'

In his diary, Mohammed reports several other cases of adulterous liaisons leading to the birth of children:

1 SH married Bt. S, but on the day of the wedding, he did not consummate the marriage, nor for the following five years. But the woman got pregnant [nonetheless] and had a child, HS. SH went secretly to the Sheikh and said to him: 'I ask you, I married a wife, I have not had intercourse with her even once, and she has had a child, HS.' The Sheikh replied: 'The law says that the child is yours, after all, you have the woman to this day, it's all the same, the child is yours.'

Mohammed added:

He [SH] was previously married to another woman, whom he divorced. He was impotent all this time, he was just a shadow (*kivuli*) going by the name of a man. So HS cannot be his son.

2 JA and his sister Bt. A were both born when their father was away. He returned to find them there, but the law says that they are his, both of them.

3 AZ and his sister Bt. Z were also both born when their father was away. He saw them only on his return, but they are his children.

According to Islamic law, the children of a legally married woman belong to her husband, regardless of who the genitor is, and will inherit his property. But if such a child suffers misfortune in the future, people may say that this is because of the illicit nature of his or her conception:

> MS married a wife who was already pregnant, and she had a boy SM, and the husband acknowledged the child as his own. MS died, and SM inherited the property, but it has no blessing (*baraka*), it is accursed (*laana*).

Thus adultery does not necessarily lead to illegitimacy, unless a married man has an affair with a divorced or widowed woman. In such instances, if she bears a child, it is considered illegitimate (*mwanaharamu*), and this is a matter of some shame, as Mohammed notes in Chapter 2. Much worse, however, is for an unmarried girl to become pregnant. There were few such cases in the 1960s, when most girls were secluded between first menstruation and marriage, but Mohammed's diary does contain one particularly notorious instance, which resulted in a murder case:

> A girl in southern Mafia got pregnant. Her father and mother got together and killed it [the baby]; they dug a grave and buried it. Above the grave they placed coconut husks and set fire to them. An investigation was made and they were arrested and taken away and put in jail in Kilindoni.

Mohammed added:

They did this because the girl was getting engaged. It is not known if they killed the child first or buried it alive. The father [of the girl] was released pending the trial because he maintained that the girl was being brought up [not in his house but] by her grandmother, and also that since she was a pubescent girl (*mwali*) who was secluded 'inside' (*kualikwa ndani*),[6] he would not have been able to see her until she got married. This case has to be dealt with by a judge from the mainland [because of its serious nature].

Although adultery not infrequently arouses violent passions, it does not necessarily lead to physical retribution, but sometimes rather to suspicions of witchcraft, particularly that involving spirits. It is as though human emotions are projected into the spirit world, where they can more easily be managed (Crapanzano 1977b, 1980, Caplan 1992a). Mohammed recalled several such instances which had happened sometime in the past:

1 Bakari of Mashariki married Bt. T of Minazini. But afterwards MM of Minazini committed adultery with her. Bakari immediately divorced her, and she married her lover. Then MM bewitched Bakari and sent a spirit after him which rendered him impotent (*kamvunja kiume mbeleni*), then he caused the spirit to climb into the latter's head so that he became possessed. And Bakari slaughters cows [i.e. participates in spirit possession rituals] to this day. MM is now dead, and so is the woman, but Bakari is a shaman (*mganga*) even today although he is now old and blind.

P. But if he had become a shaman, couldn't he then get his own back?
M. Some people are more possessed (*wanasikiwa zaidi*), that is, the spirit loves them more. The spirit loved MM more because he had been with him from the beginning, whereas Bakari had only had the spirit sent to him by MM.

Mohammed added:

Of course, all of these deeds will eventually be called to account before God.

2 BJ, an important man in Pwani, came into his house and saw a man whom he recognised. He went back out and went to his older brother's house and called out to him. The latter replied [that he was there]. Then BJ said, 'Come, there is a man in my house.' The brother got up and said, 'Leave him to come out by himself, don't confront him directly (*usimsemeze*), it is a shameful matter (*aibu*).' But they gave him [the lover] their spirit which destroyed his legs [so that he couldn't walk] nor could he speak. He died of that very illness (*shida*). But this happened a long time ago.

Mohammed added:

BJ is reputed to do such things even now – he has quite a young wife and whoever speaks to her is given to the spirit. He is a powerful witch (*mchawi mkubwa*).

In both of the above cases, jealous men are thought to use their control of spirits to cause the illness of rivals. Indeed, it is striking the extent to which sexual activity, especially if it is illicit, is thought to lead to involvement with spirits, a topic which is discussed in greater detail in Chapters 9 and 10.

CONCLUSION

On Mafia, as elsewhere, norms of behaviour may be laid down to regulate relations between parents and children, husbands and wives, but these are ultimately negotiated in day-to-day living. Where one party considers that the other has failed to behave in a reasonable way, by thwarting their authority, failing to pay due respect, and exposing them to shame and ridicule, powerful emotions are aroused. In the case of serious quarrels between parents and children, parents have the sanction of withdrawing their 'satisfaction before God', who is seen as the ultimate agent in the consequences which ensue. In the case of quarrels between husbands and wives, a husband can have recourse to Islamic law (*sheria*) which allows him to divorce his wife. But in many instances, quarrels are projected onto the world of spirits and witchcraft, a topic on which Mohammed wrote a good deal in his diary.

First, however, in the next section of the book, we see how some of the issues discussed in this part were reflected in Mohammed's own life as I observed it over three encounters between the 1960s and the 1980s.

Part III

Other texts, other voices

Three encounters 1965–85

Introduction

In this third section of the book, comprising three chapters, I turn to other voices besides that of Mohammed. I have utilised a variety of texts not only to add more information about Mohammed, but also to provide a portrait of Mohammed's wife Mwahadia, their daughter Subira, and their complex relationships with each other. Here I present a series of sketches drawn from different periods of time – my first three visits in the 1960s, 1970s and 1980s – to give increasing layers of information which reveal how their lives developed, as well as how my own knowledge of them accrued over time. In each chapter, the voice of each of the characters is heard in turn. Two themes recur in each visit: one is the often stormy nature of the relations between Mohammed, Mwahadia and Subira, and the second is the ways in which their various afflictions and problems, particularly in regard to illness and death, were dealt with. Here a belief in spirits (*mashaitaini, majini*) and their powers for both good and evil, healing and harming, is significant.

In the first chapter of this section (Chapter 5), based on my first and longest stay between 1965 and 1967, we encounter Mohammed and Mwahadia in their 30s, bearing children and struggling to make ends meet. Here I have used records of conversations with both of them, as well as my own field-notes and diary, as well as employing a few extracts from Mohammed's diary. The second chapter of this section is based on my 1976 visit of a few months, when I went to make a film with a BBC TV crew. At this time, Mohammed's and Mwahadia's marriage had just broken up, and I was called upon to act as a mediator. The texts used in this chapter are conversations with Mohammed and Mwahadia, some of them recorded on film, each giving their account of the situation, and the views of other people, including their daughter Subira, who thought they should divorce, and Mohammed's elder brother, who was keen to see them reconciled.

The third chapter, based on my 1985 visit, finds Mohammed and Mwahadia divorced, and neither has remarried. The children meanwhile are growing up; some are married and some have children of their own. Their daughter Subira, already married, divorced and remarried, is having marital difficulties of her own, and turning to shamans for help with her problems.

This part of the book, then, is multivocal: it is one in which voices 'talk with, against, and about each other' (Werbner 1991: 4). Here too the voice of the anthropologist is heard more clearly, partly because most of the texts are conversations between myself and one or other of the informants, and partly because I was increasingly drawn into their lives.

5 Encounter one
1965–7

The voices in this chapter are primarily those of Mohammed and Mwahadia, as well as my own as ethnographer, from the period betwen 1965 and 1967, when I spent over a year living in Minazini village. In the last part of the chapter, the story of the family's life is continued through Mohammed's letters to me written in the late 1960s and early 1970s when I had returned to Britain.

MOHAMMED

As already noted, I first met Mohammed when my cook, Ali, introduced him to me early in our stay in Minazini village. Mohammed became a frequent visitor to our house. In my first notebook, I record that he gave me a short account of his life, telling me that, as a youth, he had run away from Koran school in order to become a sailor on coastal dhows. Later he had been several times to Zanzibar to pick cloves. About eight years earlier, he had married Mwahadia, a distant relative, and by that time in 1965 they had had five children, the first of whom had died.

Mohammed gave me the following account of the circumstances of his marriage:

She [Mwahadia] was already married in Zanzibar and her husband was a witch (*mchawi*). My mother didn't want me to marry her because she was afraid I would be killed. But I said even if I marry her on Thursday and die on Friday [I don't care]. When I went off to Zanzibar, I didn't get any reply from the letter which I sent to my parents [about this proposed marriage], but finally when I returned to Mafia, I found [another] wedding prepared for me about which I hadn't received their letter.

I threatened to change my name, go off and never see them again. My mother was afraid I would commit suicide, so finally I got my own way. The wedding took place on the 13th day of the month. The next day I went to build a fence together with my father. He became ill and died on the 15th day, and everyone said, 'He has already been eaten' [i.e. by the witchcraft of the ex-husband].

When I returned to Pemba, I got stung by a scorpion and when I returned to Zanzibar, I met Mwahadia's ex-husband. We exchanged greetings, but later the hand he had shaken swelled up. I went to a shaman to get medicine; he said it was '*tambo*' (harmful objects believed to be sent into the body by witchcraft, see Chapter 9). By that time I was already married to Mwahadia. But the arm still hurts me to this day. Then I had a small sore on my leg and it swelled up for seven months. I had some charms which I got from Kirongwe to wear on the leg, and the same shaman gave me some medicine. One day the leg would hurt, another day it would be the arm.

At the time, I thought that the point about this story was that Mohammed had risked his life, as well as the affection of his parents, to marry Mwahadia because he loved her so much. I was therefore somewhat surprised when he revealed later during my first visit that he had already divorced her once:

Mwahadia's father, who had never wanted the marriage, said to her, 'I do not like Mohammed – tell him to divorce you.' After she had borne two children, he [Mohammed] divorced her at her own request. But then she persuaded his relatives to get him to recall her. She was two months pregnant at the time. She made a vow (*nadhiri* i.e. to a spirit) that if he should recall her she would 'do something' [i.e. make an offering], but she hasn't fulfilled it yet.

After he [Mohammed] had recalled her, her father was furious and forbade her to go back to her husband; he insulted Mohammed's father's brother, who was his own cross-cousin, until the latter told him that he had no manners (a serious insult), which was going far beyond the bounds of their joking relationship (*utani*).[1] Mwahadia said she had had enough and she went off immediately [back to Mohammed].

My understanding of this account at the time was that the divorce had been precipitated by Mwahadia's father, rather than by any problem between Mohammed and Mwahadia, and that she had defied her father to return to Mohammed because of her affection for him. Although this was probably true, I was also soon to learn from Mohammed himself that he had frequent affairs with other women:

In Pwani and Minazini there are many people who hate me because of their wives. They watched me to see which house I go to a lot and decided to put a spirit there to catch me.

On the day of the *kitanga*[2] ritual in Pwani last Tuesday, my mother's brother became possessed and said: 'My friend I have something to say to you, but I am afraid.'
'Say it.'
'They have their suspicions of you, but they have not yet actually seen you, so they have put a spirit to catch you.'
So I didn't go to that house again.

I became an important confidante for Mohammed, and was frequently told about his affairs with other women. There is no doubt that he saw himself as something of a Don Juan:

If I had had all the women who wanted to marry me, and whose parents wanted it, I would have had six or seven wives by now. When I go to the next village, the whole country shrinks. I mean they see me as a lion!

I was aware that not only was he being unfaithful to his wife, but that he gave money and gifts to his mistresses. There are half a dozen references in his diary to his own affairs, current and past, such as the following:

Mohammed committed adultery with the wife of one of the village shamans. The woman said, 'My love, I beg that I bear a child with your face, so that when I see my child, I have no doubt that I am seeing you, my love.' The woman got pregnant. After two months, Mohammed went off to Zanzibar and stayed there for three months, during which time that sweetheart's pregnancy was spoiled. [When we were together] she gave me a bread and I gave her two *kanga*. Now she runs away from me because our love is finished, and there is none left. Once she had got the *kanga* out of me, she got fed up – that is typical of what happens.

In view of his frequent affairs, it was scarcely surprising that many of the entries in my early notebooks concerning Mohammed are to do with his chronic shortage of cash. He himself recorded in his diary several presents he gave his girlfriends: cash and *kanga*, even a hen to a go-between.

Other factors also contributed to his impecunious state. At the beginning of my stay, he was being chased for a long-standing debt by a shop-keeper in a neighbouring village, who was threatening court action. At the same time, he hadn't paid his tax either, and in spite of going to work repairing the road – the usual way of paying off tax defaults – he was arrested and imprisoned in early 1966. Fortunately his older brother Kombo came to the rescue and paid the tax, for which Mohammed agreed in return to assist in completing the building of his brother's new house. The same brother also paid for the school uniform shirt of Mohammed's eldest son Seleman, without which he was not allowed to attend school.

Mohammed used to earn some cash from making thatch (*makuti*) for roofs, and he also had an income from the coconut trees which he had inherited from his parents, both of whom were dead by this time. Mohammed defined his occupation as that of a sailor, and indeed, one of the first mentions of him in my own diary is that he had gone to the district capital Kilindoni to see if he could get work on a dhow. He thus had income from a variety of sources. However, his friend Ali, my cook, always maintained that much of it went on women. He reported that after Mohammed's spell inside, he had turned over a new leaf and had started earning money by washing clothes, getting 5 shillings the first day. Even so, Mohammed told me shortly afterwards that although he and his sister were supposed to hold a joint circumcision ceremony for their sons, he had no money and therefore could not participate, a situation which was to be repeated thirty years later (see Chapter 10).

Mohammed not infrequently 'borrowed' money from me during the early months, but later in my stay, especially when he started keeping the diary, I made more regular payments to him. He sometimes accompanied me to events, and gave me a great deal of help

Plate 13 Thatching a house with palm fronds (*makuti*)

when I did a survey of the village fields. Furthermore, Mohammed was an endless source of information on spirits and their doings. He himself had inherited a relationship with a spirit which came to him in his dreams, especially after he burned incense (*kutia buhuri*) for it at night. However, although he attended spirit possession rituals, and took offerings to his ancestral spirit, he never became possessed. He regarded his relationship with his ancestral spirit as a source of protection for himself and his children and would always inform the spirit of what was about to happen, including going to see a lover.

Paradoxically, I became closer to both Mohammed and Mwahadia when I left Minazini to live in another village in the south of the island. Here I spent a shorter period of time, and found field-work much more difficult, partly because of the highly dispersed nature of the settlement. I did not make so many close relationships as I had in Minazini, and received fewer visitors from the second village. But my house was near to the main road running from north to south, and villagers from Minazini would often drop in if they were going to or from the district capital. Mohammed visited regularly, sometimes alone, sometimes accompanied by Mwahadia, and we would spend days at a time working on his diary, as well as queries I had about other texts. At the end of my stay in the second village, it was Mohammed who helped Ali and me to pack up my belongings – I still have a photo of the two of them sitting on a rolled-up bundle of mats, which I was going to ship back to the UK, and smiling broadly.

MWAHADIA

Mwahadia was Mohammed's first wife, but, as already mentioned, she herself had been married previously. She told me that she had spent three years in Zanzibar with her first husband, but had then returned to Mafia and asked for a divorce, for which she had had to pay 200 shillings, which her father raised by selling a cow and some coconut trees.

At the time of my first visit in the 1960s, Mohammed was aged about 30 and Mwahadia about 25. She had already had five children by him, three sons and two daughters, and in the summer of 1966, had an early miscarriage. Two of their children lived with other relatives in neighbouring villages – a son in Pwani and a daughter in Kisiki, a common situation in this area where a large proportion of children would be brought up by foster-parents, usually relatives such as grandparents, parents' siblings, or their own older siblings. Their eldest son, Seleman, was attending the village primary school.

Plate 14 Women's heavy workload: pounding rice

Mwahadia suffered from periodic bouts of ill-health, many of them to do with her frequent pregnancies, but also, as I realised later, with the kind of work-load that she carried, like many women in the village. In Chapter 3 there is an extract from Mohammed's diary in which he boasted that he had cleared a field which was so large that it had previously been cultivated by two people, but it was Mwahadia who had to plant and weed it. He noted shortly afterwards that she held two cooperative planting parties (*wiazi*) but much of the rest of the work she must have done alone. Furthermore, she would have had to repay the labour of her relatives and friends and, indeed, there are several references in Mohammed's diary to her going to work parties called either by other women or unmarried youths (see Chapter 3).

Mwahadia was not much better off than Mohammed in terms of wealth and property: my census for that period records that she owned one cow, but that she had not yet inherited any coconuts, as both her parents were still alive. An early entry in one of my notebooks records that Mwahadia and Mohammed came to see me, and that she asked me to give her some money to buy *kanga* as Mohammed did not give her money for clothes. Later when we were alone she told me that she was particularly annoyed with him at that moment because she knew that he had undertaken some work in the village, building a hut for someone, and that he had been paid in cash, none of which she had seen. She also told me that she wanted a divorce. I was rather shocked by this statement, as I had thought that they had a good relationship, but when I discussed the matter with Ali, he assured me that they were 'having me on' (*wanakudanganya*) as he put it. Later, I came to realise that theirs was an extremely stormy relationship, and that the source of most of their quarrels was money.

During that first visit, Mwahadia never mentioned Mohammed's extra-marital affairs, only complaining of his lack of financial support. She felt that matters would not improve as long as they stayed in Minazini, and sought to persuade him to migrate. One entry in my notebook reads as follows:

> Mwahadia is trying to persuade her husband to go to Zanzibar to live, and says that if he won't, he should divorce her. She says that they have no clothes, no hope of betterment in Mafia. She wants him to rent out his coconut trees, and get his older brother, who lives in Zanzibar, to help him get a job, and she can plait mats and do other things. But he refuses to move to Zanzibar because he says once they are there she will run away from him.

I have written elsewhere of how, during that first period of field-work, when I was in my early 20s, unmarried and childless, my relationship with Mwahadia did not become as close as it did later (Caplan 1992a). It is not insignificant, perhaps, that the full account of her first violent marriage was only given to me in 1976, when I returned as a married woman and a mother (see Chapter 6). Further-more, although I visited her often, she was always very busy, either cultivating her fields, caring for her children or finding ways to make extra cash to make ends meet in the household. Nonetheless, she was an important informant, and we discussed a number of matters, including marriage, birth and puberty rituals. On several occasions, I noted in my diary that they both came to my house and we discussed interpretations of rituals. Mwahadia came several times to stay with me when I moved to the southern village after spending a year in Minazini. An entry in my own diary notes:

Got back home at 2 p.m. [after morning out in the new village] to find Mohammed and Mwahadia asleep in my house. We talked [for a long time]. I wanted Mohammed to fix the roof because for the last few days the rain has been coming in. We talked, slept, had a meal, talked again. Mwahadia is perhaps the only person here I am comfortable sharing a room with for long periods of time. They are both so easy to be with.

I also recall from my 'headnotes' two occasions when I visited her and Mohammed. On the first, I arrived at their house one evening to have supper with them to find Mwahadia cooking fish. Their son Seleman said to his mother, 'Can I have a big piece of fish so that my body grows? They tell us at school that fish is good.' Unfortunately, a few minutes later, the cat took most of the fish, to Mwahadia's great annoyance: 'That cat! I thought it was a nice one, I've been looking after it, now it's stolen our supper!'

The second occasion was when Mohammed and Mwahadia were living in their field hut during the cultivation season. We sat inside, me on a little stool, he and she on the bed. Mohammed put his arm affectionately around his wife and said to me 'You'd better not come and sit on this bed unless you want a lot of children.' I asked what he meant. They both laughed and said 'We sleep on this bed and get a baby every year.' Maybe it was at that point that I said that I did not intend to have more than two children, a remark with which Mohammed was to tax me nearly thirty years later (see Chapter 10). This memory was a striking one as it was the only demonstration of physical affection between spouses that I had ever witnessed on Mafia, and indicated, so I thought, how fond they really were of each other, in spite of the ups and downs.

LETTERS FROM MAFIA, 1967–76

When I left the island in 1967, I gave Mohammed a pile of addressed aerogrammes, and asked him to write to me regularly, which he did for several years. There are thirty letters covering the period between my leaving the field in March 1967, and returning in May 1976. The letters were very frequent at first, less so as time went on.

Because Mohammed could only read or write in Arabic script which I could not read easily, the letters were written for my benefit in Roman script, usually by his eldest son Seleman who was then at school in Minazini, and they improve in spelling, handwriting and general literacy as the years go by. When Seleman failed his Standard

7 exam, and left school to go and train in hotel-keeping in Dar es Salaam, Mohammed had to look for other amanuenses. The first was his next son Waziri, later to be tragically drowned at sea at the age of 19 (see Chapter 2).

In contrast to the diary, which focused very much on the doings of other people in the village, much of the information contained in the letters concerned Mohammed and his family, so that I was able to follow events in their lives even when I was in London.

The following extracts are not untypical of many letters. Like those of any polite Swahili, they begin with asking after the health of the recipient, and often of all of her family too. They then detail the well-being of the sender and his family, always beginning 'we are well' (*hatujambo*) then going on to list specific items of news, for example how his second daughter Subira had reached puberty and been ritually washed, but then sent back to school rather than being secluded as was previously the custom. How his eldest son Seleman had failed his Standard 7 exam, and he did not know what to do with him. One frequent topic was illness in the household:

> 10/4/67: Greetings, and after greetings I want to know your health, and if you want to know my health, I am very well. Waziri Mohammed is ill with a chest infection (*kifua cha pumu*), and Mwahadia has a bad stomach (*ana tumbo*).

> 23/4/67: Receive this letter, beloved mama of much love and faith and sympathy Patricia Bailey [my name before marriage]. I want to know your health and well-being, and that of brother-in-law [my husband] and our elders, big and small. And how is our grandmother [my grandmother who had been unwell]? How is her illness?
>
> I am sure that you reached home safely and you were rejoiced over by our elders. And I am sure that when you go to school [i.e. University] on Monday the teachers will be very happy [to see you].
>
> If you want to know my health, I am well. Mwahadia is ill in her whole body, and her father is also ill. He has been at my place for five days now. . . .
>
> Again, I am sorry that I have sent two letters, but I have not yet had a single reply from you. . . . Again I ask that you do not neglect me (*usinitupe*). I cannot [say] much of what is in my heart [because I am overcome] if I think of the great affection we had for each other. . . .
>
> Greetings – one who is in need has no shame.

Mwahadia had several bouts of long illness after I left the field. In an early letter, Mohammed reports that she had a bad stomach, and shortly afterwards, that it had swollen up. The next few letters continue to contain references to her stomach problem, which was finally resolved by the birth of twins:

> I inform you that Mwahadia, God has opened her with twins, two babies, both girls. The big one is called Sijalowa (lit. 'I have not yet got wet') [later her adult name was Miza] and the little one Ungojewe (lit. 'wait for me') . . . but she has already begun to be called by your name, Patrisha. They were born in the 8th month, on the 24th day, on a Sunday night.

In the next letter, he informed me that the younger child had been given to me as a *somo* (namesake), which of course meant a present was called for. At the end of the letter he added:

> Mwahadia sends you many greetings. She asks you to send her an umbrella so that she may cover your somo. There has been heavy rain in Mafia – it has been raining for fifteen days now.

Mohammed, too, had his obligations as a result of the births – he was supposed to present the mother with a pair of new *kaniki* (work-clothes) after her fortieth-day purification ritual, as well as a carrying cloth for each child, but he said that he had no means of getting them 'because of the way the world is going'.

The twins were born around the end of September 1967. At the end of December, Mohammed wrote that my *somo* was unwell – she had scabies, a disease to which children are particularly prone, and one which causes intense itching, irritability, and often much crying and loss of appetite – it also often results in septic sores. Two weeks later, he sent me the following news:

> I am very sorry, I have a great deal of grief. And that grief which is afflicting me also concerns you together with my brother-in-law [my husband] and our mother [my mother]. Your namesake Patrisha Mohammed left this world last Sunday, 7th January 1968, and her illness was that of *tambazi* (swelling of the body and internal organs) and fever.

In his next letter, written at the end of January 1968, he reported that the other twin was now also sick, but was receiving treatment, both from a local Koranic healer and from the brother of a Minazini villager who worked as a dispenser in the district capital Kilindoni. Two months later he reported:

> 22/3/68 Your child Sijalowa is better from her illness; for treatment she went to the clinic in Minazini, and she was also treated outside . . . [i.e.

by local medicines]. Now she is better, she just has conjunctivitis. Mwahadia has scabies, and I have scabies, and Subira [his second daughter] has sores on her legs.

A frequent topic in Mohammed's letters is his own dire state of poverty.

23/4/67 Please, I want you to know that the *masika* [the rainy season prior to the harvest, i.e. the lean season] has got hold of me. I do not have anything to say – I only want to eat.

But once the harvest was completed that year, his thoughts turned to other monetary needs:

2/7/67 Please, Patrisha, I am very sorry, and have a lot of grief because I am giving you my shame, [since you are] my confidante. My wife and I do not have any clothes – our clothes are finished from the rain. When it rained in the night, they would rot in the day . . . My other main problem is *kitoweo* (i.e. the fish or meat bought by the husband for the daily curry). And I inform you that the circumcision of my children will take place in the 9th month. I have not got the money to pay the circumcisor. Please, I fall before you. I am in a mess (lit. I am caught), please lend me 100 shillings. Please, Patrisha, I want to buy chickens and shells [to use for trading]. One cowrie shell of first class quality costs 6 shillings and even a third grade shell costs 3 shillings. I want to get raffia, chicken and shells to go to Dar es Salaam [and sell them].

Mohammed did make this business trip, and a subsequent one shortly afterwards but the second time he went, he incurred a loss. The boys finally had their already-postponed circumcision ceremony at the beginning of 1969 (which was already very late, as one of them must have been well into puberty) but it was done as cheaply as possible, and not without the help of relatives:

I inform you that I had my children Seleman and Waziri circumcised at Kilindoni hospital on the 3rd day of the 3rd month. I was very sorry and I wept at missing your presence. I was alone in Kilindoni with [only] Mwahadia and Bwana Kombo [his brother]. I got lodging at the house of the Magistrate (*Hakimu*) of Mafia for the duration [of their stay in hospital].

His next letter, written shortly afterwards, reports

I have completed taking my children from the hospital and I went back home . . . I have not yet had the means to organise [the celebrations]. The people who helped me were my elder brothers . . .

and my wife's brother, my [classificatory] sisters and my [classificatory] daughter. I was very sorry and I wept, Patrisha, to think that you were so far away . . . I tell you everything, now I have to find a new way of earning money because I have to hold a feast [to celebrate the circumcision]. Please send me some money.

For some time after leaving the field, I used to send Mohammed small sums of money on a regular basis, but I stopped doing this when I began to be inundated with requests for similar financial help from other villagers. Tougher exchange controls were imposed, and I was somewhat thankful to have an excuse to stop, although I continued to send Mohammed and Mwahadia gifts such as clothing.

Mohammed also often wrote about his relationship with me and his feelings on the subject – sometimes he reproached me for not writing, sometimes he thanked me for money, gifts or photos. When my younger sister, who was already married by this time, had her first child, Mohammed was ecstatic to receive a picture of me holding him:

22/3/68 Thank you very much. I am very happy that you sent me a letter together with photos, you sent me your picture and one of our child. I am very happy, and so were all my brothers and sisters and friends – I showed them all the picture and they were very happy.

My feelings (lit. 'understanding') and those of Mwahadia [can scarcely be described] . . . when I got your picture I was calling you, and [it was as if] I was holding you by the hand, there only remained to call you by name, 'so and so, daughter of so and so' (*fulani binti fulani*). You filled my cup to overflowing (lit. 'you finished my understanding to the end'), and all my elders said: 'Never reject Patlisha, because she is an honest (*sawa*) person, a person of truth, and in the whole of your life you will never get a friend like her.'

Often, the affection is tempered by requests for help, or else is proffered reproachfully because I have not written to him:

6/12/67 I am very sorry, because this is not what we promised each other. I am very ready to send letters, but you are very reluctant (*mzito*). I got your letter after you returned from your journey [I had spent the summer in Canada], and I understood everything that was in it. I sent you a reply but I have not had a letter since then until today. And so I want to know, are you getting my letters, or are you not?

1/9/68 And that present [i.e. the coconut tree he gave me when I was leaving] is bearing well. Do not think that I have forgotten you. I will not forget you until I die even if you do not write me letters.

In a letter written in December 1969, Mohammed announced a bomb-shell – Mwahadia had walked out:

> Mwahadia is asking me to divorce her. What do you say? She is at her [parents'] place, she went there without my permission very suddenly. Quickly, quickly, I want an answer – I am having big problems.

However, they were reconciled again and in 1970, Mwahadia became pregnant and another child, a boy named Juma, was born in early 1971. Again Mwahadia was unwell, and Mohammed wrote complaining of their parlous state, because they had not been able to cultivate that season. But Mwahadia became ill again, and once more there was a quarrel – in an undated letter around the end of 1972, Mohammed reports that he divorced her but then recalled her. That was the second formal divorce, and a third would, under Islamic law, mean the end of their marriage.

6 Encounter two
1976

On arrival back on Mafia in May 1976 for a week's stay to prepare for filming several months later,[1] I found Mohammed and Mwahadia living in their field hut in the bush-land on the outskirts of the village, guarding their ripening crop. I spent several hours with Mwahadia, helping her cook and catching up on news. To my surprise, she told me that she intended to leave Mohammed as soon as the harvest was over. I did not take this very seriously at the time, but on returning with the film crew in July, was greeted at the airport by Mohammed's elder brother Kombo with the news that Mwahadia had indeed left him. As we travelled to the village together, he asked me if I would try to reconcile them.

In this chapter, I utilise my field-notes and 'head-notes', as well as some of Mwahadia's interviews for the film, to give an account of the breakdown of her marriage to Mohammed. Over a two-week period I had a series of conversations with each of them during which I was cast in the role of intermediary. These conversations are highly revealing not only of each of the protagonist's views about the other but also of their marriage, and the reasons for its breakdown. Other voices – their daughter Subira, Mohammed's elder brother, Kombo, and one of the village Koranic teachers – are also heard.

MWAHADIA'S FIRST MARRIAGE

During this field-trip, my relations with Mwahadia became much closer than previously. Mwahadia needed someone to talk to, since she felt unsupported by her mother, now elderly and already burdened with care of other grandchildren, and her siblings, who had problems of their own. Telling me about the breakdown of her current marriage brought back painful memories of what had happened during her first marriage. It is very striking that this story, told so emotionally, should have been given to me only in 1976, and formed part of one of the interviews recorded on camera for the film. One reason may have been that during the previous period of field-work in the 1960s, I was unmarried and childless, and, as I subsequently realised, may well have been seen as childlike myself. By the time of my return in 1976, I was the mother of two children. Inevitably we saw each other differently: in her eyes I had finally become an adult woman, with some knowledge of what being a wife and mother meant, and I in turn saw and heard things which I had not noticed before in terms of gender relations, and the work of rearing children.

Mwahadia's first unhappy marriage

Mw. The first time I got married, it wasn't here, it was in Zanzibar. His mother was from Zanzibar, his father was a man from Mafia, but he himself was living in Zanzibar. We stayed in Zanzibar for about three years. The fourth year he brought me back here by mutual agreement, because we were at the stage where all we did was fight incessantly in Zanzibar. Well, we didn't communicate, we had different ideas, I didn't want him any more, I didn't want that husband, he was trying to poison me, to drug me so that I wouldn't want to come back home, so that I wouldn't recognise anything.

He used to insult me, that first husband, and I really took it to heart and I got thinner and thinner, until I was really skinny, although I wasn't really ill at all. Anyway, he went on insulting me, saying the filthiest things, and I couldn't stand it, and I went on thinking about it and getting thinner.

Then I went to visit someone from Mafia, a relative whom I called 'older sister' (*dada*); her name was Mwanahawa and she and I got married together [to Zanzibar men] and she said to me: 'What's the matter with you that you have got so thin, what's the trouble?' And I told her my trouble was in my whole body. But that trouble which was making me get thin was words, insults which I got, and I couldn't stand any more, I was taking it all to heart, and it was making me thin. So she said: 'Who is doing this to you?' And I told her it was my husband and she said to me: 'Well, don't you have a natal home, weren't you born there, don't you have elders there?'

So she said to me, 'There's a simple remedy, when he insults you you do the same to him, and as for taking it to heart, well I'd send word home.' And really I could have died. I was as thin as a stick by this time. And I was not really ill so as to need to stay in bed, but nor was I well, I was just about managing to get around. Well, from the day that my cousin said this to me, I started giving him some of his own medicine back, and we quarrelled, and yelled at each other the whole night until the morning; and I didn't spare his parents either. Well, he said to me 'You don't even know how to give birth on your own.' Well if he insulted you in that way, wouldn't you have sent him packing? He said, 'You don't even know how to give birth.'[2]

So we went on like that, with that Hemedi [her husband's name]. There wasn't a single day when we didn't fight at bed time. He wanted to sleep with me, I didn't want him to, until [one night] he got up and slapped me three times across the face, here [indicates]. I was in bed at the time, I was asleep, and he hit me with his fist, once, twice, three times. I got up and my brain wasn't working, my head was going round and round, I didn't know what was happening, because he had hit me three times in the same place. It was night then, and people had already gone to sleep, and my husband had locked the door. Well there was a *panga uziwa* (a sharp shell) there, you know, that thing they use on the coast, you put those little whatsits in it, well, I emptied it and I got up and dressed myself and crushed my other clothes around my chest [so that she could take them with her] and then I took that thing, and I gave him a good one with it right on the shoulder, and I split it [the shell] open. Well, he bled that night, alright.

Our neighbours woke up and came into our courtyard and said, 'Hemedi, what are you doing hitting that child?' And I realised that my face was swollen right up around the eye, in fact, I couldn't see, my face was so swollen. Then I began to cry, 'How can I return home like this? I left my home healthy, beautiful, with my face intact. I wasn't disabled (*kilema*), I had nothing wrong with me, I didn't have a lump on my face. Now I have a lump on my face, where can I go? I shall be laughed at.' Well I was crying all the night, and we were yelling at each other. . . .

And then that relative of mine, that woman from Mafia, she asked him: 'Hemedi, what right have you to hit someone's daughter? Open the door.' And Hemedi opened the door. Hemedi was my husband you know, Hemedi Hatibu. Well, Hemedi opened the door. And when he had opened the door and she saw me, I was pulled out and I took my things. And she said to me: 'You can't sleep outside, because there are witches who will come and get you.' And I said: 'Let them come and get me and kill me and eat me, that's better than going back in there.' Then Hemedi was asked by the man who had arranged our marriage, that is, his uncle: 'Who the hell do you think you are? Even I don't know who the hell you are, or where you came from, but you certainly aren't anyone who is going to inherit from me – I disown you completely.'

P.   So what happened in the end? Did he divorce you?

Mw. Yes. [But first] I came here, it was in the fourth year [of our marriage that] we [Mwahadia and her husband] came back [to Mafia]. We got into a boat, and the whole way we were insulting each other in the boat, and I was like someone drunk, I didn't know myself at all. No one recognised me, so no one asked about us, we got into the boat, we hadn't even bought any food [for the journey]. Well, the others were cooking their food, and we asked them for some and we were given some, we women in the boat.

   [When we arrived] He wouldn't formally divorce me at the government office. I had to give 200 shillings to 'buy' my divorce.

P. You had to buy it? Why didn't he just give it to you?

Mw. He didn't want to divorce me, I was the one who wanted a divorce. When he came and said this at home, my father said, 'My daughter isn't going back there. I won't send her.' So I bought my divorce for 200 shillings and I got my certificate. I took my certificate, and he took his money, his 200 shillings. He divorced me right here. And then I got engaged to this husband [Mohammed] whom I have now.

P. And did your first husband give you your *mahari*?[3]

Mw. No, he didn't give me my *mahari*.

P. But you had to buy your divorce?

Mw. Yes, I had to buy it.

P. And what reason did you give at the government office to get a divorce?

Mw. I said he doesn't want me, he wants to kill me. And he knew I didn't want to go back to him.

P. And what did your parents say about all this?

Mw. Well it was my parents who decided that he should divorce me, and that if he wanted money they would give it, so that their child shouldn't be forced to go off where she didn't want to go, she wouldn't go across the sea again, it was too dangerous. They thought I might go crazy in the boat and throw myself into the sea, it was useless [to send me back], so when my father said to my husband that he wouldn't force me to go back, then he couldn't take me.

In this account of her first marriage, Mwahadia shows that a number of people supported her – her female relative from Mafia who was also living in Zanzibar, the uncle who had arranged the marriage, and the neighbours. Her husband had to agree to take her back to Mafia, where her parents, realising the seriousness of the situation, refused to allow the marriage to continue and found the money for her divorce. But she also reveals that she herself had not been prepared indefinitely to put up with an intolerable situation, a stance which she was to re-adopt *vis-à-vis* Mohammed in 1976.

In the next part of this chapter, conversations with Mohammed and Mwahadia reveal their feelings about the current state of their own marriage.

SEPARATE CONVERSATIONS: TWO WEEKS IN THE BREAKDOWN OF A MARRIAGE

Once I was back in the village, Mohammed was quick to come with his version of events. He berated Mwahadia for leaving him, arguing that her action was a contravention of Islamic law, since he as husband should have taken her back to her natal family, as a signal that the decision had been his. He also accused her of having removed much of the household equipment. Plainly, he was angry and humiliated, but, since he did not immediately divorce her, was still wanting her back.

13 July: Mwahadia's story

Mwahadia, of course, had her own tale to tell when she came to my house early one morning after she had been to the hospital to get medicine. In my notes I record how she told me that they had agreed long ago that they would part after the harvest but then he changed his mind, and said that they should not separate.

He just wants to quarrel. He has insulted me, he says of other women, 'So and so is better than you.' So am I his wife, if he talks like that? And then he threatens me and hits me.

We had a quarrel a few months ago, and I said I wouldn't go back to him. But everyone came and persuaded me, particularly Seleman, who paid my *mahari* for me – 130 shillings it was. So I went back to him, and that very day he hurt my arm, so it swelled up like a gourd. And my chest too.

Now I'm seven months pregnant – he says it isn't his child. But in any case, he is a big *mganga* (shaman), he knows a lot of things, he has put a spirit on to me, and he is trying to kill the foetus, and kill me as well. He really hates me now.

No, I don't want a case, I don't want for us to go before the VDC and insult each other – 'You went with so and so', 'You went with so and so.' He has no shame, but I have. I told the [Village] Chairman, I just want my divorce certificate (*talaka*), and the Chairman went to tell him. I want my divorce not so as to get married again, [but because] I want to be alone, I want to be my own person again (*nataka uzima wangu*), that's why I want my divorce certificate.

You asked me why I didn't go and tell his family [about his misdeeds]? Of course I did, but they should be on his side, shouldn't they? Anyway, his elder brother is afraid even to speak to him because he doesn't listen, he just goes off. And isn't he his senior? Shouldn't he [Mohammed] listen to him?

Yesterday he came to my house, but I stayed inside, I didn't see him. He came to ask after one of the children who isn't well. I don't want to see him, even my mother doesn't want to see him after the things he has done and said to me.

If we had parted amicably, then it would have been alright. I could have gone my way and he his. After all, we have had all these children together – we have always been poor, and the only property we have is the children. So if I get into difficulties, shouldn't I go to him, my partner (*mwenzangu*)? But if we have quarrelled like this, what can I do? I can't go and speak to him. As it is now, we pass each other on the path and don't speak to each other (*tunakatiana*).

I used to make tea for him each morning, and when he came home in the evening, his meal would be ready. Should he then come and insult me the way he does? You know he has already bewitched me once. I was in bed for seven months a few years ago – I gave two cows, and five trays of offerings [to the spirits]. So I got better. And this time too I'm getting better – God doesn't want me to die. But he says he wants 2,000 shillings to give me my divorce certificate (*talaka*).

It's not true [as Mohammed was alleging] that I took everything when I left. We divided the harvest equally, and I left him one of everything, although there was hardly anything in the way of cooking or eating vessels because he never buys anything. If he has money, he gives it to his women, and I have bought the crockery and things for the house myself.

Here Mwahadia's complaints again Mohammed were manifold: that he failed to support the household properly, preferring to spend his money on other women, that he did not appreciate her wifely services, that he had sometimes been violent towards her, and that he had bewitched her by sending a spirit to make her ill.

14 July: Mohammed refutes Mwahadia's accusations

The following day, Mohammed came to see me and repeated again much of what he had said before. When he had finished his complaints and justifications, he asked me what Mwahadia had said and we had the following conversation.

P. She wants a divorce.
M. Well I won't give it to her. She can stay there as long as she likes, and

I'll get married again. I told her if she wants her divorce paper she can pay me 3,000 shillings. Why should I give my property away for nothing?

P. She says you have threatened her, and also bewitched her.

M. If I had wanted to do all the things which she says I have threatened her with, what would stop me? It isn't true. And as for this business about spirits, it has been going on for five years now – she keeps going [to diviners] and getting told that she is afflicted by different spirits. How could I have bewitched (*kuapiza*) her with all of those? I'll tell you what happened – *she* tried to bewitch *me* – yes, she has spirits in her family too – but my spirit was stronger, and overcame hers, and so she got caught. That's why she is sick.

P. She says you claim that she is not pregnant by you.

M. Ha, who told her that? You go and ask her, that will catch her out. Yes, that pregnancy she got in my house, wasn't she still with me when you came before? But of, course, only she knows for certain whose pregnancy it is. She was behaving very badly – she used to go out and not ask my permission first. Is that how a wife should behave? When I go to Kirongwe, I say, 'Tomorrow I'm going to Kirongwe.' I inform her.

P. She says that you already agreed to a separation.

M. Well if I did why didn't she wait and let me take her to her parents? When she was previously sick for a long time I looked after her. I did everything – even washed her after she had been to the toilet – is this the way I am rewarded? And I don't want to abandon the children I have borne.

P. So do you send them money or food?

M. Why, I can hardly get enough for myself.

In this conversation, Mohammed sought to refute Mwahadia's claims that he had bewitched her, and he painted a picture of himself as an exceptionally caring husband who informed his wife of his own movements, which he did not have to do, and who nursed her himself when she was sick, a task usually undertaken by female kin, not husbands.

Mohammed came regularly to see me after that, always saying more or less the same thing. On one occasion, he asked me to go and see her, and put to her the following questions:

Who said I said this is not my pregnancy? Did you ever go and see my father's brother [i.e. his surrogate father since his own father was dead] if you were dis-satisfied? If I didn't bring money and other things home, where did I take them? If I went with other women, which women? And don't you know that saying such a thing could be a cause for dissension (*fitina*)? It can cause a serious quarrel – such a [cuckolded] husband would fight with me.

It was increasingly evident that he wanted her back.

15 July: Other people's views

Mohammed's elder brother Kombo came to visit me, and I asked him what he thought. He again asked me to try and effect a reconciliation, to persuade Mwahadia to go back to Mohammed:

That woman, he is her man, and that Mohammed, she is the only one for him. Yes, I know there has been a lot of bitterness, and quarrelling, but they should make up. They have borne children together. You call her here, and talk to her.

I pointed out that relations had become very soured, and that she was accusing him of bewitching her. The brother, a pious Muslim who refused to have any truck with spirit possession, replied, 'Oh, that's a lot of nonsense (*upuuzi tu*)' and left.

Shortly afterwards, I was sitting in my house talking to Mohammed when one of the village Koran school teachers (*mwalimu*) arrived, and after greeting me at some length, the following conversation took place.

Mwalimu [to Mohammed] How is it that you, with grandchildren, can behave in this childish way?
M. [getting angry] It isn't my fault but hers.
Mwalimu But you go after other women, you don't stay at home.
M. That is not true.
Mwalimu [to me] Can't you try and reconcile them? It is not good that they stay like this.

As I went to see him off, I told him that I would try. Mohammed was very angry indeed after the *mwalimu* had left:

He has no right to say that, you see he is on her side. . . . But the law is on my side – she has no right to up and leave like that unless I take her back to her family, or unless I divorce her. And her mother and brother could be taken to court for harbouring my wife.

I was very struck by the amount of support which Mwahadia enjoyed. Here, one of the village's most respected Koranic teachers, who might have been expected to uphold Islamic law in this regard, did not blame Mwahadia for leaving Mohammed, but rather Mohammed for his bad behaviour which had precipitated the rupture. Even Mohammed's family condemned his behaviour, rather than hers, although they were anxious for the separation to end.

19 July: Mwahadia loses the baby

A man sent by Mohammed came early in the morning to tell me that Mwahadia had just had the baby [at seven months] and it had died. I went to her mother's house. Mwahadia was lying on the floor near to the fire, her mother and another old woman with her. They told me that the baby had been born dead. The placenta had come out but her stomach was still hurting.

A woman came in and asked if there was any incense for the burial. Someone said: 'Go and ask Mohammed, he's the father', but the mother said grimly: 'This [the baby's death] is his work – ask someone else.'

22 July: The anthropologist attempts reconciliation

Three days later, Mwahadia again came to my house after she had been to the clinic for a check-up and we had the following conversation:

P. What do you think about going back to Mohammed?

Mw. No I am tired, I have put up with things for many years, but he is too much for me, I can't cope with him.

P. What will you do if he does not give you your divorce?

Mw. I will just stay at home, that is all. No, I won't buy it [the divorce], I don't have anything – my father died a poor man, and if I have two or three coconut trees, that is [what gives me the right to] where I live.[4] Should I sell those and then not have anywhere [to live]? Nor will I take him to court.

P. How will you feel if he marries again?

Mw. Let him, why should I care? As far as I'm concerned, he isn't my husband! Of course, he won't get a young girl, that would be too expensive, but he'll get a divorced woman like me – there are plenty around!

P. He asked me to ask you where you heard that he said that this pregnancy wasn't his?

Mw. He said it himself – he said, 'If you get pregnant, then it won't be by me!' And he brought in the other children too; he told the people to whom he talks that Juma and Amina weren't his children. But he never said anything about them to me. No, I can't go back to him. We got to the point where we were fighting on the path once – we spilled the water, and I can show you the piece of wood he hit me with. And if he hadn't bewitched me, then I wouldn't have lost this baby – that is his doing, and even now I still feel unwell; he wants to kill me.

I am still coming to the clinic to get medicine, and I am also getting medicine from a *mwalimu* who writes it out and then you drink it (*ya kuandika na kunywa*).[5] But I have to pay him [a fee of] 20 shillings, and I don't have it. I'll get it somewhere. I can't go back to Mohammed now because this has been going on for several years – he has changed towards me, the things he has done, he is no longer my partner, so how can I live with him?

In the above speech, Mwahadia spoke bitterly of the deterioration in her relationship with her husband to the extent that he was even rumoured to be doubting the legitimacy of some of their children. This was an accusation which cast aspersions on the past as well as the present, and on one of the most important bases for their relationship – that they had borne children together. She saw his feelings towards her in terms of witchcraft, claiming that he was trying to kill her through his control of a spirit.

22 July: The daughter's viewpoint

Subira was the second daughter of Mwahadia and Mohammed (the first was already married), a girl of about 15 or 16, and she came to my house to bring me some rice: 'I cultivated it myself – it is from my field. Not a bush field, a meadow field (*dawe*). I have been cultivating my own field for some time now.' I asked her what she thought about her mother and father:

I think it is better that my parents separate, and that he give mother her divorce. But of course he doesn't want to now, because she has had two divorces, and if she gets this third one, then she will have to marry someone else [i.e. it will be irrevocable]. . . . He never buys us clothes – I buy my own. I plait mats and that's how I get them. . . . He did give me a little money towards my school blouse, but it isn't enough. I need 35 shillings to buy a decent one. Why should I go in a cheap blouse when all my friends have better ones?

27 July: Mwahadia feels unsupported

A few days later, Mwahadia came to see me in a state of great depression and complained of lack of support from her own family:

Mw. I have no one on whom I can depend in my own family – my own mother even, she is not much help, and my brothers the same. They are quarrelling with me – I would like to move away from their place to the outskirts of the village where I have a few coconuts and build a little hut for myself. Some of my brothers are there. That is the trouble, I don't

Plate 15 'Her mother was now very old': old woman winnowing, watched by grandson whom she fosters

have anyone I can tell my troubles to. The other year, when I was so ill, they [her relatives] just used to go off to the fields in the early morning, and not come back until 7 o'clock at night. I would just be lying there helpless. I couldn't move – I had to have everything done for me.

P. Who did help then?

Mw. Why, *he* [Mohammed] did! Now I am still not well after losing that baby, but no one ever asks me how I feel. I want to get better so that I can begin to make some money by making mats . . . but I no sooner seem to shake off one thing than something else starts [she had a very bad pain in her tooth that day].

At the time, I was aware that her natal family had many problems of its own – her elder sister, who had just been divorced, was living there, and her mother was now very old and frequently sick. Yet paradoxically, in complaining of her own family's lack of care, she confirmed what Mohammed had said – that when she had been very ill, he had nursed her, a most unusual course of action for a man. I made her some ginger coffee and as we sipped it, she cheered up a bit and began to tease me:

Mw. You shouldn't be drinking that if your husband isn't here, it heats the body (*inachemsha mwili*)![6]

P. And what about you?

Mw. Oh, it helps my stomach, but otherwise, as far as *that* [i.e. sex] is concerned, I'm finished!

P. Perhaps you should go and find another man.

Mw. You mean get married, or find a 'friend'? Oh, friends [lovers] give you nothing here – now if it were Zanzibar or Dar. . . .

P. But you said that Mohammed is always giving gifts to his mistress. . . .

Mw. Yes, that's true, but there are very few men who give their mistresses anything.

1 August: More attempts at reconciliation

Mohammed's elder brother Kombo came again to ask me whether there were any signs of a reconciliation:

K. Did you manage to see Mwahadia? What did she say?

P. She doesn't want to go back to him.

K. Well, I have formed a plan, I will ask you to speak to her again, but with two other people – MA and that *mwalim*. The former has already agreed, now I have only to ask the latter.

P. I think that she might change her mind in time – she is already fed up with being at her mother's place. And Mohammed keeps talking about her, and has been by to see how she is. However, if only half of what she says about his doings is true, then I feel sorry for her.

K. Yes, sympathy (*huruma*) is all very well, but that isn't going to feed the children. These days it is hard enough for two people together to manage, how is one person alone going to do it?

2 August: Mohammed wants Mwahadia back

Mohammed came again to see me, and asked me to go and talk to Mwahadia on his behalf.

I want you to write this down, because I want to teach her. You asked me earlier today whether I would take her back – certainly, I can't throw her out. After all, she started the quarrel, not me. If she comes, then that is fine. But I will not send anyone for her. If *you* bring her, that is alright. You asked me if I still talk to her, of course I do. You saw me talking to her this morning. If she is sick, I go and ask her how she is, as usual, and she answers me normally. And the same if one of the children is sick.

Now I want you to tell her this: there will be no peace in the house if one of the parties does as he or she likes. If I the husband am going away, I should tell her (*kuagana naye*) and she should not go out anywhere, to fetch water, or to go to a ritual or ceremony (*shughuli*) without my permission (*amri*). Because once one does that, then the other one does the same, and so it will go on like that. I think that is how our quarrel started. If she comes back, then it must be resolved that each tells the other what is happening. Don't you think so? Doesn't your husband know where you are? Didn't you discuss it before you came? Yes, well, it is the same here as in Europe.

It is interesting that here Mohammed was offering an alternative kind of marital contract, one in which there would be some degree of consultation between both parties. This is rather different to the one he talked about on previous occasions (see Chapter 2), in which he as a male had the right, which Islamic law gives him, to do as he pleased, whereas she had to ask his permission before doing anything which involved leaving the house.

However, none of the attempts at mediation on the part of Mohammed's brother, his intermediaries or myself achieved the reconciliation so desired by everyone except Mwahadia. She was resolute and I admired her for it, as well as for her determination to manage her life on her own, a resolution to which she was to adhere for the next ten or eleven years.

7 Encounter three
1985

When I left Minazini in 1976, the situation between Mohammed and Mwahadia appeared to be a stalemate – he wanted her back, she refused to go. From Mohammed's subsequent letters, this situation did not appear to change. I arrived back in 1985 to find neither of them had re-married, although several of their children were going through marriages and divorces and had children of their own. There had been several deaths in the interim including those of their 19-year-old son Waziri, and Mohammed's older brother, Kombo, who had always been a source of great support to him, and who had tried to reconcile Mohammed and Mwahadia in 1976.

MOHAMMED

Mohammed was living in a fine new house built for him by his eldest son, Seleman, whose career as a hotel waiter had progressed well. He told me that the house was meant for himself and Mwahadia jointly, but that she had refused to live there. He had one of his adult daughters, currently divorced, and her children living with him, and his daughter Miza, then 11, would stay there sometimes. Nonetheless, his financial state was as parlous as ever. He was also feeling lonely, and in our conversations, the subject of sex and marriage cropped up constantly.

One evening, he and I were talking about spirit possession, but he was complaining of not feeling well:

M. No, I don't want to go to the hospital – I'll go to one of those Wanyamwezi immigrants[1] – he has good medicine but it is expensive. I'm trying to get a load of raffia together – I'd like to get thirty bundles to take and sell in Zanzibar – I've got seventeen loads so far. I'll also be able to visit my older brother.

P. Have you finished drying it already?

M. No, because she [divorced daughter] has a lot of work to do – there's only her and the little girl doesn't help her.

P. Why ever don't you get married again?

M. Yes, for the last three years I've been having a lot of trouble. I don't get enough food because I don't have a wife to cultivate. Last year I got at most one and a half bags of rice. That will last only a couple of months at best. I should try to get some money together and get married again.

A few days later, he visited me in the early evening to tell me he was unwell again, and had been working non-stop for the last few days:

P. What have you been doing? Cutting raffia?

M. Not only that, I've also been planting some coconuts. And I lost some of the raffia I had cut in all this rain. . . . I feel so cold these nights on my own.

P. So why don't you get married then?

M. Yes, I want to – if I can sell my beast. I thought that from our herd I would get a bull to sell, but I have only got a cow and its value is less.

A few days later, I got a message from Mohammed to say that he was still sick, and to ask me for some medicine for diarrhoea. I went to see him and give him some medicine, and the next day I met him on the road and he said he felt better.

One striking aspect of this period was that Mohammed, much to his sorrow, was not involved in any sexual relationships. He kept thinking of re-marriage, but had been unable to raise the necessary cash. It is perhaps no coincidence that he appeared untroubled by spirits. In spite of the fact that he was ill several times during my stay, he did not attribute the cause to affliction by his own ancestral spirit or any other.

MWAHADIA

This time, Mwahadia was living in a hut belonging to Subira built by the side of the big marsh where they were both cultivating that year, but she was planning to build a hut of her own. She had some of her younger children with her, as well as Subira herself, recently separated from her husband, and some of her children. The conversations which I had with Mwahadia on this occasion concerned not only family news, but also topics on which I was focusing for research on this trip: food, health, fertility and gender relations. I went to visit her there:

P. Why don't you get married again?

Mw. I was engaged [a few years ago] to someone in Baleni – but he was killed by a spirit. One night he went outside and saw a hippo – he came back in to look for his gun, but he couldn't find it. When he went out again, the hippo had gone, but it must have been a *jini* because he got sick immediately. He went to Dar for treatment, but he died there.

P. What's happened to the children who are not living here?

Mw. They are staying with their father at the moment. The boy [Juma] says he doesn't want to come and live here 'in the bush' as he says, but the girl [Miza] will come and live here.

P. So what is your daily routine at the moment?

Mw. I get up and get the fire going. Clean my teeth and wash my face. Have some tea, and left-overs from the previous day. Then I go to the field until 4 p.m. – I don't eat at midday. I come back and pound rice, fetch firewood if I need it, and several buckets of water, then cook. At the moment, Subira and I cook together, but when I've built my own hut, we may cook separately. Subira washes up.

P. When do you rest?

Mw. Only after the evening meal, but then I usually go to sleep. If I need to rest, I take a day off. Now that the work in the field is slackening off a bit, I want to start cutting raffia and send some to my daughter [Amina] in Zanzibar when her father goes there.

Plate 16 'I want to start cutting raffia': woman stripping raffia from dried palm frond prior to selling

P. So will you get married again?

Mw. Who will take the children of someone else? I have my children to think about – but I'd like to. But I won't be deceived by a husband over other women or over money, him claiming he has no money every evening, when he's said he's been working and you know perfectly well he's been felling coconuts. I won't put up with that again.

P. Could you live with a co-wife?

Mw. Yes, even two! But it's hard. The husband only takes food (*kitoweo*) to the place where he sleeps, [yet] the men all want two or three wives these days. Yes, I'd like to get married, but no one has come forward.

Mwahadia, like Mohammed, was uninvolved in any sexual relationship during this time, and also appeared untroubled by spirits. Indeed, in spite of her professed wishes to marry, and complaints about the difficulties of managing on her own, she seemed to be enjoying her independence, and had been on trips to visit two of her daughters Asha and Amina, both now married and living respectively in Dar es Salaam and Zanzibar.

Mwahadia and Subira: a conversation

Mwahadia and Subira had an ambivalent relationship. Like most divorced and separated women, Subira had been forced to turn to her mother for assistance, but they did not always get on. On another occasion when I visited their hut, which was newly built in Mwahadia's coconut field, Subira was also there. So too was Subira's husband – he had been felling some coconuts for Mwahadia, but he left soon afterwards. Mwahadia was cooking fish and rice, after asking Subira how she wanted it done, 'as it is her house and her fish'. Subira's two little girls were pretending to pound rice with sticks. The following conversation took place:

S. [looking at her children] The older one already knows how to pound. One day when I was late coming back, she had tried to start cooking.

Mw. Last year, when he came to ask for Subira's hand, her husband helped out a lot – he cleared a bush field for me. He had no wife at that time, and I helped him by planting rice for him. But this year I cultivated meadow land which I got from Mohammed's side.

S. I did not cultivate last year because I was pregnant with that boy who died. Well, anyway I don't want my husband back – I'm his fifth wife, and he has divorced us all. He has refused to buy clothes for the children, even though they were the ones who guarded the field, and it was his field as well as mine.

Plate 17 'One can't sit doing nothing': woman winnows rice while a neighbour's son looks on

P. But do you think it is better to have a husband or not?

S. Better to have, because otherwise, you can't afford [shop-bought] food like flour. But if you can't get anything from your husband, it is better that you manage on your own. Look at my husband, he gives me nothing. But today I got some fish in exchange for the rice I gave to that man yesterday. I manage well on my own. I cultivated cassava myself, about an acre. I paid 400 shillings to have the field prepared [and did the rest myself].

P. Where did you get the money from?

S. I get it here and there from men [laughs] – do you think if you aren't clever (*mjanja*) you'll get anything?

Mw. See now that I've eaten I start plaiting – a person can't sit doing nothing. I usually make eight mats a year, and get 200 shillings for each.

P. [to Subira] Tell me about your pregnancies.

S. I had a daughter who is now 7 [born before marriage], then I got married in a southern village – I was there for three years and I had another daughter – she is now 6. I got divorced and lived for a while with father [Mohammed] – during that time I had a son, the one who died.

Then a year ago I got married in Pwani. That was when my son died. I had asked my husband to look after him while I went to the well for water. But when I came back, he [the baby] was crying and he died in my arms. I cried a lot. I have no male child now. But I'm pregnant again. I never manage to wean my children [at the proper time] – I always get pregnant again immediately.

P. Do you want a boy or girl?

S. I'd prefer a boy – I can send him to look for fish at the beach. I've already got two girls to help me cook. I feel sleepy all the time and can't work much. I don't even feel like plaiting raffia.

P. Will you give your children to your mother to bring up if you re-marry?

S. No, these days she likes going about to Zanzibar and Dar to visit her children. Besides, I like to have them with me.

Mw. Last year I had to go to Zanzibar to help my daughter Amina at the time of her delivery. Her previous pregnancy was very difficult, and she didn't want to come to Mafia.

S. My mother does not want to bring up grandchildren.

Mw. That is right, I have had enough.

S. I'd like to take a trip to London.

Mw. No way, you'll be gone for months, maybe years, and forget you were ever a mother.

S. Never. I always take my children everywhere.

I was struck by the contrast between Mohammed and Mwahadia: the former complained continuously of his health and his financial state, while the latter seemed relatively contented with her lot, managing her finances, and enjoying her freedom from the care of small children, and ability to travel and visit older ones. Subira, on the other hand, was plainly having problems: her second marriage was breaking up, her health was poor, and she began to complain of being troubled by witchcraft and spirits.

SUBIRA: 'PEOPLE HERE DON'T WANT ME TO PROSPER'

Subira and I had a number of meetings and conversations. On one occasion, she brought me a gift of millet, beaten rice and cucumbers, and requested a loan. I asked her why she and her husband had separated:

S. It was because he was having an affair with another woman. He told me to take the children and go, he said the children were not his [anyway].

P. So what will you do now?

S. First of all, I am not sure if I am properly divorced – I went to see the Sheikh about it and he told me to go and see the other Sheikh, with my husband, but he refused to come with me. Second, we want to divide up our crop – he wants to divide the field into two immediately, but I want to divide the crop only after the harvest. Then he wants us to do the dividing ourselves – I think we should bring in the elders, otherwise it would be as if we had insulted them.

P. So how are you managing?

S. He refuses to give me any money. He hasn't prepared any new clothes for the children for Id [festival].[2] Last time any of us got any new clothes it was because I sold some of my coconut trees – now that money is finished. I met him on the path the other day and I told him I wanted to eat some beans, I really had a craving for them, and I asked him for just 10 shillings [to buy some] but he said he didn't have any money. Well, I'll manage without him. When I've had this baby, I'm not going to have any more for a while. I'll get some medicines [contraception]. Maybe when I find a man I can trust, I can consider having [more] children. I'll get a room in Kilindoni and stay there.

On another occasion, Subira came with one of her children who had a bad cold – they had just been to the clinic. She began to talk more about the break-up of her marriage:

S. It wasn't only the matter of the other woman, it was also partly my mother's fault. Last year, she had a common field boundary with us, but my mother said bad things to my husband until finally he said to her: 'Take your daughter [away].' Now mother doesn't want me in her house – she has asked me to move.

P. Why don't you go and stay with your father? He has a fine big house now.

S. But he is poor, he can't help – he doesn't buy me clothes or anything – he hasn't done so since the last time you were here and he bought me something for school.

P. But why is he so poor?

S. He has sold most of his coconut trees to buy food. My mother helps more – she buys clothes for me and the children. She told me: 'Come and live here – you'll manage.'

History, then, seemed to be repeating itself. Subira's relationship with her husband had been jeopardised both by his affair with another woman, and by tensions between Mwahadia and her son-in-law. A decade earlier, Mohammed and Mwahadia had also quarrelled both because of Mohammed's affairs, and also because Mwahadia's father disliked Mohammed and tried, albeit unsuccessfully, to persuade his daughter to leave him (see Chapter 5). Subira was obviously making plans for her future, considering using contraception to avoid further pregnancies for a while, and going to live in Kilindoni. She had begun to find ways of managing without the support of a husband, cultivating on her own, engaging in reciprocal exchanges, and getting cash and gifts from other men.

Subira's illness: witchcraft strikes again

Soon after my arrival, Subira began to complain of illness and being troubled by various forms of witchcraft and sorcery. One day as I was sitting with the *mwalimu* on his verandah, Subira came by. She sat down and ate an orange, then started to complain that someone had previously sold her an orange and after eating it, she felt very ill.

S. I shall go to the [government] office and complain. It looked as if it had been split and something put inside.
Mwalim Who did you buy it from?
S. I shall say that name at the office.

The conversation continued and Subira soon made it plain who it was. The *mwalimu* commented, 'Ah, that woman is involved in a lot of cases.'

A few days later, Subira came to my house with one of her daughters:

S. I've been sick ever since I ate the orange which that woman sold me. She is a witch (*mchawi*), she wants to kill the baby in my womb. She is always killing people – she gives them to her spirit – she wants the foetus to rot and come out, or to make me die.[3] So I went to a shaman in a southern village.
P. Why not one in Minazini?
S. Because although there are plenty of shamans in Minazini, they don't always tell you things – they hide them. And if you go to a *kitanga* (trance healing dance) like I did yesterday, there are a lot of people there. You need to be able to speak secretly. So I begged a lift from the [Mafia] MP when he was returning to Kilindoni after a visit to Minazini. I got to this place at 6 p.m. It is at least an hour's walk to the shaman's house and when I arrived he wasn't there – he had gone fishing. So I went to sleep and saw him the next day. I told him my stomach was hurting, but I didn't have a bean to give him. So he agreed to treat me and that I would pay him when I got better.

First he gets possessed by shaking rattles until the spirit comes into his head. Then he divines, but you can't understand a word of his language when he is speaking with his spirit. His older brother is there, and he tells me in plain Swahili what the spirit has said. And the spirit said that it was that woman [who gave her the orange].

He treated me with two kinds of medicine – he made little cuts – see here in my hands – and put things in. That is preventative (*kitu kingo* – see Chapter 8). Then he gave me medicines to drink. I have to go again in a week. [As part of the payment], I should take several packets of the kind of cigarettes he smokes and at least two packets of matches, because after all there are two of them [the shaman and his interpreter], and some money. I'll have a problem to get that money. Maybe I can get a bit from my mother. But I can't get it by having a relationship with a man – it has to be lawfully gotten.

Anyway, I came back – I thought I'd have to walk all the way, but I met a few people on the road – mates of mine (*wacheshi*) – and begged a bit of money off them. So in Kirongwe, I got on to the Pwani lorry.

I'll finish taking all the medicines he gave me on Sunday and then I want to go and see him again on Monday. It's a secret – I didn't tell my father. Only my mother knew. The shaman also gave me herbs to eat. I have a spirit in my head – it is the spirit of our ancestors.

P. Do you get possessed?

S. No, I could be if I went to the shamans and they made it climb into my head, but I don't want to get possessed, because then it will mean giving a cow or an offering tray, or a goat. And where am I to get that money? As I told you, money for the spirits has to be obtained lawfully.

The children have also been taken hold of by our ancestral spirit. It was angry because it was forgotten, and it did not have its proper dues taken to it. I went to my father, and he got ten plants from around the sea shore, and gave them to the girls. I said I would give him 20 shillings for each of them but I haven't paid him yet. . . . Now my husband has come and said he wants me back. He comes and sleeps at our house. But he will not recall me officially by telling the elders – he says it's up to him [to decide when to do so]. Nor will he give me a proper divorce. But he says if he catches any men around my house, he'll kill them. He says he's deeply in debt – he had some immigrant labourers do some work for him for 9,000 shillings and he hasn't paid them. He's relying on his own work, which is felling coconuts, to pay them. So he says even if he takes me back, he won't be able to give me anything.

My sister, the one who is at home with my father, has also suffered from witchcraft. People here don't want me to prosper – they don't want me to bear children, or to work. That is why I suffer from witchcraft. This child [her daughter who is sitting there listlessly] has been sick – it is because she was fed poison (*kibumbwi* – a form of sorcery – see Chapter 8) by someone. I saw them do it on the path when I went to get water – they covered her with a cloth and fed her.

P. Who was it?

S. I know that person – a relative. The child had a nose-bleed today – I was going to take her to the hospital, but someone told me there is no medicine for that.

Subsequently Subira did decide to seek treatment for her various problems in Minazini as well, and she and I went to a *kitanga* dance ritual together. After the cow had been slaughtered and the blood drunk, she went with one of the still-possessed shamans to the side of the house, where he sat down with the drummer, his interpreter, and she asked him the reason for her illness:

Shaman Didn't you go north one night at 7.30 p.m.?

Drummer [repeats question more clearly]

Shaman And didn't you eat something when you were coming back? And didn't it hurt you?

Shaman's sister [to shaman] Don't take on this case – it will be expensive. Neither she nor her parents can afford to pay.

Shaman It's your stomach that's hurting you, isn't it?

S. Yes, that's true.

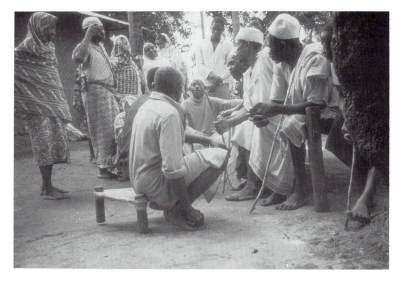

Plate 18 Divination at a *kitanga*

Shaman You thought you were alone, but there were others [that is the spirits] there with you. . . . The sun is coming up – I [the spirit possessing him] have to go. . . .

Drummer [to Subira] So go and find someone to treat you.

S. It's true, I did feel something in my stomach for three days.

Later, Subira and I listened to the recording of the divination session together:

S. Now that I come to think of it, a bit of the fruit stuck in my throat and for three days I could taste it every time I salivated. But of course, that wasn't the *real* reason for my illness – he hid the real reason.

P. Did he know the real reason?

S. Of course he did. A spirit (*iblissi*) sees everything. But he prevented the drummer from telling me – he said, 'Let it be as it is.'

After this, I did not see Subira for some time – Mwahadia told me she had gone back to visit her shaman for a few days. But then she turned up at my house, wanting some money to try another treatment. Her southern shaman could not function because his brother, who interpreted for him, was sick. But Subira by this time was feeling even worse, and had pains in her stomach:

S. And my child is sick. My husband is a shaman – he could treat both of us. I saw him and I asked him. But he won't.

P. Does he get possessed?

S. Yes, they all do in that family.

She told me that she wanted to try yet another forms of treatment, this time consulting a Makonde[4] woman who lives in the village and gets possessed by a spirit. A few days later, however, she was feeling much better and went to a disco (*dansi*) organised by some of the village youths and reported that she had had a nice time.

When I went to say a final goodbye to Mwahadia and Subira, the former had made me a farewell gift – a rice cake. We drank tea and ate some of it together, and the rest was packed up for me to take on my journey. I offered to take their photos. Subira wore her only pair of *kanga*, but Mwahadia produced a very elegant dress which she said her son Seleman had sent her from Dar. Subira asked me to let her have some kerosene, saying that she would come back to my house with me to fetch it. On the way, she wheedled a pair of plimsolls and some socks off me, saying, 'I'm sure to get a fiancé now.'

Subira's life at this period was extremely problematic. She was pregnant but with an uncertain marriage, in need of money to buy food, pay for treatment and support her children, but had little means of earning it other than by engaging in relationships with other men and getting gifts from them. Her relations with both her parents were ambivalent: she did not want to discuss things with her father, although she did want his help in claiming her share of marital property; she did confide in her mother to some extent, but blamed her for the break-up of her marriage. In this situation, she invoked affliction by both witchcraft and sorcery, which she attributed to the malevolence of other people, and the unwanted attentions of spirits, both ancestral and otherwise, which were seeking to possess her. The next section of the book deals with these issues in greater detail.

Part IV

The search for knowledge

Introduction

This fourth part of the book, consisting of three chapters, deals with various kinds of affliction: illness, misfortune and death. I have entitled it 'The Search for Knowledge' because it deals with explanations for affliction, means of treatment and methods of prevention. Two kinds of text are used: the first two chapters (8 and 9) are again drawn from Mohammed's diary, and the third and final chapter consists of my fourth encounter with Mohammed, Mwahadia and Subira in 1994.

In Chapter 8, Mohammed describes how people with affliction seek knowledge of its cause through consulting diviners, either those using Islamic methods, such as astrology (*falaki*) and geomancy (*ramli*), or those who divine through spirits (*kwenda pachironi, kutazamia*). Diviners may use a range of explanations: various forms of sorcery (*uwanga* and *muhanga*), the evil eye (*jicho baya*), being 'seized' by an ancestor (*kushikwa na maiti*), being the victim of magical spells (*mazingera*), or being troubled by a spirit (*pepo, jini, shaitani*), perhaps because of witchcraft (uchawi).

There are a range of treatments available in the village, including not only a clinic dispensing allopathic medicine, but also experts (*mafundi*) of various kinds: those knowledgeable in Islamic treatments (who are usually *walimu*), cupping (*kutia chuku*), burning (*kutia moto*), herbal medicines (*dawa ya miti*) and shamans (*waganga*) who can deal with spirits.

As on other parts of the East coast of Africa, and indeed, throughout much of Africa generally, there is a belief in spirits and their ability to intervene in human affairs; arising from such beliefs are numerous cults of affliction, based on drumming and trance dancing.[1] We have already seen from earlier chapters that spirits may need to be propitiated in order, for example, that crops may grow well (see Chapter 3), and that one form of witchcraft is the sending of a spirit to attack someone (see Chapter 6). In Chapter 9, there is a detailed consideration of spirits and their doings, as explicated by Mohammed in his diary.

In Chapter 10, which deals with the 1994 encounter, we find that each of the main characters has a large number of problems: Mohammed is still unmarried since his separation from his wife in 1976, Mwahadia has made a belated and rather unsatisfactory new marriage, and their daughter Subira has been in and out of relationships. All of them are suffering acutely from poverty, and also from the grief of multiple bereavement, with the recent deaths of two adult children. Mohammed, who has long had a relationship with an ancestral spirit, has now become fully possessed, and is about to be initiated into a cult. Subira is afflicted by several spirits and seeking a way of dealing with this problem. Much of this chapter, then, is about the part that spirits and their cults play in their lives.

SPIRITS AND THEIR DOINGS

It would be useful at this point to explain a little more about the cosmology on Mafia, and particularly beliefs in the spirits which have already been mentioned several times in the preceding chapters. Spirits are of many kinds – some live on the land, some in the sea, a distinction which, as will be seen in Chapter 9, is important in terms of cult practices. Spirits can afflict humans for a variety of reasons, and in order for the affliction to cease, some kind of bargain will need to be made. Usually this consists of an offering of some kind, ranging from a few sweetmeats to the holding of a full-scale initiation ritual into a cult. Spirits which are known usually have shrines (*panga*) to which offerings can be taken, and if they are possessory, they will have shamans (*waganga*) who can control them, and mediums (*miti*) whom they possess at regular intervals.[2] Some people are believed to have hereditary relationships (*asili*) with spirits, others are given to spirits as children to be 'brought up' (*kulewa*) and thus protected. Sometimes spirits are thought to seek a relationship of friendship with a human, or to punish someone for annoying them.

SPIRIT POSSESSION AND ISLAM

Beliefs in spirits coexist uneasily with Islam. All villagers agree that spirits exist, and know that they are mentioned in the Koran. Yet for many orthodox Muslims, engaging in trance dances (*ngoma ya kupungwa*), slaughtering animals and drinking their blood, ascribing illness and death to spirits, and making offerings at spirit shrines, is a form of polytheism (*ushirika*) which is anathema to Islam, and they refuse to have anything to do with such practices. Thus I can in no way claim that Mohammed is 'typical' of northern Mafian villagers in his interest in spirits and their cults, because there are many who have nothing to do with them including Mohammed's own brother (see p. 131). In Chapter 9, Mohammed explains that some treatments are considered lawful (*halali*) by Islam, such as cupping, burning and Islamic treatments. Others, however, such as the use of local medicines (*dawa ya kienyeji*) are condemned by the orthodox and pious as unlawful (*haramu*).

What is in dispute between spirit cult adherents and the ultra-orthodox is the amount of power which such spirits possess, particularly their ability to intervene in human affairs, and hence what action should be taken by humans to deal with them. Some, and this would include Mohammed, argue that, ultimately, the power of life and death rests with God (Allah, Mungu), and that the spirits are only instruments. Furthermore, they see spirit possession cults as aspects of custom (*mila*), from long ago (*ya kizamani*), and linked with ideas about the fertility of crops and humans, the well-being of children and the quality of human relationships.

It is, however, not possible to delineate clear categories in discussing Islam and spirit possession. Some have argued that, in much of Islamic Africa, there are different and clearly discernible systems of knowledge, with typically Bantu cults, on the one hand, and Islam on the other. However, as Gray points out, references in the Koran to the existence and status of spirits are contradictory (1969), and Janzen, too, notes that the distinction between Islamic and indigenous African therapy is ambiguous and fluid (1986). Lewis, who has written widely on Islam in Africa (see Lewis 1966, 1986, Lewis *et al.* 1991), attacks the notion of core and peripheral Islam, and notes the need for a greater recognition of Islam's own magical and astrological lore, seeing Islam not as a religion of *the* book, but as a religion of the *books*; this judgement would hold well for East Africa, where several authors show the importance of Islamic magic (Becker and Martin 1968, Parkin 1985, 1995, Lambek 1993, 1995). Giles has argued that for the Swahili, spirit cults are a central aspect of culture (1987).

ANTHROPOLGICAL APPROACHES TO SPIRIT POSSESSION

There has been a long-running debate in anthropology about the best way to analyse and understand such cults. One school of thought, led by I.M. Lewis, has taken a sociological, indeed epidemiological view, focusing on the categories of those who are most likely to get possessed, and arguing that cults of the kind found on Mafia may be described as 'deprivation cults', attracting the dispossessed and marginal, particularly women.[3] A second approach involves a consideration of the extent to which such cults allow for the expression and alleviation of stress, and re-adjustment in the social relations which may be causative of this stress (Obeyesekere 1970, 1981, Crapanzano 1973, 1977, 1980, Kapferer 1983). Many authors have noted the extent to which spirit possession cults provide an explanation for illness, affliction and death which is *causative* and thus satisfying, as well as a means of both curing and prevention (e.g. Turner 1968, Crapanzano 1973, Janzen 1978, 1982, 1992). For the participants, especially for those undergoing cures, their cost and preparation involve the coming together of what Janzen (1978, 1987) has termed a 'therapy management group' of relatives who support and reassure the patient.

In addition, it has been shown in a variety of settings that the rituals of the cults are dramatic, providing a form of theatrical entertainment to their audiences. Lewis has drawn attention to rituals such as a form of 'psychodrama' (1966a), and Beattie and Middleton have referred to the cathartic nature of the cult dramas (1969). Bourgignon has noted that spirit possession cults allow people to play with identity (1965), and Crapanzano (1977) has argued that the cults he studied in Morocco are particularly concerned with sexual identity.

A third and more recent approach takes a more phenomenological and hermeneutic stance (Boddy 1990, 1994, Lambek 1981, 1993, Kapferer 1991), examining the phenomenon of spirit possession on its own terms. Boddy, for example, sees spirit possession as a form of relationship to the world, and a reservoir of cultural knowledge which is therefore intellectually empowering (1994). Lambek argues that spirit possession is a system of communication (1980) and a form of knowledge (1993).

All of these approaches are useful, and far from mutually exclusive.[4] Here I propose to focus upon the cults primarily as systems of knowledge, and particularly as ways of dealing with basic human dilemmas and the emotions they arouse – illness, loss of loved ones, especially children, and the fact that humans quarrel with one another, and feel envy, anger and frustration. Spirits, witchcraft and sorcery are, however, not only about major life crises – they are also about the everyday nature of people's lives. In writing this book, I did once, fleetingly, contemplate separating out all the texts which contained reference to the supernatural from those which did not. I quickly realised that this was a ridiculous idea, born of my own world view, not that of Mohammed and many of his fellow villagers. For this reason, spirits and their doings need to be incorporated quite as much into the understanding of such a mundane activity as growing crops as they do in comprehending how people deal with the death of a child.

8 Dealing with affliction

Explanation

On Mafia, as elsewhere, there is a diversity of local beliefs about the reasons why people suffer misfortune. In order to establish what has caused illness or other problems, people often have recourse to diviners, who will suggest not only the reason for the situation, but also the most suitable treatment. In this chapter, Mohammed first explains how divination is carried out, and what kinds of explanations diviners may produce for affliction. These include sorcery, the evil eye, ancestors and spells.

Just as there are many explanations about the agents responsible for affliction – God, spirits, ancestors, humans – so there are many ways of treating it. Mohammed next discusses methods of treatment such as herbal, Islamic and bio-medical, as well as other remedies such as cupping; another important form of treatment, through spirit possession, will be discussed in detail in Chapter 9. In a case of affliction, people may use more than one form of treatment, either simultaneously or consecutively. Decisions about which experts to call are usually taken by the therapy management group of close relatives, for once someone has adopted the sick role, they are not thought capable of taking care of themselves, but must be cared for.

The third major topic in this Chapter is that of prevention, particularly the use of magical inoculation. People who take precautions through use of local or Islamic magic, charms and amulets, or the performance of suitable rituals, can avoid many of the pitfalls lying in wait for the unwary. As Mohammed explains, some people are thought to be more vulnerable than others, but can reduce their vulnerability in a variety of ways.

SEEKING AN EXPLANATION: DIVINATION

When someone becomes sick, a decision has to be made about what kind of treatment should be followed. In order to do this, not only the kind of illness but also what has caused it must be diagnosed. People may decide that it is simply '*maradhi*' (illness) which is caused by God's will (*amri ya Mungu*), or that another agency may be involved, such as some form of witchcraft and/or a spirit. I asked Mohammed under what circumstances witchcraft might be suspected:

P. How do you know when it is witchcraft (*uchawi*)?

M. You suspect it if the illness is very sudden or very prolonged.

P. Can you recognise what is the matter by the type of illness?

M. That is unlikely, except that sorcery (*kibumbwi* – see below p. 160) always leads to a swollen stomach, but then a swollen stomach is not always *kibumbwi*.

P. So how do you know whether someone is bewitching you or it is just illness (*maradhi tu*)?

M. You can only know by divination. But I may hear reports [of other people's illnesses], and not know how people know it is witchcraft.

Thus in cases of sudden or prolonged illness, recourse may be had to a diviner[1] to seek the cause. There are two main forms of divination (*kupiga ramli*): one utilises astrology (*falaki*), and is practised by some Koranic teachers (*walimu*) and others who have learned how to do it; the other form is carried out by shaman-diviners (*waganga*), who seek information from their spirits; this is known as *kwenda pachironi*. Mohammed explained the difference:

For divination, K takes I shilling. He uses astrology and makes marks in the sand. But if you go to Ali, who has a possessory spirit (*mzuka*), it costs 5 shillings, as he has to become possessed, i.e. to fumigate himself (*kutia buhuri*) and call on the spirits.

Not all Koranic teachers practise divination. HM is the main one, and there are two others who do it secretly, using books or a divining board (*ubao*). These methods are all unlawful (*haramu*).

The diary has relatively little information on Koranic diviners, possibly because Mohammed himself usually went to shaman-diviners, but also because orthodox Muslims condemned all such practices, so, if carried out at all, they were often done secretly. But Mohammed gives a good deal of information on how shaman-diviners work:

You are sick, and someone calls Ali [the main shaman-diviner in the village]. He fumigates himself and tells his spirit that he is going to examine this person. When the patient arrives, he may do it again, calling on all the spirits by name. He is seated, covered with cloths, and has his censer (*kiteso*) under the cloths with him and he fumigates himself. Then he begins to sing *kitanga* songs, and the people who are there also sing and clap until he

Plate 19 Father brings a sick child to shamans after a *kitanga*

becomes possessed. Then he throws off the cloth and says: 'What is going on here?' [The people there reply] 'We have called Ngwali [Ali's spirit name] here to divine for this person (*kiumbe*, lit. creature).'
'And what will I get?'
'Money (*shami*)'
'Let us not quarrel [i.e. about payment of the fee]. And who has called me?' [The patient's companion replies:] 'I have done so. This woman (*mwanakasi*) has been caught [and made sick], I do not know by what, whether the evil eye of a human, or the will of God, or a spirit. Perhaps it met her on the path, and it caught her because of pollution (*uchafu*), or perhaps the spirit was sent by someone who passed by here and said, "Catch her, she is yours." And I will give you a cow or an offering tray (*chano*) [if you cure her].'[2]

In Mohammed's hypothetical example, the person speaking for the patient adduces three common sources of agency in illness: the will of God (*amri ya Mungu*), the evil intention of a human being utilising either the evil eye (*jicho baya*) or a spirit (*shaitani*), or a chance encounter with a spirit which is possibly angered by her state of pollution (particularly likely to be as a result of having had sexual relations). The shaman-diviner will suggest which of these explanations is most likely. Other explanations might include being afflicted by an ancestor (*kushikwa na maiti*), sorcery (*uwanga* and *kibumbwi*), and the casting of spells (*mazingera*). In the next section, Mohammed discusses all of the above explanations, with the exception of affliction by spirits, which is dealt with in detail in the next chapter.

EXPLANATIONS AND AGENCY: SORCERY, THE EVIL EYE, ANCESTORS AND *MAZINGERA* SPELLS

Sorcery: *uwanga* and *muhanga*

Illness can be explained by a form of sorcery[3] known as *uwanga* which is believed to involve both the giving of poison (*kibumbwi*) by the sorcerer, as described by Subira in Chapter 7, and the learned ability of the sorcerer to transform his or her bodily shape, and to compel other people to do their bidding while the latter are asleep at night. The following account was given to me jointly by Mohammed and Mwahadia in 1966.

Yesterday a man was buried in Kisiwa village and this is how he died. He had two wives, one of whom, A, who was a local woman, had borne him children, while the other one, B, who was from the Mrima coast of the mainland, was barren. [In consequence] wife B was jealous of wife A. Wife B is a sorcerer (*mwanga*). One night as the husband was leaving her to go to the other wife, she told him not to go. He said he must – it was his day for sleeping there.[4]

So he set off but wife B [went after him and] took another path and came out in front of him, growing to the height of a coconut tree. The man fell down unconscious with fright. Wife B returned home and was waiting there when he finally arrived back, never having got to wife A's house. He became ill and stayed in bed. He told people what he had seen, although he did not recognise [that it had been] his wife.

One night he woke up wanting water, but his wife B had gone out to practise her sorcery (*kwanga*). He called and called and eventually got up to look for it himself. He fell over the still hot fire and was too weak to move or call out. He remained there until dawn when wife B came back and pulled him off, put him on the bed, and called other people, but he died [soon afterwards]. Thus he had been killed by his own wife, so people said. But they did not think she could be [formally] accused, because she would just say she had gone out [of the house at night] to defecate. But all the neighbours know she is a sorcerer.

Mohammed and Mwahadia added:

Sorcerers kill by putting poison (*kibumbwi*) in food or drink – they keep it under their fingernails. They also know medicine to make themselves invisible, to fly and to become giants. And they can compel people to work for them at night, for example by sewing or driving a car. Sorcery is a matter of knowing the right medicine and one can go to a sorcerer and buy medicines. One can also be taught.

But some people know preventive medicine (*kingo*) and if you have this, you either will not take the food or drink [they offer you] because your hand shakes so much, or the glass or plate will break, or if you eat the poison you will immediately vomit. The preventive medicines his father prepared for him protect Mohammed against this (see pp. 168–9). Kisiwa village and other villages in the south of Mafia are the worst places for sorcery [in this area] but there are also a few sorcerers in Minazini now. However, there are also people here who know [how to make] preventive medicines.

The notions of sorcery expressed in the above passage have much in common with classic accounts from other African societies: the use of some form of poison, extraordinary powers and evil intention. As elsewhere, *wanga* sorcerers on Mafia are believed to be associated with night, with graveyards and corpses.

Another form of sorcery, albeit much less frequently mentioned, is termed *muhanga*. Mohammed told the following story:

A long time ago, the shaman Juma was sleeping, and he was told by his spirit: 'Get up and go to Pwani.' He did so and went by the coastal path. When he got to the salt flats of Pwani village, he saw people digging a hole, and there was a goat there. Their intention was to put out its eyes and bury it alive. Their purpose was *muhanga*. They buried the goat.

Mohammed added:

The people he saw digging were the sons of a man called Abdallah in Pwani who have the habit of putting out the eyes of any kind of animals from goat to hen. *Muhanga* is a form of witchcraft. The purpose of burying the goat like this is that the spirit [being called upon] should do the same to a human [i.e. kill him or her]. So, when a person is given to this spirit it makes him blind. A shroud is buried with it. Some use pigeons or hens. Some say prayers and use all the ingredients of a funeral [to ensure the death of the victim].

P. So what is the difference between witchcraft (*uchawi*) and *muhanga*?

M. *Uchawi* means either giving *kibumbwi* (poison) or sending a spirit to attack someone. *Muhanga* means putting out the eyes of a creature and burying it alive – it is [also] a form of witchcraft (*uchawi*) which is done by shamans who are Koranic teachers – such as BJ and JK. For example, in building a ship or a house, you take a hen, put out its eyes, and bury it alive. And you do this so that you stop anyone coming with the evil eye: 'Let him be a fool, like this one, let him be blind, let him die just as I have buried my hen.' You could also use a goat or a cow, and even [bury it] with a shroud.

It will be noted that this form of sorcery is not said by Mohammed to be prevalent in Minazini, but in a neighbouring village, just like *uwanga* sorcery. Furthermore, *muhanga* is said to be practised by people who are Koranic teachers, which makes it even more reprehensible, and yet at the same time, gives them even greater power.

The evil eye and being seized by an ancestor

Mohammed reported in his diary that during my absence from the village, one of my neighbours had held a Koranic reading at his ancestral graves because his son had been seized by an ancestor (*kamshika mtoto wake maiti*). The child in question had been ill on and off before I left:

> The ancestor who had seized him was the one after whom he had been named because he wanted the first chapter of the Koran (*fatiha*) to be read to his namesake (*anataka fatiha apeleke somoye*).

Here the ancestor wanted remembrance in the form of a Koranic reading. Sometimes, however, an ancestor 'takes hold of' a child, because he or she has been 'forgotten', as happened with Mohammed's son Waziri (see below). In such a case, the remedy is to change the child's name to that of the offended ancestor, who then becomes the *somo* (namesake) of the child, and vice versa.

Another form of explanation for misfortune is the 'evil eye':

P. What is the evil eye (*jicho baya*)?

M. It is when someone says to him or herself, 'Why does such a one do well and I don't get anything?' An evil eye means an evil heart. Someone has many children, or donkeys or cows. Someone sees that Mohammed has a fine child, Waziri, and he says, 'Oh, that God would take away this child' – he has a bad heart, that is a thing of hatred (*chuki*).

There are various preventive measures against the evil eye, some of which are discussed below. *Muhanga* has already been mentioned; another is to read a *halbadiri*:

> MO read a *halbadiri* with the intention of protecting (*kingo*) the door [to his house], himself, his children, and his cattle and donkeys from the evil eye. 'May God give him [anyone] trouble, if he tries to send a spirit after me.'

The evil eye can thus either involve the agency of God ('Oh that God would take away this child') or that of spirits ('May God give him trouble if he tries to send a spirit after me'). Mohammed went on to give an instance of the illness of his own son, who was diagnosed as suffering both from the evil eye and from being seized by an ancestor who wanted him as a namesake (*somo*):

My son Waziri was in a terrible state because of the evil eye of three people – he had a prominent stomach and he was skinny. I went to the Kisiwa shaman-diviner, and he said [the reason was that] three people were bewitching him, and second, the name by which he was called was not right. He had been called after his mother's father . . . but it had to be changed to that of his father's mother's father.

Mohammed asked the shaman how he could do this [i.e. let the deceased know about the change of name] when the man was already dead. The shaman burned incense (*ubani*) and went to the rubbish heap and talked to the ancestors (*amegongolea*) and said: 'I went to divine and I saw that you have got hold of him, you want this child, so I want you to know that his name is now Waziri, let him get well.'

Such changes of name are not uncommon in the village, and the reason is almost always illness which is diagnosed as having been caused by an ancestor who wants a *somo*.

Casting spells: *mazingera*

In Mohammed's account of his life, he describes how as a young man, he left employment on a particular dhow because he had been told that a *mazingera* spell had been put on it to cause harm. But there are other kinds of spells, such as love magic at which Mohammed himself was expert:

The ingredients are honey because it is sweet, spittle because it never dries up in your mouth, tobacco because it is addictive (*hamu*, – lit. longing), and a sticky thing you get on the beach which is difficult to remove. [If you use these things] the woman will want you and will stay with you, she will never get tired of you and will think there is no one in the world like you.

The lover should put this mixture on his penis just before going to his assignation with the woman, then he penetrates her without satisfying her, promising to return later. Then whenever he returns, she will want him.

Like many other forms of supernatural power, however, *mazingera* can also be used for harm:

There is also medicine to cause impotence. You take the faeces of the man you want to bewitch, put them into a clean new white cloth, and then put this into an underground stream and leave it there. If you just want to teach him a lesson, you leave it there a couple of days before the cloth becomes too rotten, then blood or water will come out of the man's penis. But if you really want to finish him off, you leave it there and the cloth rots and he becomes quite impotent.

Explanations for affliction thus involve four agents, God, spirits, ancestors and human beings, or a combination of these. God, spirits and ancestors may afflict people for a variety of reasons, while humans who feel envy or hatred can call on God to afflict their enemies (as with parental curses), they can utilise spells (*mazingera*) or physical substances (*kibumbwi*), or they can send a spirit, one with which they have a relationship or one which is controlled by a shaman who agrees to act for them, in order to harm their enemy.

TREATMENT OF AFFLICTION: THE PERMITTED AND THE FORBIDDEN

Mohammed divided treatment of illness into two categories – *halali* (lawful) and *haramu* (unlawful) under Islamic law:

Those which are *halali* are as follows: applying fire (*kuchoma moto*), which is done by two men in the village, writing charms (*kuandika hirizi*), being encircled by the Koran (*kuzingua kwa Korani*), and cupping (*kutia chuku*), which is done by five men in the village.

Medicines which are *haramu* because they are not in the [Islamic] books include using herbs, roots and leaves (*dawa ya miti*, sometimes called *dawa ya miti shamba*, lit. 'medicine of field plants'), going to the spirit shrine (*kwenda pangani*), slaughtering cows [in spirit possession rituals], taking lighted coals [i.e. fumigating oneself – *kutia buhuri*], divination (*kupiga ramli*), and saying that people died for any reason other than the work of God (*kazi ya Mungu*).

Thus *halali* medicines are those 'of the books' (writing Koranic charms and using Koranic knowledge protectively), as well as applying fire and cupping, while medicines which are *haramu* are those which rely on knowledge of herbs and roots, and control of spirits; these are often known collectively as 'local medicines' (*dawa ya kienyeji*).

Mohammed himself was an expert in treating certain kinds of problems, particularly swellings. He noted one case he treated in his diary:

> Bt. F had a bad foot which swelled up. This illness is called *mnyama*. Mohammed was called and treated it with the leaves of the *mdumba* tree. You put them on the swelling, and then put three fibres above the swelling. This will quickly lead either to the swelling subsiding, or bursting completely. She gave him a measure of paddy as his dues.

In another part of the diary, he gives a slightly different version of this treatment:

> The plant Mohammed uses to treat swellings is called *mteja* and works well unless the reason [for the swelling] is a spirit (*feli*).[5] His father taught him this medicine. The tree is called *mdumba*; you take strips of its bark and tie them round the affected swollen limb four times. The leaves can also be pounded and put on the swelling.

Another treatment he knew was effective against the bite of a *katwa* (stingray) to which fishermen are particularly prone:

> You take the leaves of the *mkasili* or the *nzima maradhi*. Chew them together with tobacco. Place them on the spot where the person has been bitten, then suck and spit. And the sick person should not be put inside a house or hut. When he says he wants to urinate, you know the dirt in the wound has come out. Then you take the fibres (*wigo*) of an *mdumba* tree and tie them twice around the ankle. If the wound becomes a sore, you take the roots of the *mtoe* tree, grind them, and put them on the wound.

Mohammed explained how cupping and burning work:

> M. [For applying fire:] If an organ (*mshipa*) is hurting, the specialist (*mganga*) finds the central spot and then touches you lightly two or three times with a hot iron. Then the organ quietens down (*unalala*) and you get better. It hurts a lot, but then many hospital medicines are bitter too.

With cupping:

The bad blood gathers in a bad place, especially if you work too hard, or you have banged yourself and it swells. Then you cut it, and put the cupping horn on, and the specialist sucks, and the bad blood all comes out.

P. [And if you use herbs] How do you know which plants to use?

M. The healing properties of a plant are a matter of knowledge, whether of a person or a spirit. Spirit, God, has created anything that is required in this world, and he can get it. But you have to treat the cause.

P. So suppose you cure the cause of the illness, do you get rid of the illness at the same time?

M. No, then it becomes sickness (*maradhi*) and you need medicine for sickness (*dawa ya maradhi*).

Mohammed's comments here very closely fit in with much that has been written on African forms of healing[6] – the idea that cause as well as symptoms of illness must be treated. He also makes it clear in the above passage that God is the creator of all spirits and all knowledge. Our conversation continued with a consideration of the power of diviners and spirits:

P. But it doesn't always work, does it? For example, [you remember] Abdallah's child was suffering from malnutrition, but the diviner said '*amelishwa*' (it has been eaten, i.e. by a spirit). Can a diviner make a mistake?

M. Yes, of course, he can. He is a human being.

P. What about a spirit?

M. Sometimes it will be defeated. Its plants do not work (*miti hazimfai*).

Mohammed then went on to point out that the issue is not just one of power, but also of specialisation:

For example, AJ has a powerful spirit, and AS has a little spirit, but AS knows more about herbs. But then again there is no one better than JK [the Kisiwa shaman and Koranic diviner] whether for herbs, books, and all spirits. But even he can be defeated.

On Mafia, there is the complication of different forms of treatment – Islamic and non-Islamic. In Mohammed's view, the former are actually more powerful:

M. The spirit and the Koran are different things and the former runs away from the latter.

P. So why don't people use Koranic charms (*hirizi*) more often against spirits?

M. We like to use our ancient medicine or herbs, and/or our own spirits, and then we also go to to the hospital.

P. But why doesn't everyone get [Koranic] charms?

M. Some don't believe in this as much as *migoda* (local charms) and spirit things. Only if you are defeated [at home] do you go outside [for remedies]. Even in the household of AJ [the chief land spirit shaman of Minazini], people are treated outside, perhaps because things get worse, perhaps because it's not his luck [to be successful in treating that particular case]. [For example] His sisters . . . have both been initiated (*kupungwa*) into the *mkobero* (sea spirit ritual)[7] cult by one of its shamans.

P. But why doesn't AJ prevent such spirits from coming and afflicting them?

M. He does have medicine, but he can't always be successful. He told me once that the late YA took bad things (*tambo*)[8] out of him, and I myself have given him love medicine to get Bt. M, wife of JH who was a member of his guild (*mteja wake*), and became his mistress, but finally abandoned him on account of his meanness.

Although Mohammed does not mention them in the above list, *halali* medicines also include allopathic medical treatment. In a later conversation, I asked him about this:

P. What is the difference between hospital medicine and local medicines?

M. There is a difference. At the hospital, you will be given medicine to drink or apply. But local medicine you might be asked to put on outside, when your illness is inside, and then it [the source of the trouble] comes out. Another difference is that hospital medicine is already prepared, but local medicine has to be pounded and boiled. And we are told by [allopathic] doctors that we are destroying people by this latter medicine, but it is no good giving hospital medicine until you have got rid of the spirit. Such medicines do nothing for a spirit (*hazihusiani na iblissi*).

Again, Mohammed makes it clear that it is essential to treat cause, as well as symptoms.

PREVENTING AFFLICTION: INOCULATION

There are several ways of preventing illness and witchcraft striking: first, the use of Koranic measures, such as amulets of Koranic verses (*hirizi*), reading a *halbadiri*, or encircling (*kuzingua*) something or someone in need of protection (see Chapter 3); second, being 'inoculated' (*kuchanjwa*) (see Chapter 5) by local medicines, and third, giving someone into the guardianship of a spirit (*kupewa ulezi*). Mention has already been made of Koranic measures, and in this section, I consider inoculation: spirit guardianship is dealt with in Chapter 9.

Mohammed himself attributed much of his well-being to a variety of modes of protection. He wrote in his diary of occasions where he knew he was threatened by the relatives of a woman with whom he was having an affair, and so took preventive measures:

Mohammed has been given *hirizi* by K because he had a dream in which he saw the husband and relatives of his current mistress in the place where he usually meets her. The dream continued that he [Mohammed] went on and found some money and put it in his pocket. As it happened, the next day he met you [PC] near that spot and you gave him 10 shillings, so the second half of the dream came true. He was afraid that the first part would as well, so he avoided his mistress that day.

The first person to whom he told this story was a shaman who was a relative of his. He said [the dream meant that] it was probably the woman's husband who had given her a spirit to guard her and prevent her from committing adultery and that if she did so, the spirit would take the lover. [The shaman went on to remind him that] Mohammed's protection (*kingo*) is his ancestral spirit KC and its spirit friend KZ. So the day before going to see his mistress, he should fumigate himself and ask the spirit to go with him and guard him.

But Mohammed still felt uneasy, saying: 'A spirit is like a human, it can go off somewhere' (*shaitani binadamu, anaweza kwenda kutem-bea*) [i.e. leaving him unprotected]. So he went to K and got a Koranic charm from him, which he is to wear. If he has sex, he takes it [the charm] off and puts it in his trouser pocket until he has washed. If these charms get polluted, e.g. because of sex, then he has to wash them.

Mohammed, however, is still worried, so he has made himself a medicine which brings clarity (*dawa ya mbayana*) which he knows how to do himself. He once bought it [the recipe] from a man now dead for 12 shillings. This consists of plants and enables him to know anything his rival does because someone will be sure to tell him. To make this charm he does as follows:

He takes weeds from near a cross-roads, because that is the place where people meet, for good or bad. Then he takes a small incense burner (*kiteso*) or a broken pot and a hot charcoal and puts the weeds into the container, then the charm, but not so that it burns, saying: 'I have taken the weeds from this path. The path is a big one, it gets used by everyone here, by night and by day. Anyone with good intentions, I want them, anyone with bad intentions, you will know yourself.' This makes anyone who has evil intentions towards Mohammed become good. It inoculates him (*inamkinga*); it even helps his spirit to be more effective. Also Mohammed himself will become much more popular and required in rituals of every kind.

On one occasion Mohammed told me that he intended to be 'inoculated' (*kuchanjiwa*) again:

I got a little from my father, and some more from a man from Tumbatu Island, and now I want more. Because you may have perhaps seven herbs [to protect you] but if your enemy has ten, won't he defeat you?

Thus 'inoculations' have to be periodically renewed and strengthened to be sure of their efficacy.

Mohammed also described another method of 'inoculating' by making cuts with a razor on the face, shoulders, arms, legs and knees – two or three cuts in each place. Into each cut is rubbed a medicine made from the roots of certain trees, as Mohammed explained:

There is a tree called *mwinga jini* (lit. 'the chaser away of spirits') to which no one returns, because it just chases them away. You dig up the roots with a hoe. When you dig up the roots of the *mwinga jini* tree, you dig in its shade. So you dig in a different place according to the time of day. There is also another tree called *mlemea chuma* which he used as medicine on the day of his case in Kilindoni and another bush called *kuku mweupe* and you couldn't penetrate it if you tried, even if someone offered you 1,000 shillings, even [a creature as small as] a hen couldn't do so, its thorns are so thick.

All these trees you have to talk to before cutting them – you might use the bark or the roots. But for 'inoculation' (*chanjio*) you use the roots and sesame (*uto*)[9] oil or honey. You fry them all, then mix them together and rub this mixture into the cut. This recipe cost him 12 shillings and some cigarettes, and he gave the man a few shillings extra because he was so pleased with it.

P. Why those ingredients?

M. The *mwinga jini* because it wards off spirits just like its name, the *mlemea chuma* because it prevents sorcery (*sihiri*) getting in from below, that is bad objects (*tambo*) can't get in [to your body]. [You use] the *kuku mweupe* tree because no one can get through it (*hakupigi mtu kifua kwa kifua*) thus an enemy will step to one side on seeing you, just as he would [have to do] for this tree, and honey because a bee eats from the flowers of all trees, bitter or otherwise, and so it represents a kind of synthesis of all trees, and you use sesame oil beause it is heavy. But Mohammed himself prefers honey.

Similar preventive measures can be taken to 'inoculate' someone against the bites of a *katwa* or a poisonous spider:

Take some roots of *mkasile* trees and the roots of another tree which is used against poisonous spiders, some honey, and some sesame (*uto*) oil. Take a small potsherd (*kigae*) and fry the roots in it, then split them up, and finally grind them in a coconut shell with the handle of any implement such as a hoe. Add the honey and sesame oil. Make three cuts below each ankle bone, and between the big toe and next one, then over the whole body if you want to prevent the spider's bite. Then rub in the medicine.

Knowledge of such measures can either be given to someone, most likely a child by a parent, as in Mohammed's case, or be bought for money, or else exchanged for a different remedy as in the following case:

The other day Athman came to see Mohammed and asked him for medicine; he wanted him to show him the plant which would make it [his finger] better, and in exchange he would show him a plant for making a child walk if it is slow.

Mohammed attributed a large measure of his safety up to that time to the fact that he had been 'inoculated':

If [you have been inoculated and] you are asleep, you will begin to shake because the spirits in your cuts come out to protect you against the approaching enemy. In each cut are three spirits, therefore in the whole body are a huge number of spirits. They are not possessory spirits, nor do you know their names. They are the kind that live in trees, and they will drive away those coming with bad intentions. If a spirit is sent against you and you are an inoculated person, it can't look at you directly because you have your jinns protecting you. Nor can it pass in front of you, only to one side. Then the [enemy] jinn will return to the person who sent it and say, 'I didn't see him' and if he has any sense, he won't send the spirit again, or the spirits [in the inoculation] will turn against him (*watamvuruga mashaitani wale*) and he will die.

P. Will this be effective against *wanga* (sorcerers)?

M. Yes, very much so. Your enemy puts *kibumbwi* into a glass of water and brings you the glass, but the water begin to fizz and bubble – then you know he is trying to poison you.

P. What about medicines put in your path?

M. You won't walk on them, or you will feel a tingling in your body and know that there is a danger in front of you – a sorcerer (*mwanga*) or a spirit or some buried medicine. Similarly if a man has the evil eye put on him it won't get him.

Linked to the notion of being inoculated are the concepts of relative vulnerability and invulnerability:

If you yourself are *mzito* (lit. 'heavy', i.e. powerful, relatively invulnerable) and try to make witchcraft against an inoculated person, you will both remain in the same state. But if you yourself are *mwepesi* (lit. 'light', i.e. not powerful, relatively vulnerable), you will get hurt.

Mohammed added:

Patricia, never hate me, because if you do anything against me, it will hurt you. I tell my mistresses the same thing. And I am warning you now because I am fond of you.

I return to these concepts of vulnerability and invulnerability in the next chapter in which I consider how affliction by spirits is dealt with.

9 Dealing with affliction
Spirits

In this chapter, the focus is on relations between spirits and humans. On Mafia, as elsewhere on the East African coast,[1] there are various categories of spirits, which are collectively termed *mashaitani* or *iblissi*. The first category is spirits of the land, known as *mizimu* or *pepo*, some of which guard fields, and some of which are possessory (*mizuka*). Similar kinds of spirits (often with similar names) are found throughout much of Bantu Africa[2] and are the focus of cults of affliction and healing, as they are on Mafia. The second category is spirits of the sea (*majini*),[3] which may also be possessory, and which mainly afflict women; the cults which surround these spirits have much in common with those in other Muslim areas, particularly the *zar* cults of Somalia, Ethiopia and the Sudan, and similar cults in North Africa.[4] I will first deal briefly with the cult of sea spirits, about which Mohammed did not write much in his diary, before discussing relations between humans and land spirits, in which he was much more interested, and about which he wrote at greater length.

AFFLICTION BY SEA SPIRITS

Sea spirits (*majini ya bahari*), unlike land spirits, rarely have individual names, but are grouped in 'tribes' such as Mabedui (Bedouin) and Marohani. They are not usually controlled in the same way by humans as are land spirits, but they do afflict humans. Some are also known as *majini ya mahaba* – love spirits – and the afflictions which they cause are primarily concerned with reproduction.

Such spirits are dealt with through two cults known as *mkobero* and *tari*. *Tari* cults are not practised in Minazini, and there are no diary entries about them, nor did I ever get the opportunity to witness one.[5] There are, however, several *mkobero* guilds in the village, although Mohammed did not often write about them, since neither he nor his wife were involved, nor did he attend their rituals. There are however, a few references in his diary:

1 An *mkobero* ritual was held at the house of Ali [the shaman-diviner]. They killed a goat. The *mwali* (initiate) was the daughter of his wife Bt. H. Two shamans were from Kisiwa village and one was from Minazini.

2 MM held a *dhikiri* [i.e. *mkobero*] for his wife, Bt. K, and cooked rice. In the morning they killed a goat. The shaman was HM from Minazini.

Sea spirits, like land spirits, have guilds into which afflicted people, in this case women, are initiated. The first stage is the offering of a tray of food, known as *sinia*,[6] the second is the slaughter of a goat and the consumption of its blood. Sea spirits are thought to need 'things of the book', thus much use is made in *mkobero* rituals of Arabic written texts, and 'things of the shop', such as rosewater, incense, spices, dates and other delicacies which are often particularly associated with 'Arab' culture. Furthermore, the rituals themselves utilise many features of the Sufi order rituals, particularly the chanting and over-breathing (*dhikiri*); sometimes this word is used instead of *mkobero*.

Some of the sea spirits are thought to look like Arabs (see Subira's account in the next chapter), and people possessed by them are thought to be able to speak Arabic. There seems little doubt that in this area, the cult has been intimately associated with Arab colonial rule, and the subsequent hierarchy of Arabs, freeborn and slaves which has long characterised much of coastal society. Reports from other areas where the *zar* cult is found also note that spirits are often thought to originate outside the society concerned, in this way reflecting historical changes and the impact of external forces. At the same time, these are particularly women's cults, dealing with women's issues of sexuality, fertility and reproduction, although on Mafia, all of the sea spirit cult shamans are male, in contrast with other areas, such as the Sudan, where they are female (see Constantinides 1977, 1985, Boddy 1990).

Male sea spirits are often thought to be 'love spirits' (*majini ya mahaba*) which can cause their human mistresses to constantly miscarry or be infertile, and their husbands or lovers to be impotent, as Mohammed explains:

Bt. M, wife of MA, was taken by a *jini* of the sea, which is called *uziwa* in spirit language, when she was quite small and was going to look for oysters (*chaza*) on the beach. That jinn is a male. When she sleeps, he comes to her. He comes and takes her into the sea and shows her houses there and then wakes her up with a start. This is known from the other day's *kitanga*. The shaman-diviner AS told her father that the woman herself knew the cause of her trouble, and she was told to go to the shaman of this [sea spirit] cult, who lives in Kisiwa village, as he would know how to read the Koran and how to prepare the spirit's dues (*ada*).

But the *jini* has not yet possessed her – when the Kisiwa shaman returns from a trip to the mainland, he will treat her so that it either possesses her or goes away. It is preventing her from getting pregnant. This does not mean that she will refuse her husband. She may have intercourse with both [i.e. her spirit and her husband]. But she may not get pleasure [from sex with her husband], or perhaps the spirit will render the woman's husband or lover impotent. For if she has normal relations with a man, she will not give pleasure to the *jini*, but wake up before her love-making with him is over. . . .

Both spirits of the *mkobero* and the *tari* live in the sea, and many are love spirits. Jinns are both male and female. Men are taken by female jinns, women by male jinns and they have sex with them at night while they are asleep. They appear in the form of an Arab who is handsome or beautiful. When the man or woman gets married the love spirit gets jealous. A female *jini* will render her man impotent, and cause him not to desire any women. A male *jini* would render the husband of his beloved impotent and if she does manage to become pregnant, he causes her to miscarry before three months are up, or if she does manage to have the baby, he kills it. To prevent this, the *jini* is given a *sinia* (tray of sweetmeats) or a goat. But this is not infallible.

Most of the women who participate in this cult have borne few or no children and have had many miscarriages. Mohammed could not think of any examples of men who were themselves afflicted, although he did himself once become temporarily impotent during an affair with a woman afflicted by a sea spirit. All of the shamans of this cult are male, including the most powerful one who lives in a neighbouring village; they are said to be able to control sea spirits through their knowledge of Islamic books, but are not usually possessed by them.

The sea spirit cults have, as already noted, borrowed many Islamic features: the use of the 'Arabic' language and Arabic texts, the *dhikiri* of the Sufi orders, and the 'things of the shop' associated with Arab culture such as rose-water (*maharashi*). Several *walim* in the village are involved themselves in these cults, and although others refuse to participate, condemnation of the *mkobero* by the very orthodox is less pronounced than of the cults of the land spirits, to which we now turn.

AFFLICTION BY LAND SPIRITS

The cult of land spirits is different in many ways from that of sea spirits. Aside from the fact that, as their names suggest, the latter live on land, and the former in the sea, land spirits are linked with ancestry. People inherit relationships with them, which may be activated in the case of affliction. They also come into contact with them in the course of cultivating subsistence crops on the bushland, especially that on the low ridge which lies to the east of the village.

On one occasion, I asked Mohammed what types of illness might lead someone to suspect spirits were the cause:

M. Heat, fever and cold, or illnesses that come and go, sometimes sick, sometimes well. Intermittent fever (*homa za kipindepinde*). . . . No matter what illness you have, the spirit will take [your] blood. Sometimes you will be sick (*utaaguka*), sometimes the spirit will always be with you and take a bit at a time, so that you will be sick now and then, you will be told on divination that you had *ugonjwa wa kimwimwa*, that is, you are neither ill nor well. . . .

The spirit does not always intend to kill, nor is it always sent for that reason. It may be to teach a lesson. All spirits can kill, but some spirits are the kind who need feeding (*wanazolishwa*) [regularly], they regard people as if they were cigarettes, each year they need [to use] three or four. The worst for catching people is a female spirit in Pwani village.

Spirits, then, are believed to be powerful and capable of killing people by taking their blood; they also consume the blood of animals which are sacrificed in rituals.

Land spirits may afflict humans for a variety of reasons. The first is if they have an ancestral connection with such a spirit, but have neglected it by failing to take offerings to its shrine. Second, people who have promised offerings to spirits and failed to deliver them may be punished. Third, anyone may have a chance encounter with a spirit who is 'walking about' or 'on the path', and who may, if displeased, decide either to 'consume' the human, and thus make them ill, or it may want to 'become friends' and possess the human, making him or her its medium (*kiti chake*, lit. 'chair' or 'seat'). Fourth, a spirit may wish to punish someone for offending it, to 'teach him or her a lesson'. Finally, someone may be afflicted by a spirit because of witch-craft sent by an enemy who either has control over a spirit, or who has consulted someone else who does. In the following section, each of these forms of spirit affliction is considered in turn.

Ancestry

Where someone who is persistently sick has an ancestral spirit, it is often suggested, as in Mwahadia's case in Chapter 5, that this is the reason for the illness. It is suspected that the spirit may want an offering, or it may want the patient to become possessed and initiated into its guild. Mohammed gave the following account of one of Mwahadia's numerous bouts of illness in connection with one of her pregnancies:

After her first pregnancy, she had a lot of trouble [it will be recalled that this baby had been born dead, see Chapter 2] and it was eventually decided that she had the spirit of her mother's mother. They followed up this ancestry, and went to the shaman AJ who is friendly with that spirit, but she got no better, so the diviner said to go to HH for divination (*kwenda pachironi*).

They said that the spirit was offering friendship (*amempa mkono*) and that it wanted to possess her (*kupanda kichwani*, lit. 'climb into her head'). So Mohammed was told to take her to all the spirit possession rituals, but she didn't become possessed, and she got better through other medicines.

But HH said that nonetheless, he should get some money from them as his fee (*ijara*) – 2 shillings for 'the money of the cup' or 'the rice of the cup' as his fee for fumigating himself and for invoking the spirits to communicate with them (*kugongoa*) as well as some money for the spirit. The fee is an amount agreed upon before starting, after which the diviner lights the censer and asks the help of the spirit, or he tells the spirit that they must agree, as it and his ancestors did, and he gives a time limit, and says that if the patient gets better [within that period], then the spirit will get a certain present.

Debts to a spirit

Diagnosis of sickness being caused by a spirit may often mean that the patient's earlier case history is invoked to explain the current illness, most commonly an unpaid 'debt' to a spirit whose shaman treated an earlier bout of illness. Such unpaid debts are one of the commonest reasons given in divination for sickness in Mohammed's diary:

AH has a promise [of an offering] to his spirit, but he has not yet paid it. Now he has a swollen finger and on divination, it was found that it is indeed his spirit who is 'teaching him a lesson'. The shaman is WH, and AH has already been to him and promised an offering tray.

Even shamans themselves may become sick if they have not paid their dues to the possessory spirit. Mohammed wrote in his diary of one such occasion when his father's brother, a shaman, became ill:

> WN went to a *ziara* (Sufi ritual) on the 7th day of the first month and has been sick ever since. The reason is that his spirit has taken hold of him, it wants him to dance the *mwingo* ritual (*mkiki*) (a land spirit ritual, see Chapter 10), and furthermore he has neglected its [shrine in its] house in Karibu village for a long time. So now he has to go to Karibu and sleep there.

P. But doesn't his house in Minazini belong to the spirit too?

M. It does, but the usual one is over there [in Karibu].

P. What is his trouble?

M. It is a swollen penis (*pusha*). Next month a date will be fixed for the dance (*machezo*) when he comes back from Karibu. He will also have one in Minazini, and he has already got a young bull which he has castrated to make it whiter.

P. Does it matter whether he uses a cow or a bull?

M. It doesn't make any difference what kind of animal is used.

Later in Mohammed's diary, there is a further entry on the same topic:

> WN is sick still with *mshipa*.[7] He has been caught by his spirit for neglecting his house in Karibu. Now he has to go and sleep in Mrali and dance a *mwingo* there.

P. Was he divined?

M. No, he knew it himself and from being dreamed about (*kuoteshwa*) by other people. First of all, Bt. A dreamed that her mother said to her, 'Let us go to Karibu village to a *mwingo*.' She replied, 'No, I am waiting for my child to come back from school.' Then she woke up and was surprised to have dreamed this, but as the shaman WN was already sick and he is her classificatory mother's brother, and her mother used to be possessed by the same spirit as the shaman, she recognised that the spirit wanted a *mwingo* performed.

And another man also dreamed about this [Mohammed was not sure who it was] so this reinforced the shaman's intuition. The spirit usually causes *mshipa wa mtwana* (bladder problem). WN is now better and goes to Karibu on certain days.

P. Couldn't he move there if he wanted to?

M. Yes, if he informed the spirit first.

P. So why hasn't he done this?

M. He hasn't done this only because his Karibu wife is not here, she is in Zanzibar.

Shamans have to pay proper attention to their possessory spirits if they are to remain friends – they should take care to live in the house where the spirit is thought to spend part of its time, and to take regular offerings, as well as holding a full-scale ritual annually, either a *kitanga* or a *mwingo* as appropriate. Failure to fulfil these obligations is likely to result in illness. In the above instance, WN suspected the reason for his illness from its very nature – the kind of problem he was having had been caused before by the spirit. His opinion was confirmed by the dreams of two other people.

Interpretation of dreams as a way of receiving messages from spirits is not uncommon and Mohammed himself utilised it frequently, as he mentions several times in his diary:

> On Sunday night I was asleep and I dreamed that my spirit told me that he wanted his present, and the other spirit (his friend) wanted his money. I woke up right then.

P. What did you see?

M. A man and his friend. It [the present] is for their help in guarding me from all harm.

P. Do you have to give this every year?

M. No, not regularly. I haven't taken them anything for two years now. I usually take the present for my ancestral spirit myself [to the shrine – *panga*], and give the money for the other spirit to two men who are possessed by it.

On several occasions, Mohammed notes in his diary that his spirit gave him information about me in his dreams:

> Mohammed's spirit came and told him in a dream that Patrisha was sick.

When he came to see me that day, he found this was indeed the case. Another time he told me that he dreamed that I was coming back when I had been away and I duly arrived as he woke up. At this stage of his life, Mohammed, like others who had an ancestral relationship with a spirit, communicated with it primarily through dreams, and was not yet a spirit medium in the sense of being fully possessed.

Chance encounters

Sometimes when divination takes place, it is found that someone has met up with a spirit by chance:

TA had stomach problems and was examined by a Koranic diviner, who saw that he had been taken by a spirit in the field. The spirit said: 'Well, creature (*kiumbe*), can you bring me something nice to eat (*vimemeno*, lit. sweet things) in my town?' So on Sunday or Monday he had to take them to his shrine (*panga*) and FM, the shaman of that spirit, was given them. So he took them, and then it was alright (*salama tu*).

Mohammed added:

It was not that TA had cultivated in that spirit's fields, but they met on the path while the spirit was walking around.

Mohammed himself had a similar encounter with a spirit:

KT is the possessory spirit of MJ, but now its presents are taken by WA [Mohammed's father's brother] because he has been entrusted with it (*amekabidhiwa*). It is a very fierce spirit (*anaganda kweli*, lit. 'it sticks to you really hard'). One day Mohammed went to an area of the village . . . to prepare a field and coming back met with this spirit. When he got home, he felt cold and went to lie down on a mat. His sister came [to visit him and when she saw his state] went to fetch his mother since at the time his wife was with her parents because she was pregnant.

Later his sister's daughter came to see him, and found him kicking his legs and muttering. She ran to fetch his mother again. He was talking in his sleep saying: 'Let's go, *bwana*.' He dreamed he was with other young men playing in a particular area of the village. But he wanted them to go somewhere else. The meaning of the dream was that the spirit had come from there, from its [main] shrine to its second home (*bandari*, lit. 'harbour'). He remembers this dream quite clearly.

So they fetched WA, his father's younger brother [a shaman], and he came and asked Mohammed what had happened, then sent for some medicine he had at home, and also went to get some from the forest. He pounded the medicines, mixed them with water and threw them at Mohammed's face, so that he started. WA told the spirit, 'Go away from here, it is not your place, it is my place. Each one has their place. If you have been sent, go back [to where you came from] and tell that person who sent you that if he wants a youth (*kidume*), if he wants a young girl (*tigina*), or if he wants a young cow (*mbuguma*),[8] let him give it to you.'

Although WA had already been entrusted to look after this particular spirit, apparently he hadn't recognised it, since the spirit hadn't told him of its intention, nor had Mohammed been possessed and mentioned the name of the afflicting spirit. He then said to the spirit troubling Mohammed: 'Ah old person (*kongwe*), are you here? Calm down, calm down (*mweka, mweka*)', because Mohammed was rushing around as if he were possessed. WA put medicine all over Mohammed's body, then he put charcoal into a censer and added grass with a strong smell called *mafusho* under Mohammed's bed to drive the spirit away. But when WN left, Mohammed was doubled up so that his chin touched his knees, and then WA was quite sure that Mohammed had been taken by this particular spirit.

He [Mohammed] put his knife under the sleeping mat, and when he was asleep heard someone saying, 'Can I come in?' (*Hodi, hodi*), but he did not reply. So the spirit went away. WN knew that the spirit was now angry with him for stopping it from getting Mohammed.

[Meanwhile,] Mohammed's mother sent his brother to see a Koranic diviner, and he confirmed that WN was indeed correct in thinking that Mohammed had been taken by this particular spirit. But he said that all it wanted was an offering of sweet things (*vimemeno*). So WA burned incense (*kutia vumba*) and said to the spirit that if Mohammed got well within two weeks, the third week it would get its present.

Mohammed got well before the time was up and went off to Zanzibar to pick cloves. The very night he arrived, he developed eye trouble. He went to the countryside to pick cloves, but after two days he [was so ill that he] had to go back to town. He called a boy named MH, the son of Mwalim HM the Koranic diviner, [who was on his way back to Mafia] and sent a letter to his brother telling him that he was ill and he thought it was because he had not paid his debt to the spirit.

Meanwhile he bought incense and fumigated himself and told his own ancestral spirit that if he had broken his promise, the letter had already being sent, and if the trouble was being caused by an enemy, human or spirit, he wanted his help. The second day, he started to get better. In fact, his elder brother had already got his letter and given the offering to WA to take to the spirit.

After this everything was alright and he never had any trouble again. The reason for being caught [by this spirit] was that they just met on the path. There was no special reason for this spirit to get angry with him.

Punishment for annoying a spirit

Spirits may also afflict humans when they are angered by the latters' behaviour. Spirits are thought to dislike the pollution of sexual intercourse, and may punish people if they have sex in their territory:

Committing adultery is called *kuzinga*, *kuzini* or *kufanya fuska*. If you do this near a spirit shrine (*panga*), it is inevitable that you will be harmed and caught. You will have to give a cow as a punishment for being 'dirty' (*chafu*) in its 'town'.

In another part of the diary, Mohammed describes how he was 'caught' for just such a reason. His diary entry concerned the re-marriage of a woman who had been widowed, but he then added some further information:

> This woman had been Mohammed's mistress some time before, and they had had intercourse between Minazini and a neighbouring village. He was caught by the spirit whose 'town' this is. He was ill for a long time. If this spirit gets hold of someone, it is not often they escape with their lives, but we are all 'one', because he [Mohammed] has the ancestry of this spirit through his mother who was the elder sister of its shaman. He was treated by this shaman and the spirit said, 'It will be all right as this is my child (*kengeja wangu*).'

Mohammed added:

This fact is not always sufficient, some even 'eat' their own children (*wengine wanakula kengeja wao*).

Given that affairs can usually only be conducted in the bush-land, illicit sex can often mean an encounter with one of the spirits which lives there. Such spirits also have other rules of good behaviour:

> The shaman-diviner Ali divined for Bt. M, who was sick, and he saw that she had been taken by a field spirit; she was cultivating on its land, but did not have the ancestry of this spirit. [The reason for her afflic-tion was that] she had eaten sweet foods (*vimemeno*) and not invited it. [On this occasion] the sweet food was the first fruits (*mlimbu*) of her crop, which she ate last year without throwing some for the spirit whose field they were cultivating at the time. Now she must take an offering tray to the shaman so that he may speak to the spirit.
>
> Furthermore, [the shaman suggested that] she has an enemy with whom she has quarrelled at a ritual, although Bt. M said: 'It is not my habit to quarrel with people.' The illness is that her whole body is sick because her punishment was to be afflicted by the spirit.

P. So was the shaman wrong in saying she had quarrelled with someone?
M. No, there was a quarrel with someone [which started off by them] joking with each other (*maneno ya masihara*) until the owner of the field [i.e. the spirit] got angry in its heart and caused her evil (*anambaza*) with the evil eye. So in the divination, the origin of the problem was shown, that she had used bad language and quarrelled.

Although there are certain rules of behaviour on land controlled by spirits (no sexual relations, no quarrelling), spirits of this kind tend otherwise to be amoral and capricious; their behaviour is uncertain, hence the best way of dealing with them is propitiation through offerings, and making sure that they are not offended. They cannot be got rid of, and people are likely to run into them in the course of their daily lives.

Witchcraft through the invocation of spirits

Another reason for affliction by a spirit is the agency of another human practising witchcraft as in the following case:

> Mohammed's father's brother, who lived in Kisiki village, had a mistress, but another fellow came along and she did not want him any more. He went to talk to a shaman and said, 'Bewitch him and I will give a cow.' So the shaman bewitched the second lover (*kamwapisa*) and he died, then the first lover gave a cow to the shaman.

However, in several instances recorded in the diary, such a deed may backfire; a spirit sent by an enemy to harm a particular person, may end up 'catching' another:

> A spirit had been sent that day to get MH, a man from Pwani village, but it missed him because of MH's ancestral connection with a very powerful spirit as well as his possession by a second one; both of these protected him, so MM of Minazini got caught instead.
>
> This second man, MM, was walking along the beach with two others, and he heard a car coming along the road, but the others didn't hear it. In fact it was not really a car, but this spirit, which lives in Karibu village, coming to get him. But his ancestral spirit possessed him for the first time and fought off the attacking spirit, then said 'I will stay with this medium (*kiti*, lit. chair)' and so he is possessed by it until this day.

P. What about the other [attacking] spirit?

M. It was defeated, and it turned back, but if it is not given someone else, it will catch you [the person who has sent it]. It is owed its dues (*haki*): 'Give me my fee (*ada*) or you people will have a funeral (*mtasikia mlio*).' So you must give it what you promised, although perhaps you may get away with just an offering tray instead of the cow you promised, if it still hasn't been sucessful in what you wanted it to do. But when the spirit has done some work and has tried [but not succeeded] so the person [who sent the spirit] will say, 'You did not get what you wanted and I did not get what I wanted, but take this, *mzee*', and you will give it half of what you promised.

As the above passage makes plain, some spirits want to consume humans, as well as cows and offering trays. If they do not get the one they want or have been sent to get, they will look for a substitute, and indeed, if the situation is one of witchcraft, whereby a human has invoked a spirit to harm an enemy, the situation may rebound on them – the thwarted spirit can turn on the human agent and take him or her instead:

> Bt. M of Kisiwa village, daughter of Bt. H, had a spirit come to her and say: 'I want a human.' She gave it her own mother who bore her. One of Bt. H's other children doctored her and cooled (*kapoa*)[9] that spirit [so that it went away from her]. So the spirit came back to Bt. M and took hold of her, and blood began to come from her vagina and from her ears.

Mohammed added:

This is a spirit which uses a white cow and the *kitanga* ritual, and which they inherited from their father. The spirit had gone to Bt. M and said it wanted a human to eat. She went and told her brother, who is often referred to as a witch, but he said he had none to give. So she gave her mother, who became sick. But another child of the sick woman cured her, and then the spirit returned to Bt. M and she herself became ill.

Shamans, then, who have the power to control spirits, are very much feared, both because they can send their spirits to afflict people who anger them, and also because it is thought that some spirits require regular 'offerings' of humans. Spirits want to consume blood, and some 'use' or 'catch' or 'eat' humans for this purpose, resulting in illness because of 'lack of blood' (*upungufu wa damu*). It should be noted that consumption of blood marks the spirits as the antithesis of good Muslims, for whom blood is forbidden (*haramu*).

Furthermore, some of Mohammed's other accounts indicate that where spirits require human sacrifices, it is insufficient always to give whoever happens along, it may have to be someone near. This is particularly the case if one seeks the power to harm others through a spirit:

If you want to acquire the work of witchcraft or healing (*uchawi au uganga*), the shaman will say to you: 'Prepare yourself first (*ujitenegeneze mwenyewe kwanza*). What kind of witchcraft do you want?' [I might reply that it is to acquire the power to deal with such situations as] for example, if a man seduces my wife, or deceives me, or I want a woman who is refusing me, or I want to kill my father.

The shaman replies: 'You must first kill your own child, then I have no doubt that you will get it, the power of *uganga* (healing or harming) will come forth, I believe (*halafu sina shaka utapata, uganga unatoka, naamini*).'

Here Mohammed uses the term *uganga* which is an ambiguous one. It can mean either the power of good, as in healing/curing, or the power of evil, as in witchcraft. Such power, if one does not already possess it through control of a spirit, can only be obtained through sacrificing someone who is close.[10] Mohammed's diary contains several such cases; the first is that of a shaman who attempted to sacrifice his son-in-law:

> When the children were in the big *jando* in Pwani, HM called over his son-in-law and told him to slaughter the cow. Then he was reputed to have said to the spirit: 'When it is slaughtered, he is yours; when he leaves, follow him.' This was on a Saturday. On the following Wednesday, returning from a *kitanga* in Pwani, the son-in-law fell ill with a headache and sickness. He was taken to his elder sister's place, and examined by one of the Pwani shamans who recognised that he had been taken by this particularly fierce spirit. He returned to Pwani and JM, who is a powerful shaman, gave him medicine and he got better.

In this case, the man was only saved by the intervention of a powerful shaman. In the second case, a woman was said to have sacrificed her son:

> A man named WK was called from Kisiki by Binti N to the killing of the cow in an area of Minazini guarded by a spirit. He went to place the offerings (*kuweka ada*) and the same day when he returned home he became ill, died and was buried. The witch (*mchawi*) who called him [to take the offering] was his own mother.

In the third case, a woman was said to have sacrificed her brother's daughter:

> Bt. F died on 6/2/66 in the afternoon. She was married to NJ the year before last, and had had one child which died soon after birth; since that time she has been unwell. She went to stay at the house of her father, a Karibu village man cultivating on the outskirts of Minazini, where she died and she was buried in Karibu.

Mohammed added:

The shaman of my ancestral spirit told me that her father's sister has an ancestral spirit and it was she who killed the woman. It's like I told you the other day, if you want [the power of] witchcraft you have to kill people. And she has already killed an unrelated youth, but you can only go on giving outside people for a certain period, then you will have to give someone who is near and dear to you.

In these accounts, power associated with spirits is used for immoral purposes, the killing of other humans, even those to whom one is linked by the most sacred ties such as parent and child. Mohammed himself was reluctant to probe such matters too deeply:

M. I [myself] wouldn't go and divine the cause of a death because I might be asked by the shamans, 'What is the reason for the funeral (*kilio*) which just passed?' [And I would reply] 'I do not know, whether it was because of the agency of a human (*kiumbe*) or the will of God, you know yourselves, *wazee.*'
'So this man . . .' [and then the diviner may tell you enough for you to guess the reason].
P. So what do you do then?
M. Nothing. Or perhaps you can pay the witch back by killing his or her child or in some other way.
P. Do the diviners tell each time it is a case of death by witchcraft?
M. No, not often.
P. Do they charge for this?
M. Not necessarily, it is up to them. If they [the patient's family] have already been for divination, then the witch will not go because he is afraid that he will be accused. But otherwise he may go.
P. If he doesn't go?
M. That is because of his wickedness – it doesn't necessarily lead to suspicions. . . .

This section has explored, through Mohammed's words, local beliefs about harnessing spirit power, whether for good or evil in which the notion of sacrifice, especially the blood sacrifice of an animal or even a human, is important. The powers of healing and harming – *uganga* – are two sides of the same coin, and in order to acquire or retain that power, it may be necessary to sacrifice someone to whom one is bound by the closest ties, thus infringing the most sacred bonds of kinship. Witchcraft, then, is about personal relationships which have gone wrong, about morality, and about the ambiguity of power. All of this can be known through divination, but it is rarely spoken openly. Mohammed notes that the diviner 'may tell you enough for you to guess', but he also states his own reluctance to divine the cause of a death. Some knowledge is just too difficult and painful to seek.

BARGAINING WITH SPIRITS: OFFERINGS AND INITIATION

When affliction by a spirit has been diagnosed, there is usually a process of bargaining at the divination, during which the shaman-diviner may try to suggest that a large offering (usually a cow) be given, possibly in a ritual (*kwa machezo*), which is very expensive, while the patient's relatives will try to scale down the offering to something more manageable such as a tray of sweetmeats. Mohammed writes of what the latter would involve:

> WA and NH went to the shrine of their spirit to put an offering (*sadaka*) there of sugar, dates, cinnamon (*dalasin*), raisins (*zabibu*) and nutmeg (*kungu manga*). This was because Bt. M, the wife of WA, was possessed by their spirit.

Mohammed added:

> She was ill during the time they were living in the fields and it was decided that she had been taken by the spirit. However, he [Mohammed] himself did not know whether this had become known by asking the spirit during a dance (*mzuka machezoni*) or by Koranic divination (*kupiga ramli ya kitabu*). [He only heard that] she said that if she got better, she would take an offering.

Mohammed explained in another entry how his wife's sister took an offering to the spirits:

> Miza took a present to a field spirit because it got hold of her and she was ill. The present was sugar, raisins, cinnamon, cardamom. The ones who took it were Bt. J and the shaman-diviner Ali. This spirit was not one of her ancestors, it just happened, a case of [the spirit's] hunger.

In the diary, Mohammed describes in detail how he himself takes offerings to the shrine of his ancestral spirit:

> You prepare a hen which is either white, white and black, or red and white and you make bread (*kuchoma mkate*). This is a religious offer-ing (*sadaka*). He [Mohammed] takes spices, sugar, bread, a hen and dates and puts them [for the spirit] and says: 'That's enough then, let our quarrel be ended (*Baasi tena, magomvi iishe*)', and he breaks the bread, keeping the bits which fall and says: 'Do not let me down (*usini-tupe*), let there be peace (*salaam salimi*), you are my eyes, you know what is evil (*shari*), *mzee*.' Then you leave everything except about a

quarter of the left-over bits of bread which are called *miondoro* [and you go away]. And even if you remember you left your purse there with 200 shillings in it, you don't return that day, but burn incense and inform the spirit (*kutia buhuri*) and then you can go. But if you go back [without telling the spirit], it is dangerous, because it will have invited all its friends to the feast. When you reach the outskirts of the village, you can sit down and eat the *miondoro* (left-over bread).

In some instances, however, treatment involves not only giving an offering tray or an animal to the spirit (cows in the case of land spirits, goats in the case of sea spirits), but the afflicted person has to become initiated into the guild of the spirit which has possessed him or her through a full-scale ritual. Mohammed once told me, 'Spirits are like humans', thus they can be negotiated with. Most people try their hardest to negotiate down the offerings to spirits, while the shamans attempt to negotiate them up. A process of bargaining then takes place, although the commonest outcome is a smaller initial offering, with a promise of a larger one if the problem is solved. This may include initiation into a guild. In the next section, accounts of such rituals as they appear in Mohammed's diary are given and discussed.

SPIRIT POSSESSION RITUALS: DANCES AND DIVINATION

Most of the entries on spirit possession rituals in Mohammed's diary concern the two cults of land spirits practised in northern Mafia – *kitanga* and *mwingo* – although *kitanga* rituals are held far more frequently. *Kitanga* and *mwingo* rituals fall into three stages. First of all, there is the all-night dancing, with drums (only in the case of *kitanga* rituals), hand-clapping and singing, during which people become possessed and are frequently restrained by others. Second, there is the slaughter of the animal, a cow or bull, which must be either black or white depending upon the preference of the spirit for whom the ritual is being held, and the consumption of the blood by those who are possessed by the spirit of the appropriate colour.[11] Others who are possessed but who cannot drink the blood will eat the contents of an offering tray. The third stage is that of divination, which may last several hours into the morning, when people who are sick consult the still-possessed shamans.

There are fewer references to the *mwingo* cult in Mohammed's diary, which is scarcely surprising as only one or two rituals a year are held in the village. It is, however, the cult of Mohammed's ancestral spirit. For this reason, he was always acutely aware of cult rituals taking place in other villages:

A *mwingo* ritual was held in Mashariki village, followed by divination. The spirit was one which uses a white cow, and it was the usual [annual] ritual (*ngoma ya kawaida*) for the shaman AO.

Sometimes Mohammed and others who were involved with *mwingo* spirits would participate in a *kitanga* and persuade the drummers and singers to play *mwingo* songs, as happened in a *kitanga* attended by Mohammed and his father's brother, a *mwingo* shaman, in 1966:

A *kitanga* ritual was held at the house of WP, and they cooked rice and fish. They caught the blood [of the slaughtered cow] in cups and basins, and those who served it [to the possessed people to drink] were WN and Bt. H, the wife of the shaman-diviner. The initiate (*mwali*) was Bt. W, wife of AM. The spirit was one from Karibu village (through her father) . . . which uses a white cow.

Mohammed added:

She was ill after being taken by the spirit, so they said that if it left her alone and she got better, they would hold a *kitanga* since the spirit wanted her to become its medium (*kiti chake*) . . .

WA [Mohammed's father's brother] was watching the ritual, and JM of Karibu village was possessed and took WA over to the bed [where the people who are possessed sit]. Mohammed told WA to sing the *mwingo* song 'It is finished again, that foolishness' (*Umekwisha tena, ujinga weneywe*), so he called the singer who sang the song and WA [also] became possessed and danced on the bed. . . .

Nearly thirty years later, Mohammed was to recount a similar event, in which he himself turned a *kitanga* into a *mwingo* (see Chapter 10).

Mohammed gave another account in his diary of a *kitanga*, this time held in Minazini at the end of 1966 when I was away from the village for a few weeks:

[A *kitanga* was held] At the house of AJ [the chief shaman of the village] with a cow; the initiate (*mwali*) was Bt. UA who was previously married to AJ's now-deceased father; she had also been his initiate. After their marriage, the spirit (*mzuka*) climbed into her head – no doubt she had already given an offering tray at a *kitanga* prior to this, when she had [first] been ill and AJ's father had treated her. At that time, the spirit had climbed into her head. But it had just 'caught hold of her' (*kamshika*) – she did not have its ancestry. So when his father died AJ inherited her as his initiate. Also present at the *kitanga* were other members (*wateja*, i.e. people who had already gone through full initiation – *kupungwa*) of AJ's guild. The spirit was that of AJ which uses a white cow.

Mohammed also gave an account of the divination session which was held at the end of this *kitanga*, and in particular, he discussed the case of a man who had a bad leg:

> After the *kitanga*, the shaman-diviner Ali looked at HM who was sick with a bad leg and said: 'HM made a field in Mlimani [the ridge area of the village] and it [the illness] has to do with a cow, it is due to M, the spirit of that area. [It is because] HM got up and gave out [bad] words. The field spirit heard, and took hold of his leg.' Ali divined and said, 'To teach him mannners, he must give a cow', but another man said said 'HM doesn't have a cow.'
>
> **Shaman-diviner**: 'So what will he do now?'
>
> **Spokesman for patient**: 'He will fall on his knees [and ask forgiveness].'
>
> **Shaman-diviner**: 'How will he fall on his knees?'
>
> **Spokesman for patient**: 'He will say "Cool down, cool down (*mweka, mweka, mzee*). I, your child, have done wrong."'
>
> **Shaman-diviner**: 'So let him give a tray, then the quarrel will be over. Let him go to the shaman of that spirit, and let him light his censer (*kutia buhuri*) and contact his spirit (*agongoe*), let him give medicine (*migoda*), and when he is better, he will take the tray. He should ask that shaman which day he should take it to the spirit shrine, and he should go together with the shaman, and he can tell the shaman-diviner Ali [i.e. himself], because they have one ancestry.'

Mohammed added:

This spirit M is old (*pevu*), with a white beard, it does not climb into the head, but it does slaughter cows [i.e. requires cows to be sacrificed to it], and it catches people, it is dark (*jeusi*) and tall (*refu*).[12] The explanation of this divination is that several people were cultivating there and most of them decided to leave because they were all on the borders of the cultivated area, and they thought monkeys would come and eat their crops. So several of them left this area and went off to cultivate elsewhere.

P. What were the words he said [to make the spirit angry]?

M. His companions did not say anything to him, they just left (*wameinuka*). But he said: 'Monkeys will eat your rice and I will have given money for the boundary cow (*ng'ombe ya kipako*) for nothing.' And yet he is a child of that place [i.e. he has the ancestry of that field spirit]. So it was as if he had said that the spirit was not guarding his field properly. So it said, 'I will teach him manners, he will have to give a whole cow himself!'

Here a man who was afflicted sought an explanation from the shamans during the time when they were possessed at the end of a *kitanga*. He was told that he had insulted a field spirit by implying that it did not guard the fields properly, and that he regretted having

Plate 20 The 'therapy management group' of relatives brings a sick child
to consult shamans

participated in making the initial offering to it (see Chapter 3). As a
result, the spirit was 'teaching him a lesson' by causing him to have a
bad leg. The man was told he would only recover if he gave an
offering tray and apologised to the spirit.

Given that most people in the village cultivate bush-land at some
time in their lives, and quarrel with other villagers, and that many
have ancestral links with land spirits, it is not surprising that affliction
by such a spirit is a frequent diagnosis. Furthermore, such a diagnosis offers the opportunity to resolve or at least improve the problem
through communication with the afflicting spirit. In the course of this
treatment, the patient is surrounded by relatives who give support,
both emotional and material, in seeking the reason for the sickness,
and who, as Janzen (1978, 1987) suggests, may play an even more
important role in curing than do the healers themselves.

BECOMING A SHAMAN: 'SPIRITS BRING NO HAPPINESS'

In considering Mohammed's life, it is clear that he himself resisted
full possession by his ancestral spirit for many years. On one
occasion, he spoke about spirit possession and shamanic powers in
the following terms:

It is not something good (*jambo la kheri*) [becoming a shaman], in reality, it is a bad thing (*jambo la ubaya*). Spirits have [bring] no happiness (*kheri*), and a shaman does not have happiness from God. Of course, some shamans want their task – [for example] there was a man in Mashariki village who made a vow that if he got possessed he would read a *maulid*, and he did. But some are reluctant.

Indeed, people who seek powers over spirits are precisely the ones who should not have such power, as the following story, told by Mohammed about a famous but by then deceased shaman and his sons, illustrates:

When [the *mganga*] Kirembezi had become an old man, he called his two sons and said that he would die soon: 'I want to give the shaman's basket (*mkoba*, i.e. his shamanic power) to you, but there is one condition (*sheruti*) – you must first eat a milllipede (*jongoo*).' One son replied that he would accept the *mkoba* but he would not eat the millipede, nor would he kill a person for money or for a cow. 'If you want to give it [the *mkoba*] to me, do so, but I will not do these things.'

'And what do you say, B. [the other son]?'

'Give me the *jongoo*', and he ate it immediately.

Then his father said, 'You cannot be a shaman, you would kill your own brother let alone strangers.' So he gave the *mkoba* to his first son who was [then] possessed by the [father's] spirit, and so he became a shaman who treated people (*aligangia*).

Meanwhile, the other brother [who had not got the *mkoba*] sold his cows and went off to the Mrima in search of shamanic power (*uganga*). He had the [inoculatory] cuts in his whole body (*kachanja mwili wake wote*) and he got hold of a special shamanic power (*uganga kamili*), then he came back to Mafia. [At that point] the [same] spirit climbed into his head and he was possessed, he used the blood of a cow (*anatumia ng'ombe*) and was initiated (*kupungwa*) into the *kitanga* cult. And the spirit showed him [medicinal] plants.

Mohammed explained that a shaman could choose whom he wanted to succeed him by handing over his *mkoba* but he could not be sure that this person would become possessed. In this instance, however, both sons eventually became shamans, although the younger one, who had wanted the *mkoba*, was refused it precisely because he would do anything to get it, and so he had had to acquire the power by other means. Once he had done so, he too became possessed by his father's spirit.

Mohammed also told the story of how AJ, the most powerful shaman in Minazini, achieved his status, also unexpectedly:

When his father died, no one knew who would be the successor. SM's mother hoped that it would be him, and JH's mother that it would be him. Both of these men were already possessed by their respective spirits, while AJ didn't even dance in rituals. . . . One old man said, 'It will be AJ who will become possessed', and he did.
P. How did he know that?
M. Because he was from olden times (*ya zamani*) and a man of that place (*mtu wa pale pale*).

In both of these stories, it is the unlikely candidate who becomes the shaman; those who seek it are thought to do so for dangerous reasons. Yet, it is difficult for a shaman to refuse his or her calling as is shown by the following story of a shaman in a neighbouring village who had tried to get rid of his possessory spirit after he had studied in Zanzibar:

You can't get rid of *uganga* or possession. JK was possessed by [his ancestral] spirit and then in Zanzibar he learned the art of [Islamic] healing through books (*uganga wa vitabu*) and decided that he would get rid of his ancestral spirit. He went to consult some local shamans (*waganga wa shamba*), but one of them said, 'Your spirit is too powerful, I cannot take it out of your head.' The spirit was very angry [at this attempt to get rid of it] and made JK sick, so he had to return to Mafia and give a *kitanga* with a cow as punishment.

JK has KZ as his ancestral spirit, and he also controls sea spirits (*mashaitani ya bahari*). . . . People know that he has weapons (*fimbo*, lit. 'stick'), if war were to break out. He has no less than seven charms, each valued at more than 100 shillings.

In the case of this man, his religious learning and the expensive charms which he had bought were less powerful than his ancestral spirit, whose guardianship is one of the most effective forms of protection, as in the following case told by Mohammed:

Bt. Musa has borne and lost six children. The only one now alive was given to the protection of the spirit JM (*kupewa ulezi*) and to the spirit of her brother. For this reason the man who wished her ill (*alimdhamania vibaya*) . . . couldn't kill it.
P. Why did that man want to kill her children?
M. A case of evil eye, what he felt in his heart (*moyo wake*).
P. Why her?
M. He had just decided that he didn't want her to have any children.

Indeed, Mohammed insisted as early as 1966 that I should myself have relationships with spirits to ensure my safety:

Don't forget that you [PC] 'have' [the powerful spirit] JM, because you made a friendship with him. You also have [my spirit] KC because when I light the censer, I mention you.

Spirits, then, are capricious and somewhat unpredictable. However, they can to some extent be controlled by those who are powerful enough, such as shamans (*waganga*), and to a lesser extent by mediums whom they possess. They can also be controlled by some *walim* (Koranic teachers) and Sheikhs, and it is to a consideration of Mohammed's view of Islam's attitude to spirits that we now turn.

VULNERABILITY AND INVULNERABILITY

The relationship between Islam and a belief in spirits is complex. Mohammed himself was ambivalent: he knew that orthodox Muslims, such as his own brother, who prayed five times a day and attended the mosque regularly, condemned beliefs in spirits and distanced themselves from all activities connected with them as *ushiriki* (polytheism). When this brother became sick, Mohammed wrote in his diary:

> JM got sick – he did not use any local medicines, but generally he goes to hospital, or has cupping or herbs from Mohammed – he never uses spirit medicine, which he regards as *ushiriki*.

When he was listing medicines which are *haramu*, Mohammed mentioned 'slaughtering cows', noting that anyone who did so 'will inevitably be accused before God; the cow will ask "What was the reason for killing me?"'[13] He also noted that: 'It is forbidden to say that people died for any reason other than "*kazi ya Mungu*' (God's work), for example, to say that someone has used the evil eye on me (*mtu fulani ananifanya jicho*).'

His choice of topics in the diary, and our many conversations stimulated by its entries, make it plain that Mohammed was fascinated by spirit possession. Yet he himself, as already mentioned, described it on several occasions as 'not a blessed thing' (*si jambo la kheri*).

> Many people like to have a spirit possession ritual (*ngoma*) for their children but they are fools; it is not a blessed thing, they will be punished.[14]

On one occasion we were walking together to Kirongwe village, and I asked him about the limits of a spirit's power:

The word of a Sherif, of a Sheikh, or the blessing (*radhi*) of a father or mother. All of these come from God, or if you are seized by an ancestor – a spirit can't help with these matters.

He went on to explain that some people are considered more vulnerable (*wepesi*, lit. 'light') to spirits than others, who are considered relatively invulnerable (*wazito*, lit. 'heavy'):

P. How do you know if someone is *mzito* or *mwepesi*?

M. It depends on your guardian angels, on whether you have a *shaitani* who brings you up (*ulezi*), and on whether you have been inoculated (*kuchanjwa*) or not.

Sheikhs, because of their religious knowledge and closeness to God, are considered *wazito*, and cannot be easily harmed or frightened, although they can see supernatural beings, as in the following story told to Mohammed by a friend of his:

Makungu was walking with the late Sheikh Hamis to Pwani where the latter had a wife. It was evening, and the Sheikh, because of his learning (*elimu*) discerned troops of spirits (*majeshi*), but also realised that his companion had not seen them. He knew that Makungu was *mwepesi*, and that if he did realise their presence, he would be scared (*atastuka*).

When they got to Pwani, the Sheikh asked Makungu to stay the night, but he refused, as he was living out in the fields and his wife and children were alone there. So the Sheikh asked him to wait while he went into his house. He remained there for a long time, but the man thought he was just keeping him waiting, and did not dare say anything or go away because he was a Sheikh. But in fact, the Sheikh was keeping him there until the spirits, on their way to a feast, had passed. Finally, the Sheikh came out and told him to go, but to say certain prayers as he went. This he did, but he became ill as soon as he arrived at his hut. Obviously, if he had gone straight back, or had not recited the prayers, he would have died.

Some Sheikhs are believed to have miraculous powers, as in the following story told by Mohammed:

One day a long time ago, Sheikh Salum Abdallah, two men and a child were returning [to Minazini] from a *maulid* given by a man in Pwani. The Sheikh was holding a book in his hand and reading, until, when they got further ahead, there was a rain cloud. One of the men said: 'Sheikh, it is raining.' The Sheikh replied: 'Let us carry on.' The rain came down so heavily you could not see ahead, but they passed through the middle of it, and they did not get a single drop on them until they reached Minazini and the rain stopped. This demonstrated the gift of God in response to the prayer of Sheikh Salum Abdallah of Kisiwa village.

However, it is thought that some people, who are particularly well versed in the Koran and Islamic books, may use their knowledge in ways which are forbidden. When discussing the Kisiwa shaman and diviner JK, Mohammed and I had the following conversation:

M. His pupils include two men from Minazini, but he is checking them out thoroughly first (*anawapeleleza*) because if their souls are bad, he will not give them all his knowledge, in case they will use it badly.
P. And does JK himself use his power in this way?
M. I haven't heard that he does.

   Mohammed also noted, as already mentioned, that it is forbidden for Koranic teachers to practise divination:

There is only one *mwalimu* in Minazini who does divination openly, although there are two others who also do it, but secretly. They divine using *ramli*: books (*vitabu*) or divining board (*ubao*), or write on the ground. This is all forbidden (*haramu*) and I do not think that the other Koranic teachers do it.
P. What about *nyota* (stars)?
M. Every human being has a number of stars. The one who looks at horoscopes (*nadhiri*) is an astrologer (*falaki*). You can kill someone by changing their horoscope, or their future, or their intentions. Because [since it is written in a book] it can only be changed by another book. There is no one in Minazini these days who can do that, but formerly there were several in the area – now there is only one man, that shaman JK in Kisiwa village, who can do that. To be able to do this you must have [considerable] knowledge (*elimu*).

   It is clear that both Sheikhs and *walimu*, as well as shamans, have power which can be used for good or evil. Generally, as already stated, power which emanates from God ('the word of a Sheikh or Sharif') is shown as stronger than that of spirits, but this is not always the case, as was seen when the shaman JK tried unsuccessfully to use his Islamic learning to get rid of his possessory ancestral spirit.

   In Mohammed's diary, and in my conversations with him, there was a good deal of ambivalence about the relationship between Islam and spirit possession. Sometimes he categorised them as completely different, as in his discussion in the previous chapter about medicines which are *haramu* (unlawful, forbidden) and *halali* (lawful, allowed). On other occasions, it seems that the two are not so different after all: *walimu* and sheikhs also control spirits, but their book learning makes them more powerful (*wazito*) and also renders them less vulnerable (*wepesi*). This ambivalence is further discussed in the next chapter.

CONCLUSION

The world of spirits has been termed a 'separate reality' (e.g. Castaneda 1973), yet it may be questioned whether this is the case for the people of Mafia, like Mohammed, for whom spirits and their doings are in many ways part of their daily lives. It is true that in times of crisis, beliefs in spirits and their power are activated, but people have regular dealings with them as they go about their daily business of growing crops or fishing. Because spirits are everywhere, it would be impossible to ignore them, and because of their amoral and capricious nature, it is difficult always to know how to avoid offending them. They thus provide an important reservoir of explanations for afflictions of various kinds, as well as a theory of care.

Obeyesekere argues that such cults allow for an expression of problems in a public idiom shared by the whole culture, facilitating communication between patient, ritual specialist, family and wider community (1970). Although only a minority of people on Mafia are possessed by spirits, many more seek treatment from shamans, take offerings to spirit shrines and attend rituals.

As many authors have pointed out, spirit possession and its rituals are highly ambiguous (see e.g. Middleton 1992, Boddy 1994). On the one hand, they are entertaining, theatrical, celebratory, sometimes even comic; on the other, they are concerned with pain and suffering. To become a curer, a person must usually first suffer and be afflicted; he or she should not deliberately seek the role. Becoming a medium, and particularly a shaman, involves taking on a heavy burden, and may be resisted for this reason, as we will see in the next chapter, which returns to 1994, and Mohammed's own possession by his ancestral spirit.

10 Encounter four
1994

This chapter is about my last encounter with Mohammed, Mwahadia and Subira in 1994, when I returned to Mafia for a two-month stay; it considers particularly the ways in which they dealt with affliction. Each was having problems which included acute poverty, poor health and difficulties with personal relationships. All were involved with spirits in different ways.

I found Mohammed was still living in the big house built by his son Seleman, who had, however, died in the interim, as had his daughter Amina (see Chapter 2). He had still not remarried. Two of his daughters, Asha and Miza, were currently divorced and living with him, together with their children (see Figure 3). In spite of his poverty, he was making plans to get married again. Mohammed had become fully possessed by his ancestral spirit and was about to be initiated into the *mwingo* cult.

Mwahadia was living on the outskirts of the village with their one remaining son, Juma, then in his mid-20s and not yet married, and two of her granddaughters. She had finally re-married some eight years earlier to a man who already had two other wives, and who gave her little support. She was in poor health and rather depressed, complaining that she was afflicted by spirits sent by people who wished to harm her.

Subira's marriage with the Pwani village man had indeed ended, and she had finally gone to live in the district capital, where she was having a rather unsatisfactory relationship with a man who was not a Swahili. Her eldest daughter was living with Mwahadia, while the remaining children lived with their respective fathers. Subira too was not very well, and complained of affliction by spirits.

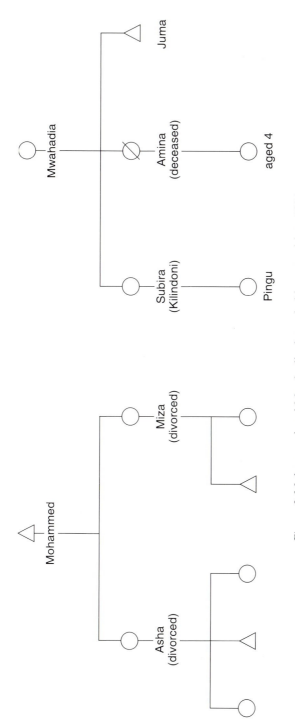

Figure 3 Mohammed and Mwahadia: household composition, 1994

MWAHADIA:

I saw Mwahadia on many occasions during this visit – mostly she would drop into my house when she was in the village for other purposes, or she would come expressly to see me, sometimes to bring a small gift of food, sometimes to make requests for help. On one occasion, I spent an afternoon at her house. In this section, I have condensed our meetings into two conversations, utilising my field-notes to highlight her financial and health problems, her worries about her remaining children, her grief over the loss of Seleman and Amina, and her affliction by witchcraft.

Meeting One: catching up with her life

My first meeting with Mwahadia on this visit was when she arrived at my house with her grandchild, a small girl who sat silent and mostly unmoving for at least an hour. This was the daughter of Amina who had died recently in Zanzibar. Mwahadia looked terrible – she had a big swelling on the side of her left eye. She told me that she had been very unwell. A couple of months ago she had fallen out of bed, causing the injury to her eye and cutting her mouth:

My eye keeps swelling up, it [the swelling] bursts, appears to get better, and then comes up again. It's been like this for three months. I can't cultivate. And my wrist is hurting [she makes the movement of wielding a hoe].

Like many middle-aged people in this area, she had hardly any teeth left now, a fact which she mentioned, and she looked her age. She talked about the recent death of her daughter Amina in Zanzibar, whose funeral she had attended and whose child she was now raising. Amina's two other children were still in Zanzibar and she had only managed to get this child after a struggle with the husband's relatives. Another close relative of hers also had died that year. Plainly all of these deaths had knocked her sideways; she had lost most of her old sparkle and rarely smiled. She was bitter about so much bereavement – first the death of her son Waziri several years ago at sea, then that of Seleman on whom she depended a great deal. 'Now there is no one to help, I get nothing. I've no clothes.' She asked me for some money for soap to wash her clothes. 'I can't bear it any more, they are getting hard with dirt.'

There were other problems too. At that moment she was the last person still living in her field hut at the end of the agricultural season. She wanted to move back to the village but needed to build another hut, and had no money with which to do so. She told me that 1,000 shillings would get her the poles she needed to buy to build a house, and she could get people to help with the rest. I gave her the money.

I asked about the other children. She told me that Juma wanted to get married but she had no means of paying for the costs of a wedding. It would be a total of 5,000 shillings for the *mahari* (payment of 3,500 shillings to the bride) and *mkaja* (lit. 'belt', payment of 1,500 shillings to the mother). On top of that, there would be the trousseau (*sanduku*, lit. 'box') for which the groom has to pay. We discussed how much this would cost – twenty *kanga*, three or more dresses, and other items – plus the cost of the proposal letter. Apparently someone had recently offered a match for him but the money had to be provided immediately so it fell through.

She also told me that Subira was having a relationship with a man in Kilindoni who was a 'real drunkard' and would beat her, 'But she wants him.' Asha and Miza were both currently divorced and living with Mohammed, together with their children. The youngest girl, Habiba, had married a man in the village by whom she had had a child.

Once again, Mwahadia blamed her poor state of health on witchcraft, saying she was being eaten by a spirit: 'My whole body aches, and I have no blood.'[1] She had been to shamans but, 'How can they cure me if they have been the ones to bewitch me?' She attributed this witchcraft to people wanting to harm her only remaining son, Juma. He had taken to keeping dogs and going hunting for bush-buck (*chesi*). She did not want him to do that, because it involved going into the bush-land on the ridge to the east of the village, the abode of spirits which might harm him.

As it happened, at that moment in our conversation, the younger brother of one of the village shamans arrived to see me. She greeted him and went to sit on the back verandah while I talked to him. When he had gone she told me that it was 'that lot' who had bewitched her. 'Did you hear what I said to him? I said "I am still here (*Ningalipo*)" meaning "You haven't killed me yet."' Then she revealed that the reason why the shaman and his brothers bewitched her was because she had told Juma not to hunt bush-buck, one of which was needed for their annual ritual of an offering to the spirit which guarded their fields (see Chapter 3).

Meeting Two: some surprising news

One afternoon I went with Mwahadia, who had now moved from the fields back to the village, to the house of her son Juma, where she was currently living. They had the daughter of the deceased Amina, and Subira's eldest girl, who was then about 13 or 14, living with them.

I sat on a mat (*jamvi*) in the separate kitchen hut and we talked while Subira's daughter plaited away with her raffia. Mwahadia again brought up the subject of her ill-health. Her left eyebrow was still swollen and continuing to get infected, but she was in better spirits today than on the previous occasion. Much to my surprise, Mwahadia revealed that she was married. Earlier, a man whom I recognised had come into the courtyard and greeted me; he then asked Mwahadia for some money and she, Juma and Subira's daughter scraped together a few shillings to give him. I was a bit surprised to see him go into the house without being invited but thought he must be a relative. Then she told me that he was her husband:

After Mohammed divorced me, I stayed alone for eight or ten years, although I was betrothed once . . . but he was killed by a spirit [she repeated the story of how he died which she had already told me in 1985 – see Chapter 7]. I married this husband eight years ago – he has two other wives, with one of whom, incidentally, Mohammed had an affair once which led to fighting. My husband has had several children by one of his present wives and also by another wife who died, but his present second wife has no children. He has divorced and recalled me twice – if he does so again that will be the end of our marriage. I told him, 'I don't want a divorce. We got married to live together until one of us dies. I don't care if you don't bring me anything, but I want us to stay married.'

P. So does he bring you anything?

Mw. Barely – he has nothing. His mother bewitched him (*kamwapisa*) because he stole his younger sister's trousseau, so she withdrew her blessing (*radhi*) from him [see Chapter 4]. He is a sailor but he has just been sent away from the dhow he worked on after a row about wages not being paid for the last trip. Do you know why he came just now? To ask me for money for cigarettes!

She produced a tray with tea in a flask and some cooked pumpkin which she gave me to eat. Mwahadia drank some tea herself, and her daughter Habiba, who had just dropped in with her baby, had a cup as well, but soon went off. I ate the pumpkin and drank a cup of tea which, unusually for the village, had milk in it.

P. Where do you get milk?

Mw. Juma goes to buy it because he has just opened that tea-shop (*hoteli*) which you saw on the way. He really needs some capital to get his business going. I advised against starting the tea-shop without any capital, but he would not listen. So he only has enough to buy around a kilo of sugar a day and the same amount of flour to make buns, whereas he really needs 5 kilos of each a day, if he's to get any profit.

I said I would think about whether to let Juma have some money, as she had requested.

Juma appeared and greeted me. There were several dogs around which belonged to him and which he used to hunt *chesi* with half a dozen other people. Mwahadia complained about the dogs: 'They are fierce, they even bite.' There were nets hanging up – I asked whether he went fishing as well. 'No, those nets are for hunting *chesi*.' I asked him if there were many *chesi*, and he replied that there were plenty; if he caught one he would sell some of the meat. He collected up a bucket and some dirty clothes and went off to wash them.

Mwahadia wanted to give me some rice to take home, so she began to thresh paddy with her feet, standing on top of a big pile and using a long stick as a support. Then she put it out on an old mat to dry. But threatening clouds appeared and it was quickly cleared away. Amina's orphaned daughter was sitting with only a cloth tied around her. Mwahadia pointed to her:

You see this child? She doesn't even have a single dress. None of us have any clothes. When I go to Mohammed's house I sometimes borrow a dress for her [from one of the girls]. Seleman used to bring us clothes, now we don't have him any more. Food I can manage myself – I have food, but these children need clothes for the Id coming up – they didn't get any for the Id festival of the 1st month [i.e. the end of Ramadhan] nor for that of the 3rd month. Now it is the New Year (*Mwaka*, see Chapter 3), they should get something.

I offered to pay for a dress for Amina's child and asked her how she managed to get any cash.

I have plaited a lot of raffia strips this year, but I don't have money to buy the dyes for them – it is very expensive now – 20 shillings for a tiny packet and you need at least 50 packets [to dye a year's production of raffia strips].

We agreed that I would supply the money to buy the dyes in exchange for her making me a mat to take home at the end of my stay. This reminded Mwahadia of my first visit:

Do you remember those mats I made specially for you on your first visit? You asked for them to be of two colours only and to be as big as a *jamvi*.[2] Everyone laughed at me, but I said I don't care – it's my work, I'm not

Plate 21 'The children of poor people have to learn to pound at an early age'

asking anyone else to do it. I'm used to supporting myself. Mohammed never cultivated, he never did anything. And this husband is the same. Yes, mats, when Seleman came on his last visit I was sewing mats and he said he must have one. So I gave it to him, and poor fellow, he never got to use it except to be wrapped in when he died.

She told the little girl to pound some rice. I asked if she could really pound when she was so small. 'Yes, the children of poor people have to learn to pound [at an early age].' The teenager continued to plait until her grandmother told her to go and do some pounding as well: 'Do it nicely, not just any old how, it's for her [PC].' The girl said she would do so as soon as she had finished the strip of raffia she was plaiting. Mwahadia and I continued talking:

I don't want to stay in this house because it is far from my husband's other houses. I said to him, 'You should build me a house there.' He said, 'Wait until I have finished a fortieth-day ceremony for a relative who died and then I'll start building.' If he doesn't build it, then I'll move somewhere else anyway. I want to move from here – you see the state of this house? First of all, it is not mine, it is Juma's. And second, it is falling to bits, the hornets have got in and made holes everywhere.

She took me inside to see and we sat in her room on her bed.

This is the bed where I sleep on this mat, and with this mattress [some stuffed sacks]. The children sleep on that other bed, which actually belongs to someone else. [When he came to reclaim it], I told him: 'If you take it now, the children will have to sleep on the floor.'

There were eight or nine bags of rice stacked up and another bag on top which she told me was sesame waiting to be sold. Apart from a small table, there was only a trunk on which there were two packets of tablets; Mwahadia said that she had been to the hospital and they said perhaps she was anaemic: 'So they gave me those [iron] tablets to take – two or three times daily.'

It was while we were in the house that she told me about Subira and Habiba; perhaps she wanted to talk away from the listening ears of her granddaughter:

Subira lives with this man in Kilindoni – he treats her very badly and beats her every day. But she won't leave him. She is a drunkard now, she's not my child any more. She lives on the money he gives her and she used to sell seashells. Her other two children are with their father, and there is another she had by her Kirongwe husband who is also with that father. Subira did not send her other daughter, the girl I have here with me, to school – she never stayed long enough in one place.

She then proceeded to tell me a story I had already heard from Mohammed (see Chapter 2): how Habiba had had a boyfriend and he had made her pregnant and wanted to marry her but both his father and hers had refused. I asked why.

I don't know. Juma asked his father if he could have the right to give her away (*idhini*) and marry her off, but he refused that too. So this boyfriend of hers went to the Magistrate in Kirongwe and paid money for a case and he gave them permission to marry and a paper for a Sheikh to do so. So they are married now but they don't have a thing – I gave them my bed, and some pots, so I have hardly anything left myself now.

We went back outside and I offered to take a photograph. Subira's daughter insisted on changing and emerged wearing a very frilly dress. Mwahadia just took out a *kanga* from inside and put it over her shabby clothes. I remembered the beautiful dress sent to her by Seleman which she had put on when I took her photograph with Subira in 1976 (see Chapter 6).

After this, we set off together back to the village, me carrying the bag of rice which she had given me, bound for one of the shops where we wanted to ask about the price of cloth for dresses for the grand-daughters. On the way, we continued talking. She complained of Mohammed's lack of interest in her well-being: 'He doesn't come and see how I am.'

P. Why didn't Mohammed marry again?

Mw. Who would want him? He has nothing and he does nothing. It was always the same – he never cultivated. I always did everything. We own that house jointly – I've got half and it is there that Asha and Miza stay. Do you know that someone came wanting to marry Asha? But her father refused. Why? Because it is convenient for him to have them there. They cook for him, they cultivate. He depends on them.

P. Does he ever buy clothes or anything for them?

Mw. Not likely – he never gives them a thing.

She also complained bitterly about the fact that Mohammed, whom she always referred to as 'your friend', sold the cow without consultation when he left for Seleman's funeral (see Chapter 2). Furthermore, he gave the widow Seleman's cassette tape recorder:

He did not wait until I got there so that we could plan. He just gave it to her. And loads of other things besides. She got all the furniture and uten-sils. I have been poor all my life and now I will die poor. Between a wife and a mother, who is the better? I asked him that question. If I hadn't borne him, she wouldn't have got him as a husband. I feel very bitter – I could have had that cassette player and listened to it and remembered my son. As it is, I don't have anything to remember him by. And he had no right to do that – we should have discussed it.

The next day she came by as arranged to collect money for the raffia dye and two dresses. To cheer her up a bit I gave her some earrings and she asked me to put them in for her. She said she was hungry and asked me to buy her two of the boiled corn cobs which were currently being sold outside my house, and then took leave, say-ing she intended to go and do a bit of cassava cultivation. On her way out, she told me that Subira, who had been in the village on a visit, had gone back to Kilindoni with her eldest daughter; she did not know when she would be back but did not expect her soon.

Mwahadia had not told me on our first few meetings at my house that she was married, only revealing it when I was her guest. I am not sure why this was – I suspect she did not quite know how to tell me, and found it easier to let me see for myself. Or perhaps she wanted to surprise me. Plainly this was a less than satisfactory marriage: Mwahadia derived little support from her husband, but she was determined to remain married, even though she had to look after herself. She still talked about Mohammed, complaining both of his past behaviour during the time when he was her husband, and his present behaviour which she defined as neglectful – as the father of her children, he should have had more concern for her welfare.

Much of the rest of our conversations covered matters such as the children, their current state and her worries about them, and her financial problems. Plainly she was glad to have a sympathetic ear, and also hoped for some material assistance to ameliorate her very difficult circumstances. I was struck by the fact that once again, in the face of problems of health, she attributed her affliction to spirits. This theme was to recur in meetings with Subira and Mohammed.

SUBIRA: THREE MEETINGS

As has already been shown from Mwahadia's account, Subira had, after several unsuccessful marriages, gone off to live in the district capital, where she could more easily support herself. There she had formed a relationship with a non-Swahili man. Both parents were plainly worried about her welfare. During the period when Mohammed and I stayed near to Kilindoni to work on his life history, he had tried to find Subira but without success. He was concerned to hear that she might be going off to the mainland with her partner.

First meeting: 'My state is not so good'

In fact, it was I who saw Subira before Mohammed did: as I was walking to Kilindoni after lunch one day I heard my name being called. Looking back I saw someone running towards me, and as she approached, I realised that it was Subira. She had not changed a jot.

Mtume (lit. 'Prophet'), how I had to run to catch you! I heard you were here together with my father, and I went to the plantation to see you. They said you had left for Kilindoni. Do you know I live just down there, off to the left in that valley? I live with a man who isn't too bad – he earns a bit and we get food, he cuts me a few clothes.

She offered to walk with me to Kilindoni so that we could get a chance to talk, although we had already agreed that she would come back to Minazini with me the next day. 'So how are you Subira?' Here the story changed somewhat.

S. Well, if you want to know, my state is not so good. I don't have any clothes. Can you let me have some money – 1,000 shillings, even 500 shillings?

P. So why haven't you got married to this fellow?

S. He hasn't mentioned marriage yet – my father came once and asked him and he said, 'Not just yet.' I've been living with him for three years now. He makes a living by tapping palm wine. And I collect shells on the shore and sell them. So we manage.

P. What about children? Have you had any with him?

S. No, I haven't carried a pregnancy to term for several years. And I've *only* got four children. I want to have some more. If I'd had all the children for which I got pregnant, it would have been thirteen by now.

We arrived in Kilindoni and, in addition to giving her some cash, she managed to persuade me to buy her a pair of sandals. She asked for a lot more, but I stood firm. As I had a commission for her mother, I asked her where I could buy wooden combs and spoons and she took me to a back street shop on the outskirts of the town. As we walked together she greeted people, and they asked her who I was, how we knew each other, how on earth we understood each other. She laughed, replying that I was 'our local person (*mwenyeji wetu*) who came from Europe and has lived in Minazini and visits regularly'.

Second Meeting: 'Two spirits want me'

The next day, the Land Rover which was to take us back to the village came rather late, but Subira was waiting at the pre-arranged spot. She had on *kanga*, her new sandals, and carried a plastic bag. For the first part of the journey she talked non-stop about her children, the death of Amina and Seleman, her own illnesses, the fact that she gets possessed, and so forth. She also handed out advice freely to a man to whom we gave a lift who was going to Kirongwe to see his sick wife.

When we got to the outskirts of Minazini I suggested she got down at her mother's place. Later, when I was at home talking to Mohammed on the back verandah, she turned up with Mwahadia. Fortunately, I had just given Mohammed some clothes (*mashiti*)[3] he wanted for his daughter Asha and he had put them away safely, otherwise there would no doubt have been an argument about who got what. Mohammed departed, taking 200 shillings to buy sugar and other ingredients for the special bread which Asha was to make for me for the forthcoming New Year's Day.

I gave Mwahadia the items I had bought for her in Kilindoni; she examined the metal comb which I bought, having been unable to find a wooden one, and said it wouldn't last two days, also that it was not suitable for African hair. She pronounced the three packets of dye she had ordered insufficient, and went off saying she had to make the bread for the following day's New Year ceremony. Subira remained behind, and we had a long talk.

P. How long are you staying here in Minazini?

S. I won't stay long, probably only until Monday. That is what I agreed with my bloke. If I delay we shall quarrel. And in any case, I don't like being here much – I'm too used to life in town. I've been there three years now. I can depend on myself, not like my sisters. Do you know that Miza got taken to Dar by that woman from Pwani village. . . . She did well for herself, came back with no end of clothes.

P. How did she get them?

S. From her various 'in-laws' [*shimeji* – she means lovers].

P. Why doesn't she get married?

S. She has a fellow here who looks after her, she does alright.

P. What about Asha?

S. I don't know about her. But she must have relationships, given that she keeps having children.

Here Subira referred again to the way in which many women who have been divorced manage their lives through a series of relationships with men. There had been hints of this in 1985, but it seemed to be much more widespread in 1994, and was openly talked about; many said that in the current climate of poverty and a decreasing standard of living,[4] men were unwilling to get married because they could no longer afford to support a wife and children, whereas occasional lovers only needed to give the odd present, such as clothes. Subira talked a lot about clothes:

S. So and so wore such a *kanga* [describes]. It hasn't yet arrived in Kilindoni, but it will – it is really nice. Can you let me have a skirt? or a top?'

P. I can give you a top, but I have no skirt.

S. Even the one you're wearing would do.

P. But Subira, it's all I've got, I brought very few clothes. [Her barrage is constant and I try to change the subject.] Are you going to see your children on the way back to Kilindoni?

S. I might, I do go and see them sometimes. My eldest daughter has got really thin, that's from helping her grandmother [Mwahadia] to cultivate. I don't know what she promised to give her [in return] – we'll find out tomorrow [on New Year's Day when children should get new clothes]. I hope she didn't deceive her [into helping her for nothing]. Of my other children, one is in Kirongwe with her father, a girl, and the other two are in the south, although at the moment the girl has gone with her father to be put in a puberty ritual (*unyago*) in Lindi.[5]

P. What about this fellow of yours? Where is he from?

S. He's from up country – an Mtumbwi – he's got scarification on each side of his face. He wants to go and visit his place, but he doesn't have the fare.

P. Is he a Muslim?

S. Yes, he is. But he speaks a different language at home with his relatives.

Pulling up her chair close to me, she asked me if I had any medicine for the stomach. I asked her if she had diarrhoea.

S. No, it's when I get my periods, I have very heavy bleeding for 10–12 days. And I keep having miscarriages every few months. And I have a discharge (*usaha*).

P. You need to go to the hospital and get examined, and you may need a D&C.

S. But some people say it is a sea spirit (*jini la bahari*) – you know what they are like – it's a man wearing a turban and really nice clothes, very white, he comes and he laughs at you – he wants to penetrate you. And then you lose the pregnancy.

P. So what can you do about it?

S. You can go to those who know about such things and get medicine.

P. Don't you have to go through a special ritual for this (*mkobero*)?

S. Some people do, but not all.

P. And have you seen such a man when you were asleep?

S. Yes, I have sometimes.

Like many women in this area, Subira attributed her reproductive problems to the agency of a sea spirit (*jini la bahari*) (see Chapter 9) which she claimed to see in her sleep. But she was also afflicted by land spirits (*mashaitani*):

P. What's all this about you getting possessed?

S. Did father tell you that we went to the spirit shrine (*panga*) with a tray of offerings (*chano*)? He didn't? Yes, it's true I was possessed, but I haven't yet spoken properly [and said which spirit is possessing her]. Father and I took the offering tray to the shrine of our ancestral spirit, because I had made a vow, and we were late in fulfilling it. As a result my daughter got a sore on her leg – did you notice? We went to the shrine together, he and I, and he said that he would show me what to do. He also told me that when he dies, I must become the leader (*kiongozi*, i.e. the shaman), and that if I get any trouble at all, this is what I should do. I said 'I'm not the person for such work', but then what alternative is there? So we took the tray, and he showed me how to place all the things he had brought – eggs, sugar (you have to buy one and a half kilos), spices and so on. [She indicates on the table the position in which they are put.] And you should put some money there as well. If you forget the money, don't go back that day, or you'll encounter serious trouble.[6] You burn your censer (*kiteso*) and you tell the spirit that you have forgotten the money but that you will bring it the next day.

But the problem is that two spirits want me – that of my mother's ancestry, which uses those blue water lilies, and that of my father. The former uses a black cow and the latter a white one. They are quarrelling over me.

In this conversation, Subira suggested that she was afflicted by no less than three spirits – a love spirit (*jini la mahaba*) which was preventing her from carrying a pregnancy to term, and two ancestral spirits, of her mother and her father. While it is not impossible for someone to be the medium (*kiti* – 'chair') of both a land and a sea spirit, it is not usual for a human to be possessed by two land spirits, especially if their requirements in terms of animal sacrifice are incompatible, as in this case. Spirits use either black or white animals, and their mediums cannot drink the blood of an animal of the wrong colour. Her description of 'two spirits quarrelling over me' graphically symbolises the conflict between Mohammed and Mwahadia.

Third Meeting: 'That thing inside me wants me to stay here'

Shortly after this, I met Mohammed at the dispensary while he was waiting for medicine; he said that Subira was still in the village and was picking some baobab fruits to take back to Kilindoni with her. Later they both turned up at my house, saying that they had gone to the hospital together, he for his chest cough, she for her gynaecological problems, for which she had had an injection. On the way to my house, she had momentarily become possessed.

She explained that she had stayed on longer than she first planned in Minazini in order to collect some limes, which were currently in season, so that she could take them to sell in Kilindoni. Then she asked me if I was leaving soon so that she could get a lift since she couldn't go on the lorry because of lack of money. She wanted to take her daughter with her so that she could get her some new *kanga*: 'I don't know how I'll get them, but I will.' I told her I was not leaving for a while but would give her enough money for her fare and that of the child. But then her story changed again:

That creature (*kidude*, i.e. the spirit) inside me wants me to stay here. It does not want me to go back there. And my mother is begging me to stay here and help her to cultivate. She even cried. I can cultivate – I am strong, I am not afraid of work, I can even put up with hunger. So I want to build a hut here – my mother has made it plain that I can't stay with her. Besides she herself is moving. And I can't stay in father's house – both Asha and Miza have a room each with their children and the third is father's room.
P. But what about your fellow?
S. Oh, if he wants me, he'll have to come here. If he doesn't want me, too bad (*baasi*).

In many respects, Subira appeared to be a classic spirit possession case. She was obviously in two minds about whether to stay in the village or go back to the district capital. On the one hand, she was not oblivious to her parents' wish for her to be in the village, and here the spirit spoke, as it were, for them. On the other hand, she was bored there. The previous day she had said that no one wanted her there, no one asked after her, reminding me of her complaints ten years earlier when she said, 'People here don't want me to flourish, don't want me to bear children' (see Chapter 7). She had continuously miscarried, and had an uncertain sexual relationship. In short, her life was a series of problems and contradictions, clearly symbolised by the different spirits which sought to possess her.

MOHAMMED: 'I HAVE A LOT OF PROBLEMS'

When I taped Mohammed's life history, I also recorded a long conversation between us about his current state and numerous difficulties. As usual, these included financial and health problems, both his own and those of his family. He had been seriously ill for some time, and had had to sell his remaining coconut trees to cover daily expenses. Seleman had endured a long illness, and Mohammed and Mwahadia had visited him several times in Dar es Salaam, and returned there afterwards to settle his estate. Mohammed claimed to be supporting his divorced daughters Asha and Miza and their children, although, as we have seen, this view was contested by Mwahadia, who saw them as supporting him. He was tired of being single, and making plans to re-marry.

M. So now I have this trouble, I have a lot of problems (*dhiki*), it's not just a question of money, I get some from time to time, but it hasn't done me any good from that time to this. I have seven people in my household . . . Miza has two children, so that is three people, Asha has three children, so that is four, altogether seven plus myself eight. I can't manage it, I just put up with it (*najizuiliya tu*).

There are times when I am eating my food and my children or grand-children come and stand in front of me in spite of the fact that they have already eaten. I never finish my food – I have to leave some for them, and what is left over they scramble for (*wanadokadoka*). And when it is finished they lick everything clean. So Patricia, my friend, I tell you straight, in my state it is difficult to get sufficient food. . . .

At one time, for which I am grateful, my son Seleman was there and he used to help out a lot. He used to send money for daily expenses, he would send sugar, he would send me shirts and trousers, and things like that. . . .

P. Don't you have any coconut trees left at all?

M. I have very few. At the time when I was sick I had to sell some to look after myself. I had no one to help and I had the children [to look after]. Even to get a cup of tea, who is going to buy it [if not me]? I even stopped smoking. So I have no strength and no income. . . . I had the bad luck of losing trees because of disease, and then I was sick and I didn't have anything, and I had no one to help me, and of the deceased Seleman and Waziri, Waziri was the first to die, but Seleman used to help more.

Some of Mohammed's problems were common to other villagers: the price of coconuts had gone down, while that of food had gone up. Life had got harder for people in Mafia. But to make matters worse, Mohammed had few coconut trees left, having gradually sold off his inheritance for a variety of reasons, and had never planted any himself. Indeed, Mwahadia had told me that he had sold all his coconut trees now and had nothing left. If this were true, it was something Mohammed was reluctant to admit to me, since in the village, selling coconut trees, the main source of capital, was always regarded as a foolish move, a short-term solution which would certainly bring longer-term problems in its train.

Mohammed's view was that he had been peculiarly unfortunate to lose two of the three sons who had already grown to adulthood, especially Seleman who had provided a great deal of help to his parents.

Mohammed's illness

And now these things have got worse since I was ill. It was when I had, excuse me for mentioning it, severe diarrhoea and stomach cramps. . . . For a period of a month and a half, I didn't even get to my neighbour's house. I couldn't walk without a stick, the ground was spinning, I had to sleep with a lot of bedding. They [the children] said, 'Come, let's go to a diviner, father.' I said I won't go to a diviner, I'm just ill that's all (*shida tu*), there is nothing the matter, this trouble comes from all-powerful God. It isn't the problem you think it is [affliction by spirits], it's just illness. Because it's often the case that people think one has been afflicted by a spirit (*kuzingukwa*), but I was just ill (*naliumwa tu*). But then I got somewhat better. But I still had no one to depend on.

It is very striking that Mohammed categorised this illness as 'just sickness'; he was clear that there was no human or spirit agency involved. Whether this was because he was reluctant, in view of his parlous finances, to get involved with divination, or whether he himself 'knew', through his contact with his own spirit, that there was no particular reason for his illness is not clear.

On another occasion, I asked him what he thought had caused the death of Seleman. He replied that he had consulted diviners and they had told him it was just illness, 'God's work'. He added that he was so relieved when he knew that the agency was God's alone, not that of humans or spirits.

Mohammed's four problems

Mohammed explained that in addition to his daily struggle to make ends meet, he needed money for four things: a pair of *kangas* to give to a woman whom he hoped would marry him, a pair of *vitenge* (heavier cloths worn by women, also known as *mashiti*) for his daughter Asha, a pair of trousers for himself, and the expenses of a feast. Our conversation covered each of these at length, and here I reproduce only extracts:

Some new clothes

M. So these days, I have no means. I do have clothes to wear, thank God, but my trouble is that none of them are new – they are all at least four years old. . . . But you helped me the other day, and I've already started wearing the shirt [I gave him]. . . . I like to wear different ones. And this vest was given to me by my grandson who is now in Dar es Salaam; when my daughter Asha went to visit him, he gave it to her and said, 'Give it to grandfather.'

Mohammed had always liked to be well-dressed, and of the presents which I gave him, clothes were the most highly appreciated. He was particularly concerned to appear smart when he attended spirit possession rituals. He would wear a sports jacket which he had recently bought from the second-hand clothes stall[7] in Kilindoni. When we agreed on his recompense for helping me in 1994, one item was a new pair of trousers.

Clothes for a dutiful daughter

P. Hasn't anyone come wanting to marry either Asha or Miza?
M. Not yet. Since Asha got divorced, no one. If someone comes along, and she agrees, he can marry her. When she went to Dar, I heard rumours of an imminent wedding, but nothing came of it . . . in the end it didn't come off, and nothing has happened here either. So she's here at home, and we are managing as best we can. . . . I want to give Asha [a pair of] *mashiti* (heavy cloths). The rest of them go around all over the place, but she is the one I can depend on. She is the one who fetches me water to bath with, who will cook for me at any time, or make tea for me at any time. It is rare for her to answer me back. As for the rest . . . Miza is crazy, one minute she's here, one minute there. She has little to do with me. If I happen to be there and she is as well and I say I want something, it's, 'Oh, wait a bit', and whatever it is I want, I don't get it, I just suffer, don't I? Suppose I want water, it's, 'No, I can't', so I have to go to the well myself and get water, and either bath right there by the well, or else carry it back to the house.

A multi-purpose feast

M. Third, I want to hold a feast. It is for my late elder brother and for my sister who died, my twin Miza. And also for my deceased daughter Amina. We have already held the feasts for Waziri and Seleman. So I want to do it for those three, even though some of them died in Zanzibar, but you don't have to hold a feast at the grave itself [i.e. in the place where they are buried]. I think we will do it next year because one of my classificatory sons told me that he has children ready to put into the circumcision lodge (*jando*). We can do both things together. And when the time comes, I will let you know, and you will be already aware of the matter because of our conversation. You will decide for yourself to what extent you can help me out, or whether you aren't in a position to do so.

P. What about the costs of the feast? How much will you have to find?

M. I can't really say. First of all, we don't have any food yet nor do we have a cow to use for the meat (*kitoweo*).

P. But won't others help you?

M. Yes, they will, to the extent that they are able, they will join with me. Some will give [as much as] 1,000 shillings, some [only] 200 shillings, others will say that they have nothing – that's all right. But people will be saying that Mohammed should be giving a feast for his older brother, his sister and the child which he bore himself. So I have to give more than anyone – I can't expect the others to give as much. I could say for instance that I will provide the *kitoweo*, and they provide the food. But a cow today costs 15,000–20,000 shillings, even up to 40,000 shillings, although I am not in that last bracket.

I will make some food – either gruel (*uji*), or a feast with rice and a cow. But if you are talking about a feast, you have to cook rice.

P. So you can't just have gruel and beans – you have to slaughter a cow?

M. It's a *feast* (*karamu*). If you really can't manage, you can hold it like that, but it will show that you can't manage. Because a lot of people come to a feast, and it is a religious offering (*sadaka*). A feast is about cooking rice and slaughtering a cow. And then there are the tips (*fupo*) for the women, to give them pleasure. And these days, they expect to get something like this [holds up his fingers], they expect 500 shilling notes in their hands, especially the ones who are most involved. So if you take account of all this and the contributions of others, the total cost will be well over a lakh (100,000 shillings).

P. How on earth do you raise that?

M. You don't do it all by yourself. Others will contribute. For instance, Subira's child – all her brothers and sisters will contribute [for his circumcision]. That's how it's done.

P. And will Mwahadia also be involved?

M. Isn't she my partner (*mshirika wangu*)? She couldn't fail to be involved. Didn't I tell you that we own the house jointly? She must be involved. And that harvest (*uchumi*) we got together, we mixed our blood together, the children are our joint wealth.

We decided that in return for the help he was giving me, I would pay for the clothes and make a contribution to the cost of the cow for the feast:

M. We will set aside a special day – I will call my son Juma and my daughter Asha, and one of my classificatory grandsons, and we will write out a document with witnesses, saying that I have got this money and that it should be kept until a certain time when it will be used for a specific purpose . . . and I will tell them that this money is being put aside. And they will know where it has come from.

P. So where will you put that money?

M. I will leave it with my [classificatory] grandson who has a shop. Because I know that if I keep it with me, given the need for maize flour [i.e. daily expenses], it will get used up. So it's like putting it into a bank, and that is why I want the children to know that it is there. It will all be written down so that it is known that father has put it there. And even if he were to die, it would still be OK because we will write down that our intention is to use this money in the collection for such and such.

Mohammed was anxious to fulfil his obligations to his grandsons to get them circumcised with the due ceremonies, and also to perform his duty by organising a feast (*karamu*) for his deceased brother and sister and his daughter Amina. There was no way he could have performed ceremonies for all of these people separately, although usually funeral feasts are held for individuals, not for two people, and they are not usually combined with a circumcision ritual and its attendant feast. Furthermore, Mohammed was aware that he would have to have a partner in this undertaking, and had already been in discussion with a relative who had children in need of circumcising. In undertaking the organisation of these rituals, Mohammed would gain the respect of his relatives and fellow villagers, a respect which he was perhaps aware that he did not always have.

A pair of kanga for a potential fiancée

Fourth, with regard to the *kanga*. There is a young woman I fancy. And when I've given her a *kanga*, I want to get together with her. If she agrees, I will marry her. She is very light-skinned.[8] She doesn't live in Minazini but in Pwani village.

P. Has she been married before?

M. She has already been married and divorced. She had children by him [her previous husband], one of whom is already married, and some younger children.

P. Have you already spoken to her?

M. Yes, I have but she refused. But someone told me, 'Just keep quiet and I will sort things out with her.' So the very day after she gets this, I want to get together with her (lit. 'join hands') and let her know that this matter is in prospect. . . .

Mohammed had earlier told me that he had tried to arrange a marriage with a woman in Minazini, but it had fallen through. By this time, he had been divorced since 1976, and was plainly very tired of his single state, but had found it difficult to arrange a marriage because of his poverty. Even marrying an older divorced woman meant various marriage payments, plus the cost of the trousseau. Although he claimed that some of his classificatory grandsons had offered to help, this would not be sufficient, and there was no doubt that he saw my re-visit as a way of acquiring the means to marry again.

Shortly afterwards, Mohammed was waiting for me when I got back home in the evening. He had brought me a present of some plantains. I put the food on to cook and listened to his tale – he had told me he would go to Pwani to an all-night *kitanga* which he did. He also wanted to see his new woman friend, so he left the village at midday and met with her before the *kitanga*. He reported that she didn't want to commit herself to marriage yet, she said 'Let us just have an affair (*tucheze kwanza*)' and she would think about it. Mohammed was very animated as he told me all of this.

P. Did you give your friend the *kanga*?

M. Not likely – I had to find out whether things were going to happen first. If they hadn't, I would still have had them to try my luck with someone else.

P. And did you meet with your friend before the *kitanga* dance started?

M. Oh, yes. At 6 o'clock in the evening. The *kitanga* didn't start being danced until 1 o'clock in the morning. . . .

P. So when are you going to see her again?

M. . . . I've arranged to go and see her on Sunday which is tomorrow. . . . I'll go in the afternoon. . . .

P. So are you going to give this friend of yours the present? Have you already told her about this or not yet?

M. No I haven't mentioned it yet. When I do, I'll say to her, 'Here you are my friend, my love. Here is a present for you.' And so she will take them and she will say, 'Thank you very much', won't she?

P. Yes, I'm sure she will. So are you thinking of asking her to marry you?

M. We haven't yet agreed about that. She said, 'Let's just carry on with our affair for the moment and we'll see afterwards.' So whether she will agree to marry me or she won't agree [I don't yet know]. If she doesn't then I'll have to look for somebody else.

Thus Mohammed began another affair, in the hope that the woman concerned would agree to marry him, although he was careful not to hand over his present too quickly, in case things didn't go well. She was also cautious, perhaps wanting to see what kind of person he was before committing herself to marriage.

We discuss the prospect of Mohammed having more children

P. But that Pwani woman you mentioned, doesn't she have small children?

M. Yes, she does.

P. Wouldn't it be better to marry an older woman who doesn't have small children? Because otherwise you'll be responsible for their expenses as well.

M. She would bring at least one of her children with her, definitely. I could make an agreement with her that I am not responsible for the upkeep of her children, that I be excused that. She might say that I have children, and she has children, and that it wouldn't be possible [for me to be responsible for both. I would tell her that] 'I couldn't bring up your children.' I would say that my children are big, and they depend on themselves. But then there are my grandchildren. If I can't even leave the big ones to fend for themselves, how could I do so for the little ones?

P. No, you couldn't do that.

M. If I want to send one of them to bring you some fish or a coconut, or if I am in the shop or the *hoteli* and I want to send them on an errand, do you suppose I will get to make use of them in that way if I have sent them away (*kuwafukuza*)?

P. No you won't.

M. What kind of human being (*mtu*)[9] would I be if I did that? Don't you think that if Waziri were still alive he wouldn't have had [at least] five children by now? When Seleman died, he had already had four children, and he had not stopped having children. . . .

P. But if you marry a younger woman, aren't you likely to have more children?

M. I will get more. I have children, and if God grants me, I will get more.

P. But how will you bring them up when you have nothing?

M. But won't God already have given that [child] to me? What can I do about it? Can I divorce my wife because she's pregnant?

P. No, not at all. But if you married a woman whose child-bearing days are over, say someone of my age, she would cook for you, everything – except that as far as having children is concerned, she has finished with that.

M. Do you know how many of my children are still alive?

P. Juma, Asha, Subira, Miza, Habiba.

M. Is that six?

P. No, five – or are there others? One boy – Juma, four girls. And those who died are Seleman, Waziri, Amina and that little one. In total you had nine children.

M. But there were also two miscarriages, and one stillbirth. How many is that?

P. More than ten.

M. If you only count the ones who survived – but the total number of pregnancies was twelve.

P. But what I am saying is this. You are not a young man any more.

M. That's right.

P. I think you must be around 60 now.

M. I think I am older than that.

P. So if you start having children now, you are unlikely to be able to bring them up.

M. I don't have the strength at the moment, but I will have [when the time comes]. But how many years have I put up with [my situation]? It's not a short period of time. Aren't you thankful to hear that [although] Mohammed has not yet married, he is still alive and well, he hasn't been beaten or killed? But I have had to put up with a lot (*nimestahimili*).

P. But couldn't you marry a woman of your own age?

M. I could. But you know, Patricia, it's just *you* that doesn't want to [have more children] – if you had wanted to you could have had more children. You already told me long ago that you only wanted two children, and that was all. But if you had been born here, you would still be having children. How old are you? 52? You could still have children.

P. No, I couldn't. I am postmenopausal (*mpevu*) now.

M. You could have started when you were 9 or 10 and kept on going. But you refused. You made up your mind to have only two and finish there.

P. But in our place, it's rare to have children like that. You have two, three, perhaps four and that's it.

M. I will be back in a minute [he gets up to go outside for a moment]. But I tell you that the children you should have had will accuse you [before God on Judgement Day]!

In this part of our conversation, we were plainly talking to some extent at cross purposes. He thought that I was querying the desirability of him re-marrying at all, when he saw himself as having suffered both inconvenience and loneliness for a long period of time. My actual concern was that Mohammed should not further increase his problems by having yet more children; he, on the other hand, was acutely aware of the numbers of children he had already lost – of Mwahadia's dozen pregnancies, only five children now survived, and he had also lost many grandchildren. He made it clear to me, as he did on other occasions (see Chapter 2), that he saw having children as an unmitigated blessing and that perhaps by having more, he could to some extent make up for the many who had died.

Mohammed becomes possessed

In our conversations during that visit, spirit possession was once again a frequent theme, not only on his own account, but also because of Subira's increasing involvement. He told me that the reason why he and his family members were currently getting sick was because he had an outstanding debt to his ancestral spirit, which now possessed him.

At first, I was somewhat surprised when Mohammed told me that he had been getting possessed for the previous three years after resisting possession for most of his adult life. On reflection I decided that it was probably inevitable, especially after the trauma of the death of Seleman.

For the first time, Mohammed explained to me how his family had acquired its relationship with this particular spirit. He wrote in his diary in July 1994:

> My ancestor Mwatima had two *majini* and two *mashaitani* whose dance was the *kitanga*. All of them, both the *majini* and the *mashaitani*, use a white cow [in their rituals]. Her son entrusted all of these *majini* and *mashaitani* to our ancestral spirit, so that he [Mwatima's son, Mohammed's grandfather] and his brothers and sisters should be able to practise curing (*kugangia*); they use a white cow in the *mwingo*, which is danced on Monday nights.

P. What is the difference between *mashaitani* and *majini*?
M. The *majini* have longer ancestry (*madaraja*, lit. bigger bridges), and are stronger. Their houses are under the sea. There were times when my grandfather used to meet up with this spirit when he went line fishing.
P. Where was that?
M. Kisiki village. He married a Pokomo woman[10] . . . and their children, that is us, practise divination with that same spirit.

Mohammed continued this story on tape:

M. We all inherited it [this spirit] from our ancestors, we got our spirit by inheriting it from them, and after inheriting it, it climbed into my head as its 'chair'. I have taken trays of offerings, and I participate in dances. But so far I haven't used a cow [i.e. drunk the blood of a sacrificed animal]. When I'm ready I will know. If you leave me your address, I will let you know. This year, Patricia, I will use a cow.

P. Have you already bought it?

M. Yes, I've bought it and put it aside.

P. How does it feel to be possessed?

M. You feel as if your soul (*roho* – indicating throat area) is disturbed, and the veins (*mishipa*) in your head hurt, your consciousness (*akili*) is changed. Do you remember yesterday on the path [on our way to a *kitanga*], when I was fixing my shoe, that man asked me why my hand was trembling? That is because I already felt drawn (*kuvutwa*) towards it.

I did remember, and indeed, when we heard the sound of the drums, Mohammed had said to me, 'I hear it like a call to me (*nasikia kama wito*)', and then as we approached he said, 'I feel it like a clock ticking inside me' (*naona kama saa ndani*).

P. Do you recognise people [when you are possessed]?

M. Yes, you know if it is a person.

P. So this is the third year you have begun to be possessed?

M. No, the fourth.

P. Who is your spirit?

M. Isn't it he, our ancestral spirit? Before I left for the *kitanga* yesterday

Plate 22 Dancers at a *kitanga*

said to him that I was going and that you were coming with me. I said,
'*Mzee*, we are going [to the *kitanga*], let it be all right, and let your child
Patricia do her work as usual.' Did you take a photograph of me dancing?
P. Yes, I did.
M. Alone or with others?
P. Both, and I will let you have copies later.
M. How did I dance? Did I look good in my jacket?
P. Yes, you certainly did.
M. One of my grandchildren said to me as I was leaving for the *kitanga*
that I looked really good and later that the eyes of many of the young
women were on me.

He returned several times to this theme which reinforced my idea
that spirit possession and sexuality are closely connected, or rather
that one is perhaps sometimes a substitute for the other.

P. Why didn't you used to get possessed?
M. I did in my dreams, and I used to dance when I was young. But then
I had trouble with my legs. And my father's younger brother, who was
a shaman, gave me permission before he died to talk to our ancestral
spirit without the necessity of burning incense, just anywhere, even
walking along the path.

During my visit in 1994, Mohammed and I attended two *kitanga*
rituals in Minazini, and he went to two in Pwani which I did not
attend – one for a spirit which uses a black cow, and one for a spirit
which uses a white cow. Mohammed became possessed in all of these
events, but did not drink the blood, because he had not yet been fully
initiated by holding his own ritual with the sacrifice of a cow. He gave
me an account of the first *kitanga* he attended in Pwani:

Mohammed attends a *kitanga* in Pwani

M. There were a lot of people there, it started at I p.m. and went on until
11 a.m [the next morning]. . . . I saw my spirit several times last night –
he kept climbing into my head. I saw my cousins and my grandchildren
in Pwani. They were all looking at me.
P. Did you wear your jacket?
M. No, because I have to go to Baleni today and I knew it would need
washing after a *kitanga*, and there wouldn't be time to dry and iron it.
P. Does your new woman-friend dance the *kitanga*?
M. Yes she does, and you should have seen the way some of those people
danced and how they behaved when they were possessed! This dance
which took place the other night was for a spirit which uses a black cow.

[One of the people present] there was a brother of mine and another is the medium JJ [his classificatory brother] who lives here in Minazini. So when they were dancing the *kitanga* the spirit climbed into their heads. So people were being treated. . . . And as it happened that *kitanga* was a very strong one. Many men and many women were there. . . .

Dancing a *mwingo* at another *kitanga*

Mohammed also attended a second *kitanga* in Pwani, this time for a spirit which required the sacrifice of a white cow, as does his own spirit. Perhaps for this reason, he was much more affected by events on this occasion than in the previous *kitanga*:

P. And what was it you told me the other day that happened in the [second] *kitanga* in Pwani?

M. I was possessed by my ancestral spirit (*mzee*, lit. old person) in the middle of the dance; the bed was here and the drummers were there and some women were over here and some were over there. So there were quite a few women there and the drums were being beaten and I came away from the dance. There were two women in particular, one was Binti M and the other Binti A, and they came after me and both of them took hold of me [to restrain him]. . . .

Then along came Subira, no, I mean Miza and the dance was being performed over there under the tamarind tree and we were over here like

Plate 23 Kitanga: drummers, singer and a chorus of women

Plate 24 'We danced and danced': the *kitanga*

this and they said to me, 'Calm down. Get your breath back.' My left hand was being held by that one and my right hand by the other one. And I said to her [Miza], 'Do you love Mohammed or do you not love him?' And Miza said, 'I do love him (*namtaka*)' and so we went back to the dance. And we danced and danced and we went round and round the whole area (*kiwanja*). And then again I had to stop for a while.

Heavens no, just a minute. [I almost forgot] The son of the drummer came along when they were dancing the *kitanga* but I hadn't yet joined in. And he said to his father the drummer: 'Can you play a *mwingo* for a bit?' And so they started to play the *mwingo* and then I joined in. And he [the drummer's son] came over to me and gave me his hand and at that time the spirit had already climbed into my head and he said to me '*Mzee*, it's ready. The *mwingo* is ready for you. . . .'

And the mother of that young man came over, Binti M, she is the wife of K, she said to me, 'That's enough *Mzee*, that's enough. Just dance a little bit.' And my friend had also come and given me her hand. And this woman Binti M said to me, 'So that's enough for now until that day in the future when you'll dance until you've had enough of it [i.e. the *mwingo*].'

And so at that point I went and sat down on the bed and the women were singing. Some of them were my granddaughters and some of them were my cousins. They sang the *mwingo* songs for me. And I said to the drummer, 'My friends [i.e. the spirits] want a *mwingo* dance.' And so they continued dancing and the men danced and the women danced and they met in the middle. And I was in the middle of them and I was dancing and dancing the *mwingo*. And then Miza came over and she said to me, 'Steady on *Mzee*, steady on. Gently does it.' And so I sat down on the bed again and then they began to sing again. This time it was the son of MH whose nickname is S [who sang] and the women were singing and it got hold of me again and so I went and danced again. Then they said, 'You want a *mwingo* but wait until you've already used a cow and then we'll dance a *mwingo* to your heart's content, right until the sun comes up, until the dawn. And then we'll dance all over again and we'll continue dancing as the sun comes up [a second time] and even until nightfall.' And so they agreed that between themselves.

And so I went and sat down on the bed again and then they resumed dancing the *kitanga* and then once again I was taken by the hand and three women came after me; they came along with Miza and they said to me, '*Mzee*, enough.' And at that point the cow had already been brought and tied up and they were wanting to slaughter it. So they slaughtered the cow and when they had slaughtered the cow people were given the blood, either in basins or in cups. But those who had a black spirit refused the blood and said, 'No we can't drink this.' And so when it was finished they brought a tray which they used instead.

It was striking how clearly he remembered all the events, considering he had been in a state of possession.[11] He had, as people do when possessed, rushed around, necessitating calming by relatives and friends, including the normally recalcitrant Miza. Possession enabled him to voice feelings normally repressed, and he asked Miza if she loved him, and she replied that she did. Another person who helped to calm him down by holding his hand was his new lover. His spirit clearly articulated its desire for a proper ritual and he temporarily turned the *kitanga* into a *mwingo*, in the process obtaining a great deal of soothing attention.

Belief and scepticism

I was curious to know how Mohammed saw the relationship between Islam and spirit possession, so I began by asking him about his participation in the *tarika* (Sufi mystical order).

P. The other day I asked you if you were going to the *ziara* (Sufi ritual), you said no. So was it just that one, or don't you go to *maziara* at all?

M. Previously I often used to go to *maziara* and do *dhikiri*. . . . I was a follower (*mridi*) [of one of the village branches],[12] which is where I drank the *ijazi*.[13] I used to go to the Pwani *ziara*, it's in the 4th month – were you here then? No I don't think so. And this month on the 16th day there is another one. I used to go to that one too. And I used to go to the ones in all the villages. But these days, to tell the truth, I don't go.

P. Why not?

M. One reason is my leg is not as good as it used to be. And I used to like *dhikiri* very much. But the state I'm in now, I couldn't do it. So I thought that it is better not to go, because I wouldn't be able to complete it.

P. So how long ago did you stop going?

M. I don't know, but it is many years, perhaps seven or eight.

P. I have another question for you. Do you ever pray?

A. Pray? A very long time ago I did pray once. It was with my brother Kombo and the deceased WH.

P. Where was that? At home or in the mosque?

M. At home, we prayed at WH's house.

P. Was this every day?

M. No, just one day. And then we once went to Dar es Salaam with the late JA and HZ and the late YK, and I would go with them to the Mtoro mosque there. We used to pray at dawn, we used to pray the noon prayer. It was the time when we were staying with IB. It was at the Mtoro mosque, which is near the Kariokoo market. But since that time, once I returned to Mafia, I have never prayed again.

P. And is there a reason for that?

M. I just don't that's all.

P. But you do consider yourself a Muslim even if you don't go to the mosque?

M. Yes, I am, I just don't go that's all. I think of myself as a Muslim, following the religion of Mohammed. . . .

P. I have heard people say that Islam forbids matters such as spirits and so on. How would you reply to them?

M. What do they say?

P. They say don't do that, Islam forbids it. What would you say?

M. The Sheikhs say that a lot, in the *maziara*, and in the mosques, and if someone dies and there is a sermon, or at the Friday prayers. They say there are no *majini*, no *mashaitani* which affect humans, that it is not true that such things exist. What is left is *ushiriki* (polytheism), but there are no such things.

P. And what would you say?

M. At the time when they talk, I couldn't say anything. I don't have an answer for them.

P. But if I ask now, how would you reply?

M. You've got me there, because if you asked me 'Have you seen one?' I would say I haven't. So I can't say they exist, because you can't see them.

P. But don't you see them in your sleep?

M. Their picture comes then, but aren't you asleep at that time? Can you talk to them and say, 'I am such and such a man (*fulani bin fulani*) or such and such a woman (*fulani binti fulani*) and I have come here'? You don't see them, it's like a spell (*mazingera*). It's a kind of darkness which comes to you in your sleep. Others say that a spirit is too big, too great to be in the head of a human being, and that even though people tremble and weep and speak [when possessed], no spirit is there. [They say that] every word they say is pulling your leg. But [when you are possessed] you are beside yourself (*hujitambui*). You feel that your head is in a completely different state [from usual]. And your chest becomes heavy, your soul (*roho*) feels as if it will burst. So you are not yourself during the time that this comes to you.

P. Why do tears come?

M. Isn't it because as I said you feel yourself choking (*roho inagharabu*). It's like you and I are talking and I say something to upset you, your feelings (*roho*) will be hurt. For example if I take a dislike to something, I could do such and such. And it's the same with them (*vile vile*) and in all their dances, each one wants to be the one and only. It does not want anyone else to touch him or her, only that one.

CONCLUSION

Several kinds of misfortune infuse each character's story in this chapter. One is poverty – each of them has to struggle to make ends meet, and with the death of Seleman, all hope of economic betterment seems to have disappeared. The second is ill-health – Mwahadia's swollen eye, Subira's constant miscarriages, Mohammed's recent severe diarrhoea. Mwahadia seeks explanation in witchcraft sent against her because she has tried to protect her remaining son. Subira's explanation is that 'two spirits are quarrelling over me', that of her mother and her father, while another spirit causes her to lose her pregnancies. Curiously, only Mohammed explains his illness as 'just sickness' (*shida tu*). A third problem is personal relationships: Mwahadia has an unsatisfactory marriage, Subira an equally unsatisfactory live-in relationship, while Mohammed's problem, as he sees it, is precisely the lack of a relationship and the ensuing loneliness. Finally, there is the question of multiple bereavement: Mohammed and Mwahadia have seen the deaths of many of their children and grandchildren. Subira herself has had some thirteen pregnancies, of whom only four children are alive. Such problems need explanations and they need a means of dealing with them. For all three characters, the activities of spirits, and the cults surrounding them, provide both.

So why finally did Mohammed succumb to full possession? He could, of course, have chosen another route as did his brother – he too had had a Koranic education – and could have eschewed the spirits in the same way. During most of the time that I have known him, he attended *ngoma*, he has practised various forms of magic and medicine, he has communicated with his ancestral spirit in his dreams seeking protection and help, and he has taken offerings to its shrine. But he resisted full possession and initiation into a cult until relatively late in his life.

Furthermore, his entry into full possession was not marked by illness, as is often the case. Indeed, I found it striking that in several instances where he had been troubled by illness, and his children had suggested divination, he had refused, saying that he knew that it was 'just illness' (*maradhi tu*). It is tempting to suggest that there were other reasons precipitating this step.

Mohammed's life, especially in recent years, has been a troubled one. He has been bereaved of a daughter and two of his sons, his wife has left him and he has not succeeded in re-marrying, he feels his daughters are indifferent to him, and his poverty has increased. Is that the reason why he finally turned to spirit possession? Possibly. Mohammed thought of himself as relatively invulnerable (*mzito*) (see Chapter 9). Yet when Seleman died, perhaps this invulnerability was breached and he began to feel the need for greater protection from misfortune than he had previously possessed. Mohammed already 'had' this spirit with him, and it perhaps only needed a traumatic event like Seleman's death to precipitate him into full possession.

Other clues come from his descriptions of spirit possession rituals he attended: he enjoyed people looking at him, 'dancing and dancing', restrained and soothed by many women, feeling himself to be in the midst of a supportive group of people, temporarily turning someone else's *kitanga* ritual into his own *mwingo*.

Yet these are my explanations, not his, and indeed, he did not see a need for explanation, saying merely that the spirit chooses the medium, rather than vice versa. Indeed, by suggesting that problems and tensions are 'projected' on to the spirit world, we are perhaps in danger of suggesting that human matters are real and spirit matters only a way of expressing them. In other words, by reducing the spirits to an idiom there is the risk of denying the integrity of Mohammed's own view of the world, in which they are a part of his selfhood, and thus as 'real' as anything else.

11 Conclusion

In this final chapter I seek not so much to pull together what has gone before, since any attempt to make a tidy ending would be spurious, but to reflect on why I wrote the book, and on the voices and process involved in producing it, and to speculate a little on how it might be read.

Apart from the fact that the material was available, and it seemed a pity not to use it once I had recognised its existence, I wanted to write something which would go some way towards countering anthropology's fascination with difference and which could be read by non-anthropologists as well as anthropologists. By producing a personal narrative, I hoped to achieve a kind of humanistic anthropology which would emphasise concerns which are common to us all – relationships, misfortune, birth and death.

Writing the personal narrative of a male informant also represented a challenge. Most feminist anthropologists in the recent past have chosen to write about other women, which has been part of a process of problematising women as well as giving them voice. In this instance, although obviously Mwahadia and Subira play significant parts in this book, the emphasis is very much on Mohammed. It would have been more difficult to write so comprehensively about a woman: few women would have had the time to spend with me that Mohammed has done over the years, and none would have kept a diary of the kind that he did, so the same kind of material would not have been available. But I also felt that it is high time for anthropologists to write about men *qua* men, and to consider the way in which masculinity is constructed and performed.

Mohammed is not in the heroic mould, indeed, in an earlier publication, I described him as an 'anti-hero' (Caplan 1992a: 64). In retrospect, I would revise that rather glib description, because I do not consider it useful to think of people as either heroes or anti-heroes, any more than it is useful to think of them as typical or deviant, as some anthropologists have suggested. The point is that they are human, and thus the usual mixture of good and bad.

Mohammed, then, is presented, warts and all, or rather that is how he presents himself. This raises complex issues of ethics, confidentiality and accountability on the part of the ethnographer who uses such a set of personal narratives. In life, the presentation of the self is always carefully managed, and tailored according to circumstances and audience. Much of what I present in this book was not given to me in the expectation that I would one day put it into print. This is one of the reasons that I spent so long discussing the writing of this book with Mohammed in 1994, and why I have changed both his name, and those of his family members, as well as the name of his village, and why he decided that this should not be a jointly authored book. We share a concern that the book should not result in him losing face (*kuvunja heshima*), although his concern is primarily *vis-à-vis* fellow villagers and other Mafians who might not only learn things about him which he would prefer them not to know, but also accuse him of revealing their secrets.

In telling their tales, did our characters obtain a different view of themselves and their world than they might otherwise have done? In a widely quoted article written some twenty years ago, Watson argues that when an individual reflects on his or her experience, which is inevitable in a life history, this transforms the attitude towards the taken-for-granted quality of the world into a phenomenological attitude (1976: 99–100, see Watson and Watson-Franke 1985). Basically, in relating a life history or other personal narrative, the informant grapples with his or her own self-identity. As Watson points out, this is not always a comfortable process:

> Part of this perception includes his awareness of the disparity between his self-image, his needs, his hopes, and the reality of the world which thwarts and contradicts his intentions, thus setting up the awareness of conflict.

(1976: 106)

Mohammed liked to think of himself in a positive light, yet he was well aware that his needs and his hopes were not always met. He must also have been aware that others would see at least some of his problems as self-inflicted. In the process of selecting what to tell me, he often left things out which he did not wish me to know, for example, the happenings which surrounded the breakdown of his marriage (see Chapter 6). Such matters I learned about from other people, and he must have been well aware of what I had heard.

But any shift in consciousness on the part of the informant arises in part out of telling a tale to someone else, who thus becomes part of its construction. For this reason Fabian (1971), for example, has argued (following Wittgenstein) that through the dialectical process of verbal exchange, the anthropologist and his or her informant create in effect a *lebenswelt* of their own, an idea which has also been utilised by other anthropologists (Rabinow 1977, Crapanzano 1980).

What then of the role of the anthropologist herself, especially in the process of writing ethnography? A number of authors argue that a hermeneutic approach enables us to understand what is going on: the anthropologist is comprehending the self by the detour of the other. Crapanzano, for example, notes that by writing, he or she is 'affirming an identity, a subjectivity felt as a sense of self, by addressing and reifying thereby, an other' (1977: 72). In writing this book, I have found myself adopting a rather different intellectual stance than in my previous work. Basically, I have wanted to let the texts speak for themselves as much as possible, but in the course of interpreting them, I have had to make shifts:

> It is necessary for the ethnographer to assume a dialectical rela-
> tionship to the life history, where he moves back and forth between
> his own position and that of the text he wishes to understand, in the
> process of which he adds accumulative meanings to the text as it
> becomes transformed in his own thinking.
>
> (Watson 1976: 104)

I did not read the above passage until I had almost completed the book, but it seemed to fit in with what I had been trying to do. I had had to make substantial moves in order to grasp what I was being told. This applies particularly to the information given in the last part of the book, where I had to learn to question my own cultural understandings in a deeper way than I had attempted previously. The story of the lives of Mohammed, Mwahadia and Subira could not be told without discussing the issue of spirits, one on which I had collected a great deal of material, yet had somehow found difficulty in writing about. Working on this book seemed to open new possibilities of understanding the phenomenon on its own terms: it can be shown to be a satisfying activity which, as Boddy (1994) points out, encompasses the aesthetic and quotidian, human imagination and creativity, an interweaving of religion and curing, healing and teaching, selfhood and identity, or, as Giles expresses it (1987), mediates otherwise unresolvable contradictions between the individual psyche, public morality and social responsiblity. For the first time, I began to see the spirit possession cults as a way of making sense of the world, perhaps utilising capacities that all humans have, but not all use. By this I do not mean that I became personally involved in the cults in the way that some anthropologists have described (e.g. Stoller and Olkes 1987), for although I was sometimes made to dance at *ngoma* rituals, I never felt as though I was about to become possessed. But I did come to understand what Mohammed and others had been telling me for years, that there is another dimension, another mode of being, which has to be reckoned with and taken seriously.

I doubt if Mohammed and I would have worked on a book such as this at an earlier stage of our relationship: not only would the material have lacked the time depth, but neither of us would have been ready to perform that work which perhaps comes best in middle and old age, making sense of a life by putting it into some sort of order. Part of the reason for our willingness to do so in 1994 is probably, as Langness and Frank suggest, less to do with life than with death:

> In old age, spontaneous life review or reminiscence is a universal feature, prompted by a person's recognition of impending death and the dissolution of the self.
>
> (1981: 103)

Indeed, they go on to cite Heidegger's proposition that our consciousness in the face of death is the fundamental human condition. In the West, such consciousness is not usually achieved until relatively late in the life cycle. Yet Mohammed seems to have had an awareness of death from an early age, as is shown by his speech to his mother when he quarrelled with her about his desire to marry Mwahadia. In a society in which death is common, awareness of mortality cannot be far away, and by 1994, this awareness had greatly intensified with the loss of so many of his children, as he was quick to tell me on my return (see Prologue).

Langness and Frank also suggest that how death is conceived in a particular society should affect the life story that a person tells. Mohammed believed that death was the end, that humans, even those who had been close, would not meet again. And yet he also believed that ancestors played an active role in the lives of the living, and that having descendants – children and grandchildren – was important. Indeed, it is the very fulfilment of this need and desire which brings both the greatest joy and the greatest sorrow: joy for the pleasures that children can give, and sorrow when they die, as too many of them do on Mafia Island.

At the beginning of this Chapter, I noted that I see the writing of a personal narrative as an essentially humanistic enterprise. By this I mean that its goal is to explore the universal human condition, and in so doing, cross, or bridge the gap between oneself as ethnographer and the subject of the life history. But this goal, if it is achieved in even small measure, has also to be communicated to the reader of the text.

In their book *Lives*, Langness and Frank (1981) suggest that the anthropological life history and the other personal accounts collected by ethnographers make ordinary individuals intelligible to other people and argue that: 'To fail to understand another person's life history is, in general, to reject one's own humanity' (1981: 136). But understanding is required from all players in the game – the teller, the listener and interpreter, and the audience, or rather audiences.

There are several categories of potential reader for a work such as this. One is other anthropologists, most of whom will be familiar with the genre of personal narratives of one kind or another, although they may differ in their assessment of its usefulness as a disciplinary tool. Some anthropologists will also be familiar with some of the content of this book: they may be fellow area scholars, or they may have worked on similar themes in their own fields. A second category is more general readers, mostly in the West, who may be interested in finding out about the lives of people in a different place and culture. Here issues of sameness and difference are thrown into sharp relief. The characters in this book are, on the one hand, very different in many respects from most people in the West: they are much poorer, their language and culture are foreign, yet it is my hope that many of their most fundamental concerns have been shown to be similar, and that Western readers will find aspects of the characters with which to empathise.

A third category of potential readers are Tanzanians and other East Africans. Most who will read this book will be well-educated, although not necessarily social scientists. They will undoubtedly read it with a particular kind of awareness: that someone from the West has come and represented people from Africa, and that most of those who will read the ensuing product will also be westerners. How, then, will they view the result? Some of the most often-cited books in the genre of personal narrative are Lewis's studies of Mexico; they have been praised by anthropologists, social policy makers, even literary critics. Yet in Mexico itself, Lewis's work has been viewed with dismay, for representing Mexico to the world in terms of a poor and 'shameless' family. It is obviously my hope that Tanzanians will not adopt a similar stance to this work. It is true that the subjects are poor, as are

Plate 25 Villagers watching themselves (and the anthropologist) on film
in *Face Values*

most Tanzanians, that their practices are not always in accord with
ideals preached by some: chastity or fidelity in sexual matters, eschew-
ing of spirit possession in favour of Islamic piety. But it is my hope
that they will see Mohammed, Mwahadia and Subira as people
who grapple vigorously with adversity, using all the weapons at their
disposal, who are seekers and doers, people who are capable of
reflecting on their own situations, and attempting to improve them.

  And what, finally, of those potential readers, who are as yet few in
number, who share a background with our characters, and who,
indeed, may even recognise, or think that they recognise them? There
is no doubt that some people from Mafia will read this book, and,
in a generation from now, even more will be able to do so. From
published work of mine about Mafia which has been available to the
few educated local people who can read English, I suspect that their
feelings will be mixed. There is pleasure that someone from far away
should take the trouble to write about them, and that people 'over
there' should be interested in reading it. There is also awareness that
such work constitutes a way of preserving knowledge about a culture
which is changing. On the other hand, inevitably, there is a sense of
a loss of privacy, a risk of exposure. This ambivalence is captured
in the response of many Mafians to the work which has been most
available to most of them – the film *Face Values*. Each time it has

been screened in the village, people, who come in their hundreds, laugh all the way through – it is as though there is simply no other appropriate reaction. It is my hope for this book that, while feelings of ambivalence are inevitable, Mafians will feel some pleasure that a small part of their rich culture has been shared with a wider audience, and that the lives of three apparently very ordinary people can be shown to contain so much of the extraordinary.

Epilogue
Intercession

In the Prologue to this book, I recorded how, at the beginning of my stay in the village in 1994, Mohammed took me to see a *mwalimu* in order to have a special Islamic prayer said (*kuombea dua*) for the success of my work. At the end of my stay, he wanted me to make an offering to his ancestral spirit for the same reason.

P. What do you think? Will we ever get a chance to talk again like this? I don't mean on this trip, I mean in the future? We have talked a lot on my trips, from the first, to the second, third and now this one the fourth. Will it happen again?

M. If I am alive, it will be the same, we shall talk as usual.

P. Thank you.

M. My feelings (*roho*, lit. 'soul') haven't changed towards you, nor has my love (*mapenzi*) for you changed. As I see it, we get more and more fond of each other.

P. Yes, that's the way it is, thank you.

M. I do not have anything to give you in this world. And in the next world, I don't think we meet again, not even with our parents.

P. Why not?

A. That's what I've heard. That's what I think. [Of course] a dead person can take hold of those who are living. 'Who is it?' [people will ask]. 'Bwana so and so or Binti so and so.' According to our customs (*mila*), it means that he or she wants a Koranic reading (*hitima*). So you call a *mwalimu*, and he remembers the ancestors (*kuarehemu wazee*), he reads and reads. And then, he asks [the ancestor] what is the reason for coming to people in their sleep? For that reason I think that I have to read a *fatiha* [the opening section of the Koran] for them, it is like sending them greetings. Just as if I had seen them, or as if they were still alive. And this reaches them. So our conversations are the same. So as I said to you, I don't have anything to give you, but God is the one who provides and he will give you more and more, and I pray that you will be blessed (*kheri*) and you will be rewarded.

Do you remember what I said to you the other day? As you know, I have the ancestry (*asili*), so apart from the *fatiha* [that is *kuombea dua* – see Prologue – which we already did], what do you say [to using the other means]? Shall I contact them (*kugongoa*) [the spirits] for you? Do you want to make a vow (*nadhiri*)? You have work to do. We were to talk about these matters [privately outside the village] and since yesterday we have been here. So now that we are here we can talk about it, if you agree.

P. All right, let's talk about it.

M. We'll talk about all my *wazee* (spirits) because they carry [i.e. look after] many people. Some people say, '*Mzee*, I want you to be with me, in my work, in my travels, be with me, keep an eye on me at night, during the day. And if you do this, I will do such and such a thing.' Some of them say that they will give a cow, others give a tray of offerings.

P. How much does a tray cost?

M. You need two chickens, a kilo of sugar, dates aren't available, bananas aren't available . . . these days. Since [the shaman] MB died, we haven't taken bananas. You take dates if you can get them, but you don't have to. So it would be two chickens, raisins (*zabibu*), cinnamon (*abdalasini*), nutmeg (*kungu manga*), and cardamon (*alaichi*). [We work out the cost of these items.]

P. So the total cost will be 650 shillings for what we've talked about plus the sugar which is 600 shillings. So in all it will be around 1,250 shillings?

M. Let me tell you. I will bear 550 shillings of the costs, and going to do this will also be on me [i.e. he won't charge for his services]. The rest is up to you. Oh, and half a kilo of rice,

P. I have some rice at home.

M. Is it ripe (*mpevu*)?

P. Yes. So did you say that you would provide 550 shillings?

M. My intention was to offer you some help, this is my contribution.

P. Thank you. So I will have to find 700 shillings, won't I?

M. All right.

P. And when shall we do this?

M. After the feast (*sadaka*) of the l3th day of the month in Minazini, that is the New Year's Day.

P. Yes, I agree.

M. And you don't have to be there. We can say the words here now and I will take them [to the shrine].

P. What about the incense?

M. Ah, the incense – yes, another 10 shillings. That's it. The work of saying the words is on me, as is the work of going there.

P. So do you have to go to the spirit shrine (*panga*) to do this?

M. To get them to intercede (*kuwasalisha*)? Yes, of course I do.

P. And do I come or what?

M. No, you don't come, because the spirit will call its friends to use the tray of offerings. They invite each other.

P. All right, whatever you say.

M. For this reason then, on that day they invite each other, you should not be there. Different spirits come, some who are from far away. It's like someone in Minazini having a ritual (*shughuli*) and inviting people from Pwani, Karibu and so on. It's the same with them, they gather together. But if they see you there, they will be alarmed (*watastuka*). 'Why today are we seeing someone of a different colour? It's not right.' So many spirits (*mizimu*) are like that. They don't like it. They just want friendship (*kitu urafiki*) [with you]. One just says everything which is relevant on the day before and then takes everything there. And what you didn't take, you are forgiven . . .

P. All right, then, I will give an offering [to the spirit shrine].

M. The days for taking it there are Mondays, in which case you say it the day before and the 'feast' is the next day, or, if you want to send it on a Thursday, you tell the spirit on Wednesday evening that you are going on the Thursday.

P. But where will you get this money from when you told me you don't have any?

M. Indeed, I do not, but I am trying to reduce the costs for you. How much would the total costs be?

P. 1,260 shillings, but if you pay 550 shillings, then only 710 shillings.

M. So that is what I am doing for you, out of sympathy (*huruma*) and faith (*amini*). And furthermore, some people charge [a fee of] 500 shillings for doing this, but I am doing it for free, I am doing it for myself, as if for my sister or my child. Would I ask my child or my sibling for fees (*ada*)? I couldn't do that.

P. I thank you very much for that – it's not a small thing.

Glossary

ada fee

baba father, classificatory father

balozi leader of a cell of ten houses set up throughout Tanzania by the government

banda hut (also used for circumcision lodge)

baraka blessing, charisma

chano large locally made wooden tray

dawa medicine

dawa ya miti herbal medicine (sometimes called *dawa ya miti shamba*)

dawa ya kienyeji local medicine

dawe meadow land which floods in the rainy season

dhikiri breathing and chanting practised by Sufis

edda period of seclusion which, under Islamic law, has to be observed by a woman after divorce or widowhood

elimu knowledge, education, learning (including religious)

feli spirit

fundi (pl. *mafundi*) expert of any kind, including ritual expert

fupo small gifts of money or tips given by the holder of a ritual to its major participants

halali permissible under Islamic law

haramu forbidden according to Islamic law

hirizi charms, amulets

hitima Koranic reading

hoteli tea-shop

iblissi spirit

jahazi big dhow

jamvi (pl. *majamvi*) large coarse mat made of borassus palm

jando circumcision ceremony, seclusion hut

jicho baya evil eye

jini (pl. *majini*) spirit, especially sea spirit

kanga (sometimes *khanga*) cloths worn in pairs by women on the coast and throughout East Africa (see also *shiti* and *kitenge*)

kaniki black work cloths worn in pairs by women; these were common in the 1960s, but had more or less disappeared by the 1980s

kanzu long white gown worn by men on coast over trousers and shirt; woman's dress

karamu feast

katwa stingray

kibumbwi poison administered to victims by sorcerers

kidau small boat with sail

kilemba turban, money paid to father of bride by groom

kingo protection, vaccination

kitanga spirit possession ritual for land spirits, with drums

kitenge (pl. *vitenge*) heavy cotton cloth worn by women, usually in pairs

kiteso incense burner

kiti chair, also used to mean spirit medium

kitoweo items such as meat, chicken, fish or legumes or vegetables used to make the curry which accompanies rice

kuapiza to bewitch someone

kuchanja to cut, inoculate

kugongolea, kugongoa to speak to the ancestors or spirits on someone's behalf

kuombea dua to pray on someone's behalf

kupoa to cool down, become calm, become well

kupungwa to be treated for spirit possession by initiation

kuroga to bewitch

kutia buhuri to make a vapour for (self-)fumigation (to make contact with spirits)

kutia chuku practise cupping

kuzingua to encircle something ritually to protect it

kwanga to practise sorcery

mashua small dhow

matanga funeral wake (usually three days)

maulid formal reading of text about the birth of the Prophet Mohammed

mazingera casting spells

mbuguma young cow which has born a calf

mchawi witch

mganga (pl. *waganga*) healer, doctor, shaman

migoda local medicines

mila custom

mkaja belt worn by women under their clothes, sum of money paid by groom to fiancée's mother

mkoba basket used by *waganga* for keeping their medicines, also used to mean the status of being *mganga*

mkobero spirit possession ritual for sea spirit, utilising *dhikiri* (q.v.)

mogo stage of circumcision ritual

mshipa (pl. *mishipa*) veins, organs of the body

mteja spirit possession guild member

muhanga form of sorcery

mwali young girl (occasionally young boy), initiate

mwalimu (pl. *walimu*) Koranic teacher (also used for schoolteacher)

mwepesi (pl. *wepesi*) light, vulnerable

mwanga (pl. *wanga*) sorcerer

mwingo spirit possession ritual for land spirits with hand-clapping and singing only, no drums

mzee elder (term of respect for both men and women; also term used to address spirit)

mzimu (pl. *mizimu*) possessory spirit

mzito (pl. *wazito*) heavy, invulnerable

mzuka possessory spirit

nadhiri vow

ngoma drum, dance

panga cave, spirit shrine (may be tree, rock, hollow)

pepo spirit, also wind

pishi a dry measure of grain, equivalent to about half a gallon or 6lbs

radhi satisfaction, forgiveness, blessing

ramli divination (*kupiga ramli* - to divine)

sanduku box, chest, trunk; term also used for the bride's trousseau

shaitani (pl. *mashaitani*) spirit

sheria law, particularly Islamic law

shiti (pl. *mashiti*) heavy cotton cloths worn by women

shughuli (pl. *mashughuli*) ritual, ceremony, event

shuka cloth worn by men around the waist, dropping to the ankles

somo namesake

talaka divorce certificate given to women by husband when divorce is final

tarika Sufi mystical order

tambo objects believed to lodge in the body as a result of witchcraft; only *waganga* can remove them

tunza money given as a tip to experts at a ritual such as *jando* or *unyago*: it is usually placed in their mouths during a celebratory dance

ubani incense, also used to refer to money collected at funeral to help defray expenses

ubao board, divining board

ugali stiff porridge made from either maize flour (*dona*) or cassava flour

uganga the power or art of healing/curing

ukili plaited strip of raffia – such strips are dyed different colours and then sewn together to make mats (*mikeka*)

ukindu raffia from the raffia palm

ukoo cognatic descent group

ukulima cultivation party

ulezi upbringing, taking care of a child

unyago puberty ritual held for girls after first menstruation

upanzi cooperative work party for planting crops

ushiriki polytheism

vimemeno sweetmeats

vuvu (pl. *mavuvu*) section of land held by a descent group

wiazi cooperative planting party

ziara annual ritual of a Sufi order

zindiko protection

SPIRIT VOCABULARY

kengenja child (Sw. *mtoto*)

kidume young man (Sw. *kijana*)

kiumbe creature, human being (Sw. *mtu*)

kongwe (pl. *makongwe*) person, people (especially elderly) (Sw. *mzee/wazee*)

kwenda pachironi to seek information from the spirits

mkiki spirit possession ritual for land spirits with hand-clapping and singing only, no drums (Sw. *mwingo*)

mlanga sun (Sw. *jua*)

mlio (sometimes *kilio*) crying, funeral

mwanakasi woman (Sw. *mwanamke*)

mkwavi cow (Sw. *ng'ombe*)

shami money (Sw. *pesa*)

tigina young woman (Sw. *msichana*)

Notes

PROLOGUE: A SPECIAL PRAYER

1 Field-work in the 1960s was supported by the University of London and the Goldsmiths' Company, in the 1970s by the BBC, and in both the 1980s and 1990s by the Nuffield Foundation; some of this material was collated and translated while I held an ESRC Personal Research Fellowship in 1987–8, and the bulk of the manuscript was written while I held Leverhulme Foundation and Nuffield Foundation Fellowships in 1994. Grateful thanks are due to all of them.
2 It is unusual for someone to be addressed simply by their name in this way.
3 All of these are Arabic greetings normally only used between males.
4 The Tanzanian currency is made up of shillings and cents (100 cents = 1 shilling). In the 1960s, the Tanzanian shilling was equivalent to a shilling in British money. By 1994, the rate of exchange was roughly 800 shillings – £1, and cents were scarcely talked about.
5 I have two adopted brothers in the village, one older than me (*kaka*), and one younger (*ndugu*).
6 My children, by this time in their 20s, were to pay their first visit to Mafia that summer, a visit that had long been awaited by the villagers.

1 INTRODUCTION

1 See Caplan (1976, 1978, 1979, 1982, 1983, 1988, 1989, 1992a, 1992b, 1995a, 1995b).
2 The film was *Face Values* and it is discussed further in Chapter 6.
3 Ali was a young man from the south of the island whom I hired as a cook at the beginning of my field-work. He became much more than a cook; he was adviser, informant and friend, and his wife and daughter also spent periods of time living in Minazini with us. I was very saddened to learn of his sudden death from illness a few years after I had finished my 1960s field-work.
4 Most men, and some women, in the village are literate in Arabic script which they learn in Koran school. Until relatively recently, Swahili was written in Arabic script (*Kiarabu*), and it is still regularly used as a means

of communication between older coastal dwellers, although today, Swahili is more usually written in Roman script (*Kizungu*).

5 For a well-referenced discussion of the history of the anthropological use of life histories see Langness and Frank (1981).

6 A number of historians, as well as anthropologists, have chosen the same method. The writing of personal narratives or life histories is part of the growth of interest in social history, which is very close to anthropology (Macfarlane 1977 [1970]). This kind of social history is characterised by interest in the everyday and in ordinary people, such as is provided by the 'subaltern studies' in Indian historiography (Guha 1982, see also Arnold and Hardiman 1993) which have been widely emulated. There are also a number of historical studies focusing on the lives and beliefs of individuals which have utilised written texts, such as Le Roy Ladurie (1990a [1978], 1990b [1983]), Ginzburg (1980 [1976]), Macfarlane (1977 [1970]), Spence (1978), Foucault (1980 [1978]), Marks (1987, 1989).

7 In his study of Marcel Griaule, Clifford (1983) notes that his career among the Dogon has two halves. In the first, what Clifford calls the documentary half, Griaule is only given *parole de face*. Later, he is initiated, and let into secrets, being given *parole claire*, after which his writing is exegetical. Clifford notes that such a view of ethnography contrasts with that which sees it as a dialogical enterprise.

8 Mohammed reads and writes only in Arabic script, while his wife Mwahadia, like several other women who were good friends, and who might well have agreed to keep diaries for me, is illiterate. In later visits, some women did keep diaries for me (see Caplan 1995b).

9 He talked about land tenure and descent groups, inheritance and the domestic division of labour. She described how marriages are arranged for daughters, the way adult children care for aged parents, the story of her first unhappy marriage, and what had caused the recent break-up of her marriage to Mohammed. Unfortunately, space has precluded including these interviews in the book.

10 Subira herself kept a diary for a very short time in 1985; unfortunately, that too has had to be omitted in the interests of length of this volume.

2 A LIFE HISTORY

1 *Mshipa* is a difficult word to translate. Sometimes it is glossed as 'veins', but in general parlance, it often means some kind of problem with the organs of the body.

2 Elephantiasis is common on Mafia Island. It is brought on by a filarial infection which blocks the lymphatic channels, as a result of which the whole leg and either the vulva or the scrotum swell up permanently due to a solid type of oedema.

3 Children have both an 'official' name and a nickname.

4 Children are invariably called after ancestors, and each is thenceforth known as the other's *somo*. Sometimes a child's name is changed if another ancestor is thought to have afflicted the child with sickness (see Chapter 8).

5 *Ziara* is an annual all-night ritual held by a branch of a Sufi order. Most

villages on Mafia have at least one *ziara* a year, more if they have more than one branch, like Minazini.

6 Although children are usually given an ancestor as a *somo*, it is also possible to ask someone still living to be a *somo* if the parents want to honour that person. During my first visit to the village in the 1960s, I was 'given' four children: two girls, one of whom died at the age of 3 months, were both given my name ('Patlisha'), while the two boys were named by me; one of them is invariably called by my maiden (i.e. my father's) name – Bailey.

7 *Mkwaju* (literally 'tamarind tree') is a mixed-sex dance with lead singer, a large drum and rubbing board; *kidatu* is danced to a drum and a *zumari* (a kind of clarinet) mainly by young people who stand in a circle watching two young men dance a few rounds side by side with a young woman, at the end of which one leaves the dance floor and bows to someone who has to take his or her place; I have not seen the *zuiya* performed.

8 After circumcision, the boys are secluded until the wounds are healed, as Mohammed later explains (see Caplan 1976)

9 Uncircumcised men are thought to be unclean, and thus unacceptable as sexual partners; on the coast, they would not be considered full adults.

10 There are three stages of seclusion, each marked by a ceremony (*mogo*). The first is called *mogo ya kuiba* (lit. 'the *mogo* of stealing') and lasts for three days. The 'stealing' refers to the fact that the boys are strictly secluded and anyone who sees them is 'stealing' a look.

11 Here Mohammed seems to be arguing that just as in death one is separated from father and mother, similarly in life, an individual has his or her own life to lead.

12 Since Mwahadia had been married before, her wedding to Mohammed would not constitute a rite of passage, and would not be accompanied by the degree of elaboration of a woman's first marriage.

13 In this hypothetical argument, the wife maintains that it is 'the law' that she should be allowed to visit a sick mother, while the husband argues that 'the law' only allows her to go if her husband gives permission. It would appear that this was an issue on which Mohammed and his wife Mwahadia later fell out (see Chapter 6). For a full discussion of the various meanings of the term *sheria*, see Caplan (1995b).

14 Mohammed's view of a wife's duty to her husband is almost exactly that expressed in the well-known Swahili homiletic poem *Utendi wa Mwanakupona*, supposedly composed by a mother for her daughter (see Harries 1962: 71–82).

15 Fields in this area of Mafia are of two categories – the dry bush fields, cultivated on a shifting pattern (*makonde* or *mashamba ya pori*) and the wetter meadow land (*dawe*) in the village (see Caplan 1975: 9).

16 The children of deceased parents are commonly brought up either by grandparents, or by a sibling of the father or mother. Later Mohammed told me that this child only stayed with them for a short time, but it seemed to be the factor of another mouth to feed which pushed him back into generating a cash income.

17 *Mazingera* is a form of witchcraft by casting a spell. It is discussed in greater detail in Chapter 8.

18 It will be noted that of Seleman's four children, three have died, and in

two cases, the death is attributed to some form of witchcraft. See Chapters 8 and 9 for further discussion of this topic.

19 After a death, there are three days of intensive mourning ended by a Koranic reading on the third day (*hitima ya tatu*). This is followed by a further forty days of mourning, culminating in a further Koranic reading and a feast (*hitima ya arobaini*). Further information is given in Chapter 4.

20 Mohammed means that he would have sole responsiblity for their welfare since the boy's side would wash their hands of them. It will be noted that responsibility in the case of a crisis such as illness rests not only with the husband or wife of the patient, but with a wider range of kin, especially elders. This is discussed further in Part IV.

21 Here Mohammed gives the names of the spirits, but because of promises of confidentiality, I have omitted them, as I have in the rest of this book. For further information on spirits and their doings, see Chapter 9.

22 The term *makongwe* is an example of a specialised vocabulary which is used only in the context of talking about or to spirits. (See spirit glossary on p. 239). *Kiumbe* means 'creature' in standard Swahili, and is often used by shamans to address patients in the context of spirit possession rituals and therapy.

23 The husband uses the term *sheria* to mean Islamic law, which confers upon him the right to insist upon his wife's presence. See Caplan (1995b) for further discussion of this point, and a detailed examination of a particular case.

24 When Seleman was in Dar es Salaam and heard that his sister was ill, he suspected that she might have been 'seized' by their ancestral spirit angry at neglect, so he brought enough money to sacrifice a cow to it. In the event, it turned out to be a different spirit, but a cow still had to be given to the spirit of the shaman who had driven out the afflicting spirit.

25 Because of the complex system of cognatic kinship and descent, and the preferential marriage of both parallel and cross-cousins, many people are related to each other in a number of different ways. See Caplan (1975) for a detailed discussion.

26 It is customary to announce deaths and funerals, especially those in the towns and cities, on the local radio.

27 The bier (which is usually a locally made string bed) is received and then carried to the grave by close male relatives.

28 The grave is dug with a niche at one side into which the corpse is placed.

29 Kisiju is the nearest point on the mainland to Mafia Island. There is a very poor quality road running from Kisiju to Dar es Salaam, a distance of some 80 miles. Most islanders travel to the capital by dhow to Kisiju, because the plane fare is very expensive.

PART II INTRODUCTION

1 The system of ten-house cells, each of which has a leader (*balozi*), was instituted by TANU (Tanganyika African National Union), the ruling party, soon after independence. Ten-house cells form the smallest unit of government, and this system has been continued by the CCM (*Chama cha Mapinduzi*), the current ruling party.

3 MAKING A LIVING: THE LAND AND SEA

1 There is now a large literature about the contemporary peoples of the East African coast, including Bujra (1968), Caplan (1975), El Zein (1974), Landberg (1977), Le Guennec-Coppens and Caplan (1991), Lienhardt (1968), Middleton (1992), Parkin and Constantin (1989), Parkin (1994), Prins (1961), Strobel (1975), Swartz (1991), Widjeyewardene (1961).

2 *Kuoga Mwaka* (lit., 'bathing the year') is widely observed on the East Coast of Africa. See Gray (1955) and Racine (1995).

3 Here the numbers have special significance. Both seven and three are numbers frequently used in Islamic magic.

4 THE LIFE CYCLE: RELATIONSHIPS, CONFLICT AND EMOTIONS

1 *Maulid* readings are held both for rites of passage, and also annually by each village. The commonest version of the *maulid* is that of Barzanj. See Trimingham (1964: 95–6), Middleton (1992: 166–9), Knappert (1971, vols I and III).

2 Seventy small stones (*mbwe*) are placed on the grave at the time of the feast (*karamu*) for the deceased. Each one represents '*la ilaaha illalla* ('There is no God but Allah' spoken a thousand times). At this time too, a large stone is placed at the head of the grave, and a smaller one at the foot.

3 Sherifs are people considered to be descendants of the Prophet, and as such, imbued with special power (*baraka*). By referring to a mother as a child's Sherif, Mohammed means that she should be treated with great respect. Lienhardt, writing of the Kilwa region of the coast, also mentions the ability of a parent to 'withdraw their satisfaction' (*kutoa radhi*), noting that the power of a mother is much greater than that of a father in this regard (1968: 29).

4 This explains Mwahadia's anger when Mohammed gave away some of her deceased son's property to his widow and she exclaimed 'Better a mother than a wife' (see Chapter 10).

5 Menstrual blood is considered polluting: women do not sleep with their husbands when they are menstruating, and must bath ritually at the end of their periods before they can resume sexual relations. A woman's sanitary napkin is kept in a secret place, which should be unknown to her husband; for him to touch it is a serious breach of a taboo.

6 Formerly, girls were kept in seclusion after their first menstruation until their marriage. By the 1960s, this custom was still being practised, but not universally. It had more or less disappeared by the 1970s, largely because of the push towards universal primary education by the Tanzanian government, which meant that girls could no longer be secluded because of school attendance.

5 ENCOUNTER ONE: 1965–7

1 Joking relations (*utani*) are recognised between cross-cousins (*binamu*) and between grandparents and grandchildren. A better translation of *utani* would be 'licensed teasing'. There is a large anthropological literature on this topic, of which perhaps the best-known article is Radcliffe-Brown (1952).

2 *Kitanga* is one form of several spirit possession rituals performed in the village. It is held to propitiate a land spirit, and consists of all-night drumming and dancing, followed in the morning by the sacrifice of a cow or bull, and the drinking of a little of its blood by the participants. Further details of these cults are given in Chapter 9.

6 ENCOUNTER TWO: 1976

1 The purpose of my visit in 1976 was to assist a BBC TV crew to collect footage for an anthropological film series which was later entitled *Face Values* and screened in 1978 (see Sutherland 1978).

2 This remark suggests that part of the husband's displeasure was caused by the fact that Mwahadia had not become pregnant.

3 *Mahari* is the sum of money promised at the time of the marriage contract by the groom to the bride. It is often withheld, although technically a woman has the right to claim it any time. Frequently, a woman only gets paid her *mahari* when her husband dies and his estate is settled. Sometimes a woman who wants a divorce agrees to 'forgive' her husband the *mahari* in exchange for her divorce certificate, in other cases she pays her husband the sum of money he demands to divorce her.

4 Ownership of coconut trees gives people rights to build a house (see Caplan 1975: Chapter 3).

5 Koranic teachers will write out Koranic verses on a plate, which is then rinsed. The water is collected into a bottle and drunk as medicine.

6 Some food and drink, such as ginger, is thought to be 'heating', while other items are 'cooling' to the body. Ginger coffee is given to women afer childbirth, when their bodies are thought to need heating after being rendered cold during the birth. However, if a body is at normal temperature when 'heating' foods are consumed, it becomes 'over-heated', and desirous of sex.

7 ENCOUNTER THREE: 1985

1 By the time of my third visit in 1985, a considerable number (government officials suggested over a hundred at any one time) of immigrants from the mainland were spending varying periods of time in the village, working as contract labourers. Most were Wanyamwezi from the west of Tanzania.

2 Id (el Fitr) is the feast held at the end of the fasting month of Ramadhan.

3 Here Subira appears to be conflating sorcery (*uwanga*) in which the sorcerer gives some kind of poison to the victim (*kibumbwi*), as in the case of the orange which she ate, with witchcraft (*uchawi*) in which the witch 'gives' the victim to a spirit (see Chapter 9).

4 The Makonde are from southern Tanzania and Mozambique. During the long period of war in Mozambique, many Makonde refugees crossed into Tanzania, most settling in the south of the country, but some travelling further afield in search of a livelihood. There were Makonde working on the large coconut plantations in the south when I first visited Mafia in the 1960s. By the 1980s, some had settled in the northern villages, such as Minazini, and lived both by cultivating land, and working as agricultural labourers. Makonde culture is very different from that of the Swahili-speaking coastal dwellers, and most Makonde are Christians. The villagers regarded the presence of the Makonde, and other 'up-country' immigrants, with considerable ambivalence.

PART IV INTRODUCTION

1 See notes 1 and 2, Chapter 9.
2 In utilising the terms 'shaman' and medium, I am following Firth's definition of a shaman as 'master of spirits', i.e. one who can control spirits (1959: 141), a usage which has also been adopted by Lewis (1971). I am not proposing to get involved here in discussions about the differences between Asiatic shamanism, with its connotations of the ritual journey (see Eliade 1964, Bourgignon 1965), and African spirit possession. The point about spirit possession cults on the East African coast is that some participants are considered to be 'experts' (*mafundi*, *waganga*) who have some control over their possessory spirits, others are simply initiated members of cults, or mediums (*miti*).

   Mti in everyday Swahili means tree but in spirit language means the medium of a spirit, who is also referred to as its 'chair' or 'seat' – *kiti*. It should be noted that these two words are from the same root: *kiti* has the connotation of smallness and *mti* of greater size.
3 See Lewis (1966a, 1971, 1986) and Wilson (1967).
4 Kapferer, for example, writes of his change of stance in the introduction to the new edition of his book on exorcism in Sri Lanka (1991).

8 DEALING WITH AFFLICTION 1: EXPLANATION

1 There has been some recent interesting work on African divination: see Abbink (1993), Akinnaso Niyi (1995), Fernandez (1991), Parkin (1974, 1991) and Peek (1991).
2 In this passage, several of the words used are from a special vocabulary confined to the spirit cults: *shami* (money) instead of *pesa* or *hela*, *mwanakasi* (woman) instead of *mwanamke* (see glossary).
3 In translating the Swahili term *uwanga* as sorcery, and *uchawi* as witchcraft, I am following the distinction originally suggested by Evans-Pritchard (1937) and utilised subsequently by others (e.g. Marwick 1965) by which sorcerers are those using some form of 'medicines', and who can acquire their knowledge through instruction, whereas witches' power is innate. It should be noted, however, that others who have written about these topics on the East African coast have sometimes followed different conventions (e.g. Lienhardt 1968).

4 Under Islamic law, a polygynously married man is supposed to treat all of his wives equally, which includes sleeping at their houses in rotation.

5 *Feli* is an alternative, albeit little-used, term for spirit.

6 There is an extensive literature on this topic, including E. Turner (1993), V. Turner (1967, 1975) and Janzen (1978, 1982), which is discussed in greater detail in the following chapter.

7 The *mkobero* is a ritual to deal with sea spirits (see Chapter 9).

8 It is believed that enemies can cause poisonous substances, known as *tambo* or *sihiri*, to enter someone's body. These can be detected by healers, who remove them by sucking the afflicted part (see also E. Turner 1993).

9 It is interesting that sesame oil is specified for magical purposes; note the English use of the term 'Open sesame'.

9 DEALING WITH AFFLICTION 2: SPIRITS

1 There is quite an extensive literature on this, see Alpers (1984), Giles (1987), Gomm (1975), Gray (1969), Harries (1962: 221–32, 1965: 201–5), Janzen (1992), Koritschoner (1936), Lienhardt (1968), Middleton (1992), Skene (1917), Swantz (1970, 1979) and Topan (1972, 1994).

2 There is a huge literature on spirit possession cults in Africa; notable work includes that by Beattie and Middleton (1969), Comaroff (1986), Janzen (1978, 1982, 1992), Lambek (1980, 1981, 1993), Lewis (1969, 1971, 1986), Stoller and Olkes (1987), Stoller (1989), Swantz (1976), Zaretsky and Shambaugh (1981); Crapanzano and Garrison's edited collection (1977) also has some African case studies. Outstanding works on spirit possession outside of Africa include Kapferer (1983 [1991]) and Taussig (1987). Articles by Boddy (1994) and Atkinson (1992) provide good overviews of spirit possession and shamanism respectively.

3 It should be noted that the terms *mashaitani*, *iblissi*, and *majini* are all derived from Arabic, whereas the terms *mizimu*, *pepo* and *mizuka* are all Bantu words.

4 For the *zar* see for example Boddy (1990), Constantinides (1977, 1985), Lewis (1966a, 1969), Lewis *et al.* (1991), Messing (1958). For North Africa see, for example, Crapanzano (1973, 1977, 1980).

5 In a later diary, Mohammed mentioned a *tari* taking place in a neighbouring village. This cult is of some long duration, and must be widespread, since Alpers mentions it as being significant in Zanzibar in the nineteenth century (1984).

6 In sea spirit cults, the offering tray is always called *sinia*, which literally means a metal, i.e. manufactured and shop-bought tray, whereas in land spirit cults, the offering tray is termed *chano* which means a wooden, locally made tray.

7 *Mshipa* – see Chapter 2, note 1.

8 It should be noted that all of these are words which are only used in the context of land spirit rituals.

9 On the East African coast, 'coolness' is associated with health and a feeling of well-being.

10 In his commentary on the Swahili ballad *Swifa ya Nguvumali* ('The Praises of Nguvumali', a witch-finder active in Tanganyika in the middle

of this century), Lienhardt notes that to become a member of a witches' coven, the initiate must sacrifice a member of his or her own family (1968: 57).

11 It will be noted that such rituals thus include the typical Bantu three-colour symbolism of black, white and red (see V. Turner 1967, Janzen 1992)

12 Here Mohammed omits the Swahili prefixes which generally denote humans (*mrefu, mweusi*), and which are sometimes also used with spirits. Lack of such prefixes suggests their superhuman quality.

13 '*Lazima atastakiwa mbele ya Mungu, huyu ng'ombe atasema "Madhumuni ya kunichinja nini?"*'

14 '*Si neno la kheri, wanapata adhabu.*'

10 ENCOUNTER 4: 1994

1 Spirits are believed to take people's blood, thus causing them to become weak and ill. Compare the case of Amina in Chapter 2.

2 There are two kinds of mats in common use on Mafia. *Jamvi* (pl. *majamvi*) are large mats made, usually by men, from borassus palm, while *mikeka* (sing. *mkeka*), which are smaller but much more elaborate, are made by women, and form their main source of cash income.

3 Women on the coast usually dress in two cloths, one wrapped around the chest, and covering the breasts and body above the knees, the other is worn over the shoulders and sometimes the head. The commonest form of these cloths are *kanga*, made of light cotton and having sayings, mottoes, or riddles on them (see Parkin 1996), whereas heavier and more expensive cloths are known as *mashiti* or *vitenge*; these do not have sayings on them.

4 Since the introduction of the structural adjustment programme in Tanzania, prices of all goods, including food, had risen dramatically, while lower prices were received for cash crops such as coconuts.

5 Subira had been married to a man who originated from the Kilwa region and who took their daughter back to his natal area for her puberty ritual (*unyago*); one reason for this may have been that by 1994, few such rituals were being held in Mafia.

6 Note that Subira echoes Mohammed's words in Chapter 9.

7 During my 1994 visit I found second-hand clothes stalls in many areas of Tanzania, including the Mafia district capital; these clothes are imported from Europe and North America. T-shirts with often highly incongruous messages are widely worn by men.

8 The coastal hierarchy already mentioned is sometimes expressed in terms of skin colour – light skin is still associated with 'Arabness' and status.

9 The Swahili word *mtu*, often incorrectly translated as 'man' means human as opposed to animal, and is used of both men and women.

10 The Wapokomo are one of the two major ethnic categories in northern Mafia, the other being the Wambwera. The Wapokomo are supposed to have migrated to Mafia from their original home in Kenya 'long ago'. In Minazini, oral history has it that the two groups originally lived separately – the Wapokomo on the ridge to the east of the village, where they culti-vated the bush-land and kept cattle, while the Wambwera lived nearer to

the sea. The two groups have long been intermarried, and, since descent is cognatic, many villagers, altbough not all, claim ancestry from both groups. However, the cult of land spirits is practised only by those with Pokomo descent (see Caplan 1975).

11 This is at odds with the situation reported elsewhere: Lambek, for example, maintains that people in a state of trance cannot afterwards remember what happened during that period (1980).

12 There are two Sheikhs on Mafia who are leaders of *tarika* – both are Qadiriyya. Minazini has followers of each.

13 *Ijazi* is sweetened water given to an initiate by his Sheikh, after he has spat into it, thus transferring some of his *baraka*.

References

Abbink, J. (1993) 'Reading the Entrails: Analysis of an African Divination Discourse', *Man* 25: 705–26.

Akinnaso Niyi, F. (1995) 'Bourdieu and the Diviner: Knowledge and Symbolic Power in Yoruba Divination', in W. James (ed.) *The Pursuit of Certainty: Religious and Cultural Formation*, ASA Decennial Conference Series, London: Routledge.

Alpers, E.A. (1984) 'Ordinary Household Chores: Ritual and Power in a 19th-Century Swahili Women's Possession Cult', *Journal of African Historical Studies* 17, 4: 677–702.

Arnold, D. and Hardiman, D. (1993) *Subaltern Studies VIII: Essays in Honour of Ranajit Guha*, Delhi: Oxford University Press.

Atiya, N. (1988) *Khul Khaal: Five Egyptian Women Tell their Stories*, London: Virago.

Atkinson, J.M. (1992) 'Shamanism Today', *Annual Review of Anthropology* 21: 307–30.

Beattie, J. and Middleton, J. (eds) (1969) *Spirit Mediumship and Society in Africa*, London: Routledge and Kegan Paul.

Becker, C.H. and Martin, B.G. (1968) 'Material for the Understanding of Islam in German East Africa', edited and trans. by B.G. Martin, *Tanzania Notes and Records* 68: 52–7.

Bell, D. (1993) 'Introduction I', to D. Bell, P. Caplan and W.J. Karim (eds) *Gendered Fields: Women, Men and Ethnography*. London and New York: Routledge

Bell, D. and Nelson, T.N. (1989) 'Speaking about Rape is Everyone's Business', *Women's Studies International Forum* 12, 4: 403–16.

Boddy, J. (1990) *Wombs and Alien Spirits: Women, Men and the Zar Cult in Northern Sudan*, Madison, WI: University of Wisconsin Press.

—— (1994) 'Spirit Possession Revisited: Beyond Instrumentality', *Annual Review of Anthropology* 23: 407–34.

Bourgignon, E. (1965) 'The Self, the Behavioural Environment, and the Theory of Spirit Possession', in M.E. Spiro (ed.) *Context and Meaning in Cultural Anthropology*, London: Collins-Macmillan.

Bujra, J.M. (1968) 'An Anthropological Study of Political Action in a Bajuni Village in Kenya', unpublished PhD thesis, University of London.

Burgos-Debray, E. (1984) [1983] *I, Rigoberta Menchu: An Indian Woman in Guatemala*, London: Verso.

Caplan, P. (1975) *Choice and Constraint in a Swahili Community*, London: Oxford University Press for International African Institute.

—— (1976) 'Boys' Circumcision and Girls' Puberty Rites among the Swahili of Mafia Island Tanzania', *Africa* 46, 1: 21–33.

—— (1978) 'The Swahili of Chole Island, Tanzania', in A. Sutherland (ed.) *Face Values*, London: BBC/Royal Anthropological Institute.

—— (1979) 'Spirit Possession on Mafia Island, Tanzania', *Kenya Past and Present* 10: 41–4.

—— (1982) 'Gender, Ideology and Modes of Production on the East African Coast', in J. de Vere Allen (ed.) *From Zinj to Zanzibar*, Wiesbaden: Franz Steiner Verlag.

—— (1983) 'Women's Property, Islamic Law and Cognatic Descent', in R. Hirschon (ed.) *Women and Property, Women as Property*, London: Croom Helm.

—— (1988) 'Engendering Knowledge: The Politics of Ethnography', *Anthropology Today* 4: 8-12; 5: 14–17.

—— (1989) 'Perceptions of Gender Stratification', *Africa* 59, 2: 196–208.

—— (1992a) 'Spirits and Sex: A Swahili Informant and his Diary', in J. Okely and H. Callaway (eds) *Anthropology and Autobiography*, ASA Monographs 29, London and New York: Routledge.

—— (1992b) 'Socialism from Above: The View from Below', in P. Forster (ed.) *Tanzanian Peasantry: Economy in Crisis* Aldershot: Gower Press. Also in C. Hann (ed.) (1993) *Socialism in Anthropological Theory and Local Practice* ASA vol. 31, London and New York: Routledge.

—— (1995a) 'In My Office We Don't Have Closing Hours: Gendered Household Relations in a Swahili Village in Northern Mafia Island', in C. Creighton and C.K. Omari (eds) *Gender, Family and Household in Tanzania*, Aldershot: Avebury.

—— (1995b) 'Law and Customs: Marital Disputes on Mafia Island, Tanzania', in P. Caplan (ed.) *Understanding Disputes: The Politics of Law*, Oxford and Providence, R.I. USA: Berg Publishers.

Casagrande, J.B. (1960) *In the Company of Man: Twenty Portraits of Anthropological Informants*, New York, Evanston and London: Harper Torchbooks.

Castaneda, C. (1973) [1971] *A Separate Reality: Further Conversations with Don Juan*, Harmondsworth: Penguin Books.

Clifford, J. (1983) 'Power and Dialogue in Ethnography: Marcel Griaule's Initiation', in G.W. Stocking (ed.) *Observers Observed*, Madison, WI: University of Wisconsin Press. Also in J. Clifford (1988) *The Predicament of Culture: Twentieth-Century Ethnography, Literature and Art*, Cambridge, Manchester and London, England: Harvard University Press.

—— (1986) 'On Ethnographic Allegory', in J. Clifford and G.E. Marcus (eds) *Writing Culture: The Poetics and Politics of Ethnography*, Berkeley, Los Angeles and London: University of California Press.

Clifford, J. and Marcus, G.E. (eds) (1986) *Writing Culture: The Poetics and Politics of Ethnography*, Berkeley, Los Angeles and London: University of California Press.

Comaroff, J. (1986) *Body of Power, Spirit of Resistance*, Chicago and London: University of Chicago Press.

Constantinides, P. (1977) 'Ill at Ease and Sick at Heart: Symbolic Behaviour in a Sudanese Healing Cult', in I.M. Lewis (ed.) *Symbols and Sentiments*, New York: Academic Press.

—— (1985) 'Women Heal Women: Spirit Possession and Sexual Segregation in a Muslim Society', *Social Science and Medicine* 21, 6: 685–92.

Crapanzano, V. (1973) *The Hamadsha: A Study in Moroccan Ethnopsychiatry*, Berkeley: University of California Press.

—— (1977) 'Mohammed and Dawia: Possession in Morocco', in V. Crapanzano and V. Garrison (eds) *Case Studies in Spirit Possession*, New York: John Wiley and Sons.

—— (1980) *Tuhami: Portrait of a Moroccan*, Chicago: University of Chicago Press.

—— (1984) 'Life Histories', *American Anthropologist* 86: 953–9.

Crapanzano, V. and Garrison, V. (eds) (1977) *Case Studies in Possession*, New York: John Wiley and Sons.

Dumont, J. (1978) *The Headman and I: Ambiguity and Ambivalence in the Fieldwork Experience*, Austin and London: University of Texas Press.

Dwyer, K. (1982) *Moroccan Dialogue: Anthropology in Question*, Baltimore and London: The Johns Hopkins University Press.

Dyk, W. (1938) *Son of Old Hat: A Navaho Autobiography Recorded by Walter Dyk*, Lincoln, Nebraska: University of Nebraska Press.

Eliade, M. (1964) [1951] *Shamanism*, London: Routledge and Kegan Paul.

El Zein, A.H.M. (1974) *The Sacred Meadows: A Structural Analysis of Religious Symbolism in an East African Town*, Evanston: Northwestern University Press.

Evans-Pritchard, E. (1937) *Magic, Witchcraft and Oracles among the Azande*, Oxford: Clarendon Press.

Fabian, Johannes (1971) 'Language, History and Anthropology', *Philosophy of the Social Sciences* 1: 19–47.

Fernandez, J.W. (1991) 'Afterword', to P.M. Peek (ed.) *African Divination Systems: Ways of Knowing*, Bloomington: Indiana University Press.

Firth, R. (1959) 'Problem and Assumption in an Anthropological Study of Spirit Possession', *Journal of the Royal Anthropological Institute* 89, II: 129–48.

Foucault, M. (1980) [1978] *Herculine Barbin: Being the Recently Discovered Memoirs of a Nineteenth-Century French Hermaphrodite*, Brighton: Harvester Press.

Freeman, J.M. (1978) 'Collecting the Life History of an Indian Untouchable', in S. Vatuk (ed.) *American Studies in the Anthropology of India*, New Delhi: Manohar.

—— (1979) *Untouchable: An Indian Life History*, London: Allen and Unwin.

Geertz, C. (1977) 'From the Native's Point of View: On the Nature of Anthropological Understanding', in J.L. Dolgin, D.S. Kemnitzer and D.M. Schneider (eds) *Symbolic Anthropology: A Reader in the Study of Symbols and Meanings*, New York: Columbia University Press.

Giles, L. (1987) 'Possession Cults on the Swahili Coast: A Re-examination of Theories of Marginality', *Africa* 57, 2: 234–57.

Ginzburg, C. (1980) [1976] *The Cheese and the Worms: The Cosmos of a Sixteenth-Century Miller*, London: Routledge and Kegan Paul.

Gomm, R. (1975) 'Bargaining from Weakness: Spirit Possession on the South Kenya Coast', *Man* 10, 4: 530–43.

Gray, J. (1955) 'Nairuzi, or Siku ya Mwaka', *Tanganyika Notes and Records* 38: 1–22.

Gray, R.F. (1969) 'The Shetani Cult Among the Segeju', in J. Beattie and J. Middleton (eds) *Spirit Mediumship and Society in Africa*, London: Routledge and Kegan Paul.

Griaule, M. (1965) [1948] *Conversations with Ogotemmeli: An Introduction to Dogon Religious Ideas*, London: International African Institute and Oxford University Press.

Guha, R. (1982) *Subaltern Studies I: Writings on South Asian History and Society*, Delhi: Oxford University Press.

Harries, L. (1962) 'The Judge and the Sorcerer's Client', in L. Harries, *Swahili Poetry*, London: Oxford University Press.

—— (1965) *Swahili Prose Texts: A Selection from the Material Collected by Carl Velten from 1893 to 1896*, London: Oxford University Press.

Janzen, J. (1978) *The Quest for Therapy in Lower Zaire*, Berkeley: University of California Press.

—— (1982) *Lemba: A Drum of Affliction in Africa and the New World*, New York and London: Garland Publishers.

—— (1986) 'Drums of Affliction: Real Phenomenon or Scholarly Chimera?' paper given at the conference on Religion in Africa, Brigham Young University, Utah.

—— (1987) 'Therapy Management: Concepts, Reality, Process', *Medical Anthropology Quarterly* 1, 1: 68-84.

—— (1992) *Ngoma: Discourses of Healing in Central and Southern Africa*, Berkeley: University of California Press.

Kapferer, B. (1983) *A Celebration of Demons: Exorcism and the Aesthetics of Healing in Sri Lanka*, Bloomington: Indiana University Press.

—— (1991) 'Preface' to new edition of *A Celebration of Demons: Exorcism and the Aesthetics of Healing in Sri Lanka*, Oxford: Berg Publications and Washington: Smithsonian Institute.

Knappert, J. (1971) *Swahili Islamic Poetry* (3 vols), Leiden: E.J. Brill.

Koritschoner, H. (1936) 'Ngoma ya Sheitani: An East African Native Treatment for Psychical Disorder', *Journal of the Royal Anthropological Institute* 66: 209–19.

Kroeber, T. (1961) *Ishi in Two Worlds: A Biography of the Last Wild Indian in North America*, Berkeley: University of California Press.

—— (1973) [1964] *Ishi – Last of his Tribe*, Toronto, New York: Bantam Books.

Kuper, H. (1981) 'Foreword' to new edition of M. Smith, *Baba of Karo: A Woman of the Muslim Hausa*, New Haven and London: Yale University Press.

Lambek, M. (1980) 'Spirits and Spouses: Possession as a System of Communication among Malagasy Speakers of Mayotte', *American Ethnologist* 7: 318-31.

—— (1981) *Human Spirits: A Cultural Account of Trance in Mayotte*, London and New York: Cambridge University Press.

—— (1993) *Knowledge and Practice in Mayotte: Local Discourses of Islam, Sorcery and Spirit Possession*, Toronto: University of Toronto Press.

—— (1995) '"Choking on the Koran": And Other Consuming Parables from the Western Indian Ocean Front', in W. James (ed.) *The Pursuit of*

Certainty: Religious and Cultural Formations, ASA Decennial Conference Series. London and New York: Routledge.

Landberg, P. (1977) 'Kinship and Community in a Coastal Village of Tanzania', unpublished PhD, University of California, Davis.

Langness, L.L. and Frank, G. (1981) *Lives: An Anthropological Approach to Biography*, California: Chandler and Sharp.

Le Guennec-Coppens, F. and P. Caplan (eds) (1991) *Les Swahili entre Afrique et Arabie*, Paris: Karthala.

Le Roy Ladurie, E. (1990a) [1978] *Montaillou: Cathars and Catholics in a French Village 1294–1324*, Harmondsworth: Penguin Books.

—— (1990b) [1983] *Jasmin's Witch: An Investigation into Witchcraft and Magic in South-West France during the 17th Century*, Harmondsworth: Penguin Books.

Lewis, I.M. (1966a) 'Spirit Possession and Deprivation Cults', *Man* 1, 3: 307–29.

—— (1966b) (ed.) *Islam in Tropical Africa*, London: Oxford University Press and International African Institute.

—— (1969) 'Spirit Possession in Northern Somaliland', in J. Beattie and J. Middleton (eds) *Spirit Mediumship and Society in Africa*, London: Routledge and Kegan Paul.

—— (1971) *Ecstatic Religion*, Harmondsworth: Penguin Books.

—— (1986) *Religion in Context: Cults and Charisma*, London and New York: Cambridge University Press.

Lewis, I.M., Al-Safi, A. and Harreiz, S. (1991) (eds) *Women's Medicine: The Zar-Bori Cult in Africa and Beyond*, Edinburgh: Edinburgh University Press.

Lewis, O. (1976) [1959] *Five Families: Mexican Case Studies in the Culture of Poverty*, London: Souvenir Press.

—— (1983) [1961] *The Children of Sanchez: Autobiography of a Mexican Family*, Harmondsworth: Penguin Books.

—— (1965) *La Vida: A Puerto Rican Family in the Culture of Poverty: San Juan and New York*, New York: Vintage Books.

—— (1972) [1969] *A Death in the Sanchez Family*, Harmondsworth: Penguin Modern Classics.

Lienhardt, P. (1968) 'Introduction' to *The Medicine Man: Swifa ya Nguvumali, by Hasani bin Ismail*, Oxford: Clarendon Press.

Macfarlane, A. (1977) [1970] *The Family Life of Ralph Josselin: A Seventeenth-Century Clergyman*, New York: W.W. Norton.

Marks, S. (ed.) (1987) *Not Either an Experimental Doll: The Separate Worlds of Three South African Women*, London: The Women's Press.

—— (1989) 'The Context of Personal Narrative: Reflections on "Not Either an Experimental Doll"', in Personal Narratives Group (eds) *Interpreting Women's Lives: Feminist Theory and Personal Narratives*, Bloomington: Indiana University Press.

Marwick, M.G. (1965) *Sorcery in its Social Setting*, Manchester University Press.

Mascia-Lees, F.E., Sharpe, P. and Cohen, C.B. (1989) 'The Postmodernist Turn in Anthropology: Cautions from a Feminist Perspective', *Signs* 15, 1: 7–33.

Mbilinyi, M. (1989) '"I'd Have Been a Man": Politics and the Labor Process in Producing Personal Narratives', in Personal Narratives Group (eds) *Interpreting Women's Lives: Feminist Theory and Personal Narratives*, Bloomington: Indiana University Press.

Mead, M. (1975) 'Introduction' to the new edition of O. Lewis *Five Families*, London: Souvenir Press.

Mernissi, F. (1988) [1984] *Doing Daily Battle: Interviews with Moroccan Women*, London: The Women's Press.

Messing, S.D. (1958) 'Group Therapy and Social Status in the Zar Cult of Ethiopia', *American Anthropologist* 60, 6: 1120–26.

Middleton, J. (1992) *The World of the Swahili: an African Mercantile Civilisation*, New Haven and London: Yale University Press.

Mintz, S. (1960) *Worker in the Cane: A Puerto Rican Life History*, New Haven and London: Yale University Press.

Mirza, S. and Strobel, M. (1989) *Three Swahili Women: Life Histories from Mombasa, Kenya*, Bloomington: Indiana University Press.

—— (1991) *Wanawake Watatu wa Kiswahili: Hadithi za Maisha Kutoka Mombasa, Kenya* Bloomington: Indiana University Press.

Munson, H., Jr. (1984) *The House of Si Abd Allah*, New Haven and London: Yale University Press.

Myerhoff, B. (1974) *Peyote Hunt: the sacred journey of the Huichol Indians*, New York: Cornell University Press.

—— (1979) *Number Our Days*, New York: Dutton.

Ngaiza, M.K. and Koda, B. (1991) *The Unsung Heroines: Women's Life Histories from Tanzania*, Dar es Salaam: WRDP Publications.

Obeyesekere, G. (1970) 'The Idiom of Demonic Possession: A Case Study', *Social Science and Medicine* 4: 97–111.

—— (1981) *Medusa's Hair: An Essay on Personal Symbols and Religious Experience*, Chicago: University of Chicago Press.

Parkin, D. (1974) 'Straightening the Path from Wilderness: The Case of Divinatory Speech', *Journal of the Anthropology Society of Oxford (JASO)* 10, 3: 147–60.

—— (1985) 'Reason, Emotion and the Embodiment of Power', in J. Overing (ed.) *Reason and Morality*, ASA Vol. 23, London: Tavistock Press.

—— (1991) 'Simultaneity and Sequencing in the Oracular Speech of Kenyan Diviners', in P.M. Peek (ed.) *African Divination Systems: Ways of Knowing*, Bloomington: Indiana University Press.

—— (1995) 'Latticed Knowledge: Eradication and Dispersal of the Unpalatable in Islam, Medicine and Anthropological Theory', in R. Fardon (ed.) *Counterworks: Managing Knowledge in its Diversity*, London and New York: Routledge.

—— (ed.) (1994) *Continuity and Autonomy in Swahili Communities: Inland Influences and Strategies of Self-determination*, Wien: Beitrage zur Afrikanistik, and London: School of Oriental and African Studies.

—— (1996) 'The Power of Incompleteness: Innuendo in Swahili Women's Dress' in B. Masquelier and J.-L. Siran (eds) *Anthropologie de l'interlocution*, Paris: L'Harmattan.

Parkin, D. and Constantin, F. (eds) (1989) *Social Stratification in Swahili Society*, special edition of *Africa* 59, 2.

Peek, P.M. (ed.) (1991) *African Divination Systems: Ways of Knowing*, Bloomington: Indiana University Press.

Personal Narratives Group (eds) (1989) 'Origins', in Personal Narratives Group (eds) *Interpreting Women's Lives: Feminist Theory and Personal Narratives*, Bloomington: Indiana University Press.

Prell, R. (1989) 'The Double Frame of Life History in the Work of Barbara Myerhoff', in Personal Narratives Group (1989) (eds) *Interpreting Women's Lives: Feminist Theory and Personal Narratives*, Bloomington: Indiana University Press.

Prins, A.H.J. (1961) *The Swahili-speaking Peoples of Zanzibar and the East African Coast*, Ethnographic Survey of Africa: East-Central Africa Part XII. London: International African Institute.

Rabinow, P. (1977) *Reflections on Fieldwork in Morocco*, Berkeley: University of California Press.

Racine, O. (1995) 'Mwaka Kogwa Makunduchi ou la mise en tourisme de la culture d'une communauté rurale du sud d'Unguja', paper presented at the 4th Franco-British Swahili Workshop, Paris.

Radcliffe-Brown, R. (1952) 'On Joking Relations', in R. Radcliffe-Brown, *Structure and Function in Primitive Society*, London: Cohn and West.

Radin, P. (1926) *Crashing Thunder: The Autobiography of an American Indian*, New York: Appleton and Co.

Schechner, R. (1977) *Essays on Performance Theory*, New York: Drama Book Specialists.

Shostak, M. (1983) [1981] *Nisa: The Life and Words of a !Kung Woman*, Harmondsworth: Penguin Books.

—— (1989) 'What the Wind Won't Take Away: The Genesis of Nisa – The Life and Words of a !Kung Woman', in Personal Narratives Group (eds) *Interpreting Women's Lives: Feminist Theory and Personal Narratives*, Bloomington: Indiana University Press.

Skene, R. (1917) 'Arab and Swahili Dance and Ceremonies', *Journal of the Royal Anthropological Institute* 47: 413–34.

Smith, M.F. (1981) [1954] *Baba of Karo: A Woman of the Muslim Hausa*, with Foreword by H. Kuper, New Haven and London: Yale University Press.

Spence, J. D. (1978) *The Death of Woman Wang: Rural Life in China in the 17th Century*, London: Weidenfeld and Nicolson.

Stoller, P, (1989) *The Fusion of the Worlds: An Ethnography of Possession among the Songhay of Niger*, Chicago: University of Chicago Press.

Stoller, P. and Olkes, C. (1987) *In Sorcery's Shadow*, Chicago: University of Chicago Press.

Strobel, M. (1975) *Muslim Women in Mombasa, 1890–1975*, New Haven and Yale: Yale University Press.

Sutherland, A. (ed.) (1978) *Face Values: Some Anthropological Themes*, London: BBC Publications/Royal Anthropological Institute.

Swantz, M.L. (1970) *Ritual and Symbol in Transitional Zaramo Society*, Uppsala: Gleerup.

—— (1976) 'The Spirit Possession Cults and Their Social Setting in Coastal Zaramo Society', *Ethnological Fennica* 1–2.

—— (1979) 'Community and Healing among the Zaramo in Tanzania', *Social Science and Medicine* 138: 169–73.

Swartz, M.J. (1991) *The Way the World Is: Cultural Processes and Social Relations among the Mombasa Swahili*, Berkeley, Los Angeles and London: California University Press.

Taussig, M. (1987) *Shamanism, Colonialism and the Wild Man: A Study in Terror and Healing*, Chicago and London: University of Chicago Press.

Topan, F. (1972) 'Oral Literature in a Ritual Setting: The Role of Spirit Songs in Spirit Medium Cult of Mombasa, Kenya', unpublished PhD thesis, University of London.

—— (1994) 'Song, Dance and the Continuity of Swahili Identity', in D. Parkin (ed.) *Continuity and Autonomy in Swahili Societies*, Vienna: Beitrage zur Afrikanstik Band 48 and London: School of Oriental and African Studies.

Trawick, M. (1990) *Notes on Love in a Tamil Family*, Berkeley: University of California Press.

Trimingham, J.S. (1964) *Islam in East Africa*, Oxford: Clarendon Press.

Turner, E. (1993) *Experiencing Ritual: A New Interpretation of African Healing*, Philadelphia: University of Pennsylvania Press.

Turner, V.W. (1960) 'Muchona the Hornet: Interpreter of Religion', in J. Casagrande (ed.) *In the Company of Man: Twenty Portraits of Anthropological Informants*, New York, Evanston and London: Harper Torchbooks. Also in V.W. Turner (1967) *The Forest of Symbols*, Ithaca and London: Cornell University Press.

—— (1967) 'Colour Classification in Ndembu Ritual: A Problem in Primitive Classification', in *The Forest of Symbols: Aspects of Ndembu Ritual*, Ithaca and London: Cornell University Press.

—— (1968) *The Drums of Affliction: A Study of Religious Processes among the Ndembu of Zambia*, Oxford: Clarendon.

—— (1975) *Revelation and Divination in Ndembu Ritual*, Ithaca: Cornell University Press.

Watson, L.C. (1976) 'Understanding a Life History as a Subjective Document: Hermeneutical and Phenomenological Perspectives', *Ethos* 4: 95–131.

Watson, L.C. and M.-B. Watson-Franke (1985) *Interpreting Life Histories*, New Brunswick: Rutgers University Press.

Werbner, R. (1991) *Tears of the Dead: The Social Biography of an African Family*, Edinburgh: Edinburgh University Press for the International African Institute.

Widjeyewardene, G. (1961) 'Some Aspects of Village Solidarity among Kiswahili-speaking Communities of Kenya and Tanganyika', Unpublished PhD thesis, University of Cambridge.

Wilson, P. (1967) 'Status Ambiguity and Spirit Possession', *Man* 12, 3: 347–65.

Wolf, M. (1992) *A Thrice-told Tale: Feminism, Postmodernism and Ethnographic Responsibility*, Stanford: Stanford University Press.

Zaretsky, I. and Shambaugh, C.L. (1981) *Spirit Possession and Mediumship in Africa and Afro-America: An Annotatated Bibliography*, New York.

Index

adultery: accusations of 128; children from 47–8, 102; as pollution 179–80; village life 62, 63, 99–102; witchcraft 103–4

affliction: prevention 166–70; treatment 163–6; *see also* illness; misfortune

Amina 46, 198

ancestors 90–3, 174–5

ancestral spirits 51, 145, 161–2, 174–5, 219–21

animal sacrifice 172, 186

anthropologist: gifts to informant 122, 198–9, 201, 204, 206–7, 214–15; marital status of 117, 125; relationship with informant 6–9, 11–12, 16, 19, 21–2, 117–18, 122, 125

anthropology 7; authorial authority 12, 16–17; ethics 17, 230; life histories 9–14, 17–22, 25, 230; personal narratives 14–17, 229, 230–1, 233; spirit possession 153–5

anti-heroes 16, 229–30

Arab culture, and sea spirits 172, 173

Asha 45, 49–51, 207, 213

astrology 151, 157, 194

Atiya, Mayra 13

authorship: authority 12, 16–17; joint 2–4, 18; prayer for success 4–5, 236

autobiography 25, 26–58

babies: death 132; infant mortality rate 84; infanticide 103; stillbirth 43, 47

Beattie, J. 154

Becker, C. H. 153

Bell, D. 12, 17

bereavement 226–7

bewitching: husband–wife 129, 130, 133; Mohammed 111–12; pregnant woman 144; seed 75; wedding 89; *see also* sorcery; spells; witchcraft

blessings, parental 94, 192, 200

blood: consumption of 172, 174, 182, 186, 220; used by spirits 174, 182, 220

Boddy, J. 154, 172, 195, 231

Bourgignon, E. 154

Burgos-Debray, E. 12–13

burning, as treatment 164–5; *see also* firing for cultivation

bush clearing 70

calendars, solar/lunar 66–7

Caplan, P.: (1975) 6; (1976) 87; (1982) 83; (1988) 12; (1992) 7, 8, 63, 104, 117

Casagrande, J. B. 10

cash crops 38, 39, 66, 78–9

cashew nuts 78–9

cassava 77

Castaneda, C. 195

ceremonies for rites of passage 83, 87

charms 72, 166

childbirth, hazards 84